Working While Black

Working While Black

*Essays on Television Portrayals
of African American
Professionals*

Edited by LaToya T. Brackett

McFarland & Company, Inc., Publishers
Jefferson, North Carolina

ISBN (print) 978-1-4766-7521-3
ISBN (ebook) 978-1-4766-4234-5

LIBRARY OF CONGRESS AND BRITISH LIBRARY
CATALOGUING DATA ARE AVAILABLE

Library of Congress Control Number 2020057850

Front cover image *Grey's Anatomy* (ABC) season 1 Spring 2005,
Shown: Chandra Wilson (as Miranda Bailey), photographer:
Bob D'Amico (ABC/Photofest)

Printed in the United States of America

*McFarland & Company, Inc., Publishers
Box 611, Jefferson, North Carolina 28640
www.mcfarlandpub.com*

To my late mother,
Phyllis Marie Brackett.
I am, because you were, mom.

Table of Contents

Part VI—New Television

Looking back on *The Fresh Prince of Bel-Air* I realize for me, and probably more so for my brothers, Will Smith was a representation of us. We lived in an inner-city area up until I was five years old. My mother, and at the time my father, both decided that we needed to find our way to a safer neighborhood. Despite having a strong community of friends, people to assist us with small things, like looking after me and my brothers if my mom or dad was away, there was a crime wave due to the influx of crack cocaine and the hyper-policing the city had undertaken. Thanks to a low income-based housing program, and my mother owning a decently reliable car, we moved twenty minutes south, to a place I had never heard of, but would find out was a large part of my family's history. My parents wanted us to grow up in a safe place, just as Will's mother desired when she forced him to move from Philly.

Will was a character of laughter, of bravery, of loyalty, and of reality—well except for having an affluent and very willing aunt and uncle to provide a lifestyle of which many people can only dream. But he made me and my brothers laugh, and for me he reflected back aspects of the life I was living. I am sure my brothers felt even more connected to Will due to their age similarities and transferring into predominantly white schools after we moved.

As an adult, things have altered in my television content preferences. I look for more professional representations of African Americans, especially African American women. I used to look for women like my mom, and now I look for women that resemble my educational and occupational experiences. Upon re-watching *The Fresh Prince* I realized how Aunt Viv was a future reflection of myself, due to her profession as a college professor. For me, television still provides a space that will never be replaced. Nonetheless, I continually, as a Black female academic, seek a television space that is built for me. And I ask myself at times "where is it?" Sometimes I ask, "where did it go?" Sometimes, I yell at the screen "don't do that." Sometimes I verbally confirm, "that's it right there." And sometimes I force myself to turn off my critical lens and enjoy the Black woman, or Black man, gracing my television screen, because at least we are represented.

Filling the Gap: Scholarly Commentary on Black Professionalisms on TV Is Missing

The reality is television has grown. Representation of racial and ethnic backgrounds has grown. Yet, despite a numerical increase in representation, it is difficult to find scholarly information about more specific types of Black character representations. African American characters are one of the most prominent racial groups that are incorporated into television. Representations are moving further away from simple roles with no character depth and stereotypical characteristics with harmful implications, and toward more complex roles that peel back the layers. Despite additions of more complex Black characters, stereotypical representations and one-dimensional characters remain. As an avid observer of the complexities of Black characterizations, I became curious about several staple characters of color in the role of medical doctors. Scripted medical series cross boundaries, and are at times more stable, and as medicine continually develops in the real world so too do the fictional shows about medicine. Dr. Peter Benton (Eriq La Salle), from the series *ER* (1994–2009), was a very curious character to me. Out of all the characters in his eight seasons on the show, he experienced some of the most impactful storylines. Despite aspects of his character which maintained stereotypical characterizations, he also ruptured stereotypes of African American men. After searching for commentary about Benton, it became apparent that even with his complex and important role in the series, there was little scholarly analysis written about him (Donald Bogle focused on Benton in *Primetime Blues*). This collection seeks to fill this void, and to add to the discussions of African Americans on the small screen, yet with a unique focus on professionalism.

There are select book compilations dedicated to African Americans on television, and the most similar to, and yet very different from, *Working While Black* is *African Americans on Television: Race-ing for Ratings*, edited by David J. Leonard and Lisa A. Guerrero in 2013. One of the main similarities of these two edited volumes is the formatting of focused essays, and yet, a main difference is the focus of the essays. Leonard and Guerrero provide a compilation of essays that cover various types of television programming featuring African Americans, from talk shows, and commercials, to scripted television—scripted television is the sole focus of this collection. The editors of *African Americans on Television* desired to cover the presence of African Americans on television from its beginnings, allowing for discussions ranging from *The Jeffersons* (1975–1985) to an essay focused on a character from *True Blood* (2008–2014). Their volume analyzes how Black representation across all aspects of television can impact U.S. society, and perceptions of African Americans. Discussions of perpetuation of racism, and resistance to it, post-racial claims, and what television teaches America is a central goal of *African Americans on Television*. Such commentary can be found in select essays of this volume, but it is not ascribed to the foci of all essays. Another similarity of Leonard and Guerrero's volume is that several series they discuss are also covered in this collection, reiterating the importance and impact of some of these series in regard to African American representation. Nonetheless, the focus of these overlapping series' commentaries is different and still, both are needed in the discussion of Black representation on television.

An earlier volume, *Primetime Blues: African Americans on Network Television* also compares to this volume. Written by Donald Bogle in 2001, his work is an especially valuable reference and commentary text that is dedicated to analyzing the sort of roles that African Americans played, specifically on network television from the 1950s through the 1990s. Each chapter is broken down by decade and the major trope that prevailed in that time period for African Americans, is the chapter focus. *Primetime Blues* is predominantly a historical and survey text. It covers stereotypes and at times provides a deeper discussion of more influential TV shows. The major differences between *Primetime Blues* and this collection reside in the focus and content analysis of the text. This edited volume is not divided by time periods, but by areas of occupations. It does not attempt to cover every series with a recurring African American character, as the Bogle text does. This volume focuses on the time period from the 1990s until today, while Bogle's work finished with series from the 1990s. It was in the 1990s that African Americans became a noticed asset to television producers and 30 years have now since passed. Television content has shifted, and this collection showcases some of these shifts.

This volume explores the shifts in television content via essays dedicated to certain series, or characters within a specific career area. This volume fills a major gap in the analysis of representations of African American professionalisms on screen. When searching for scholarly work on the occupations of African American characters on television, most searches came up empty. Multiple television series covered in this volume have commentary about them in peer-reviewed articles and within books, but I have consistently come up short with work centralized on how these characters' careers influence the series, until now. This collection centers the career of a Black television character and engages with commentary that desires to see how occupation influences the Black character's experiences and representation to the show's viewers. There is clearly a need for such documentation and discussion. This is why the 1990s is an ideal time period to initiate this analysis on Black professionalisms in scripted TV.

Television is becoming a very unique and ever changing medium. Therefore, before the "sit down at primetime and stay glued to your television from 8:00 p.m. to 10:00 p.m.," completely disappears from the American definition of television viewing, this focus of Black professionalisms representation should be documented. The television medium is advancing to other delivery modes, from cable recording options, on demand options, streaming options and new creations of television series in the internet-based industries. New modes of television delivery provide for many audiences, especially African Americans, the opportunity to find content more aligned with their experiences and what they wish to see. This is a prime time to document the condition of African American representations on television due to television's continued quick evolution. We have come very far from *The Cosby Show*, which has had its fair share of academic discourse. But what else has arisen since this important representation of an upper-class African American family, with two professional parents? That is what this volume seeks to provide. It will be a resource of importance, because in basic understandings, representation is more important than intention and ideologies. Representation matters; just ask the childhood version of me.

Introduction

Defining Black-Collar Professionalisms

Did you know that Black Americans watch more television in comparison to all other racial groups? This has been a documented truth since 1990. The 1990 Nielsen report on television viewer demographics stated that TV viewing within Black[1] households was 48 percent higher than all other households (Crain Communications, Inc., 1991). More recently, the 2018 Nielsen report stated that Black Americans are the heaviest users of all media forms, and they view almost two-and-a-half more hours of television per day compared to the average adult (The Nielsen Company, 2018). But what are they watching? It was in the 1990s that television production made a strong effort to better reflect the audience that watched television the most. An extensive evaluation of the demographic changes of characters on television from 1966 to 1992, completed by Bradley Greenberg and Larry Collette in 1997, expressed this shift in new character creation for Black Americans.

> Across decades there appears to have been a steady upward trend toward increased new Black characters. The later 1960s saw 6%, this increased slightly to 8% through the 1970s, in the 1980s this increased to 12%, and the first three years of the 1990s showed increases to 14%. After decades of being under-represented, the 1980s population of new Black characters was remarkably in sync with the U.S. Census figure for 1980 (12%). In the early 1990s new season Black characters actually exceeded real world population for the first time. This is perhaps the networks' direct response to a 1990 Nielsen study that found Black households watching TV in record numbers, averaging around 70 hours per week, compared with 47 hours for non–Blacks. The escalation of new network programs specifically targeting African-American viewers was perhaps an economic reaction to this viewership phenomenon [Greenberg & Collette, 1997].

No matter the reasoning for such an increase of Black character representation, the representation mattered. It still matters today. It was in the 1990s that Black characters continued to grow, in their ideologies, experiences,

7

surroundings, and occupations. As more Black characters graced the small screen, there were more opportunities to further develop them.

A major development in Black characters was the increase in their representation in occupations that would be considered professional. This edited volume is dedicated to sharing a glimpse into these characters and the television series that showcased them. It seeks to enhance television viewers' understanding of Black professionalism, on the small screen and in the real world. It seeks to provide commentary about the ways in which these new character occupations punched through stereotypes, yet at times still held onto some stereotypes often associated with African Americans.[2] This volume in no way claims to cover all the series since 1990 which showcased a Black character with a professional occupation. This volume does cover many of the series that gained a major following in the Black community, and some that became beloved no matter the viewer demographic. Most essentially, this volume focuses on an important type of representation on television: the ways in which Black characters embody being professionals.

Professional. What images appear in your head as you read that word? I can take an educated guess as to what you see, because it has been cultivated into our society. Characterizations of professional often infer a type of dress that includes suits with ties, blazers, trousers, or knee length skirts, definitely not jeans, sneakers, or t-shirts. We often associate professional with types of professions as well, the careers people maintain in order to make a living. Often, the word professional is not aligned with folks who work an hourly wage job—a job that most likely does not have a 9-to-5, Monday-to-Friday schedule. We can guess the several professions which are thought of swiftly if we ask American[3] youth what they would like to be when they grow up; doctors, lawyers, and teachers make that list. And what do those doctors, lawyers, and teachers look like? As of 2016, 80 percent of public-school teachers were white (National Center for Educational Statistics, 2020). As of 2018, 56.2 percent of active medical doctors were white (Association of American Medical Colleges, 2020). As of 2019, 85 percent of lawyers were white (American Bar Association, 2020). These professionals are predominantly white, and thus the images that appear in our heads are of white doctors, white lawyers, and white teachers. This too is the case for all Americans, not only white Americans, who are the majority of the U.S. and would see images of themselves reflected back at them when envisioning such professions. What these images reflect for those who are not white is the fact that "professional" is associated with whiteness. Such an association does not mean there are no professionals who are not white—rather, what we see presented to us, in all media forms, is that whiteness equals professionalism. This is a major concern. Not for the dominant group in society, white Americans, but for the marginalized,

African Americans, Latinos and Hispanics, Asian Americans, and Native Americans. We cultivate what we see. And with this in mind, we should wonder what do we see? What are the marginalized seeing as reflections of themselves within the media? In particular for this edited volume, we want to know what does representation of African Americans on television look like in regard to careers and thus the lifestyles that such careers offer?

In his 1903 text, *The Souls of Black Folk*, W.E.B. DuBois introduced a concept commonly referred to as double consciousness, and a concept continually needed to understand the ways in which Black people live in the U.S. It is also a concept for readers of this text to be better able to understand why representation, even on scripted television, matters.

> It is a peculiar sensation, this double consciousness, this sense of always looking at one's self through the eyes of others, of measuring one's soul by the tape of a world that looks on in amused contempt and pity. One ever feels his two-ness—an American, a Negro; two souls, two thoughts, two unreconciled strivings; two warring ideals in one dark body, whose dogged strength alone keeps it from being torn asunder [DuBois, 1994, p. 2].

If most of the representation of African Americans on scripted TV showcases criminality, poverty and ignorance, it once again creates an internal fight for Black viewers wondering, "why don't the lawyers, the wealthy, and the educated characters look like me?" DuBois perhaps would share the recognition that one must recognize those who create the television we watch, and how those who create it view Black people in the U.S. The negative stereotypes of African Americans on scripted television came from and often continue to come from white writers, producers, and directors, who, under the American socialization of what it means to be Black, portray African Americans in ways that white America, dominant America, expect to see them. In a way, showcasing African Americans as professionals on TV is unexpected. Black viewers are seeing themselves through the eyes of the other. And seeing oneself on television can have an impact on the viewer; this has been operationalized by the cultivation theory originated by George Gerbner.

Cultivation theory explores the effects of long-term television viewing. "The theory proposes that the danger of television lies in its ability to shape not a particular view point about one specific issue but in its ability to shape people's moral values and general beliefs about the world" (Mosharafa, 2015, p. 23). Thus, what you see on television impacts how you view the world. When 88 percent of all Americans were found to have watched live or scripted television in 2018, what is shared on television, based on cultivation theory, can have an impact on our real-world interactions and understandings (The Nielsen Company, p. 3). "And what the viewer sees on the screen becomes the basis of a mental image that the individual forms about the social practical status of values, population characteristics, and the various cultural standards common by the society's classes, categories, and individuals" (Mosharafa, p. 23). Hence, the lack of representation of Black professionals on TV does align with the actual numbers that place whites as the numerical dominant, but the amount of actual representation of Black professionals on TV is not aligned. And in understanding double consciousness, those few representations of Black professionals can also be harmful to viewers, as cultivation theory would attest, because when created by white writers, producers, and directors, such Black professionalisms are created in a white dominant narrative of what professionalism is.

Representation of Black people in professionalized spaces on TV is important. Nevertheless, simply having a Black actor in a white envisioned role is not enough for the representation not to create harm. Such representation does break the overrepresentation of Black people in criminal, impoverished, and uneducated narratives, but the professional narratives often place Black bodies in white-defined professional roles. Only the African American was "born with a veil, and gifted with second-sight in this American world—a world which yields him no true self-consciousness, but only lets him see himself through the revelation of the other world" (DuBois, 1994, p. 2). African American writers, producers, and directors are the ones with this second sight, who understand what it means to be both Black and American and also both Black and professional in this American landscape. Throughout this book you will find elements of recognizing the creators of these series, and how their race and cultural lenses impact the Black representation. This double consciousness also creates a requirement of understanding that professional doesn't look the same for everyone, and thus it must be redefined for Black professionals.

I asked earlier about what one thinks when they hear the word professional. I shared statistics on the dominance of whites in several professions we think of that align with the word professional. Therefore, professional is a socialized American understanding of what professional means or how it is defined. The *Merriam-Webster Dictionary* supported me in deconstructing how definitions are often altered to fit the needs and desires of a society. I wish to reveal some of those understandings.

First, I wish to deconstruct the *Merriam-Webster Dictionary* definition of **profession**: "a: a calling requiring specialized knowledge and often long and intensive academic preparation [and] b: a principal calling, vocation, or employment." It is definition *a* which often one resigns to when asked perhaps what their future profession will be, yet it is definition *b* which reminds us that all work is a profession. The more American nuanced way of defining professional aligns mostly with definition *a* of profession. This leads to the discussion of the definition of **professional**: Under the first set of definitions it states "a: of, relating to, or characteristic of a profession

[and] b: engaged in one of the learned professions [and] c: characterized by or conforming to the technical or ethical standards of a profession" (Merriam-Webster, Inc.). It relies on the foundational word profession and its definition. It is the second definition of professional that strikes of major importance for the focus of this volume. **Professional** is "exhibiting a courteous, conscientious, and generally businesslike manner in the workplace" (Merriam-Webster, Inc.). Each of these requirements have their own dictionary definitions as well, but we return to the question: who defines them? Beyond a dictionary definition how does our society showcase such definitions? The answer: most often through the lens of a white dominant society. Thus, to be professional aligns with being courteous in a way that the dominant society defines as such, and the same applies to how "businesslike" is defined in a workplace. When dominant white society defines these terms it leaves out the cultural understandings of people of color. Throughout the essays of this volume you will find commentary that discusses juxtapositions of how dominant white society views definitions compared to the cultural views of African Americans in particular.

The final term related to profession that I wish to deconstruct is **professionalism**: "the conduct, aims, or qualities that characterize or mark a profession or a professional person" (Merriam-Webster, Inc.). It is in this term that I find space for Blackness to be a part of the definition of conduct and qualities of a professional person. This is why this book is focused on using the term of professionalisms, with an *s* to stipulate the ways in which no one definition can define all the ways in which someone can be a professional, or what a profession should look like. This also calls to television producers to not simply assign a Black actor as a white character, but to recognize that to be Black and a doctor looks different than being a white doctor, and so forth. In fact, doctor does not need to have the adjective of white before it for it to be defined in a way that white dominant society associates as being a doctor. But Black as an adjective expresses the underlying issues of being a Black person in the U.S., which alters a Black doctor's interactions with their profession. And so, I propose we add to this terminology of professionalisms with Black-collar. There's a fictitious scene in the film adaptation of *The Autobiography of Malcolm X* that showcases Malcolm learning the roots of words, and language, and in turn the roots of self-hate from which Black people suffer. In the film he reads the words *Black* and *white* from the dictionary and recognizes the association of light and purity with white and dark and evil with Black, and he recognizes such an association in the American mind that to be Black is to be a problem, and to be white is right (Lee, 1992). Such definitions reside in the same dictionary I used for the words I have begun to deconstruct in this text. Upon looking up definitions of the categories of types of professions, blue-collar and white-collar being most recognized, I found a situation similar to the one Malcolm X had. White-collar is the preferred category of profession, once again aligning white with something more desired. Even though the scene in the film *Malcolm X* was created to perhaps condense the extensive learning that Malcolm X experienced while in prison, it speaks to the realities of his ideologies that he shared as a public voice for racial justice. "This religion [Christianity] taught the 'Negro' that Black was a curse. It taught him to hate everything Black, including himself. It taught him that everything white was good, to be admired, respected and loved" (X & Haley, 1965, p. 164). The reality is, Malcolm X did spend a great amount of time with the dictionary while he was imprisoned, and as one reflects back on his language and use of specific words, one is made aware of his radical desire to redefine them. Also, one is made aware of his radical desire for Black people to also redefine the words that define them. Applying Malcolm and DuBois' guidance, this volume redefines what professional is and highlights how television has helped in this redefining or has continued to suppress such a necessity.

In defining blue-collar, white-collar, pink-collar, and green-collar, I looked to a source with more historical insight and socialization within U.S. society, a reference volume. In the *Dictionary of Human Resources Management*, **blue-collar** is defined as:

> a worker engaged in manual work, who by tradition wore blue overalls to a job in a factory. Blue-collar workers can be unskilled, semi-skilled, or skilled but they have in common their experience of working with their hands in an industrial enterprise. Blue-collar workers once formed the core of the traditional working class, but they have declined sharply as a percentage of the workforce as a result of the shift towards service-based employment [Heery & Noon, 2017].

It is the history of the blue overalls that created its associated title, and clothing is thus what established both blue- and white-collar workers. **White-collar** is defined as:

> a worker who traditionally wears a collar and tie to work and is engaged in non-manual work as a clerk, sales assistant, technician, manager, or professional. By tradition, white-collar workers were relatively privileged ... were paid a salary, rather than an hourly or weekly wage, and received an occupational pension and other fringe benefits. In many countries, they have their own trade unions, known as white-collar unions. Today, in post-industrial economies, like Britain or the USA, the majority of employees are engaged in white-collar work [Heery & Noon].

This reference volume was published in 2017, and it speaks to the realities that most Americans work in white-collar professions, yet does society know this? It was this reality that defining a job by white- or blue-collar is not so Black and white, meaning that our socialization in society does not tell us that people who help us in a clothing store are a part of the white-collar profession. Television definitely does not tell us that retail workers are white-collar professionals. Sales assistants and clerks are often shown as jobs the teenage daughter or son on a TV series will get as their first job, a job with no skill and thus not white-collar. As this book began to come together, it was imperative to defer from using blue-collar and white-collar to categorize careers, and to be careful of associating professional with either of those categories, because it is no longer Black and white as it was when the terms were first created and defined. Definitions alter, and often new terms are made to compensate for societal changes.

The realization that as society alters so, too, do the terms we use to define it, centers the importance on creating terms for specific groups of people, based on gender, race, and area of focus, to define the type of professions/careers they are perhaps more likely to have, or the ways in which they must manage their existence within them. **Pink-collar** most aligns with the demographic aspect of my proposed term Black-collar.

> [Pink-collar] is a journalistic term for women workers engaged in sales, clerical, secretarial, and other forms of office-based work. Pink-collar workers comprise a very large proportion of the modern workforce as a result of the feminization of paid employment and the shift towards a service-based economy [Heery & Noon].

Feminization was the influx of women in traditionally male dominated occupations. I would say what is missing from this definition resides in the Merriam-Webster definition which states, "of, relating to, or constituting a class of employees in occupations (such as nursing and clerical jobs) traditionally held by women." The word *pink* within the U.S. has consistently been associated as feminine, so the term aligns with gender. To continue to set the precedence for such an identifier as Black-collar, the term green-collar evolved as society saw a need for work focused on placing the earth as central in its concerns. Green-collar jobs relate to or involve "actions for protecting the natural environment" (Merriam-Webster, Inc.). And so, I propose Black-collar.

The clear-cut division of blue- and white-collar has blurred, where there are more possibilities of such lines crossing, or even being inappropriately categorized. Is a doctor's coat, or a nurse's scrubs not a uniform? Is a bullet proof vest on a detective not protective clothing? I have guided and entitled this edited book to incorporate the realization that what will be covered is not simply white-collar which many identify with the term "professionals," more colloquially. Rather, there are various professions, ones that require intensive academic preparation, and ones that are someone's calling, vocation, or employment. There are various concepts of how one can act in a professional manner, and in the case of African Americans, such concepts are defined by a white majority often pushing out any opportunity for Black people to present their own ways of professionalism. I present a definition of Black-collar. As the creation of green-collar alludes to a new type of environmental work, and the patriarchal creation of pink-collar careers are associated with women and femininity, I present the term Black-collar to associate with the various aspects of Black people in the work place, but particularly within careers that require training, a particular set of skills, yet not necessarily academic in nature. I also include the concept of salaried positions with benefits and more flexibility to be supportive to their families, with less chance of financial loss. The definition of blue-collar experiences is often active for Black people in white-collar careers. Blue-collar workers are defined as having certain characteristics like "having, showing, or appealing to unpretentious or unsophisticated tastes" and being "dependable and hard-working rather than showy or spectacular" (Merriam-Webster, Inc.). This edited volume showcases how blue-collar characteristics are consistently fueling the ways in which African Americans present themselves in professional spaces and as they discuss their professional experiences. African Americans are not quite yet able to be removed from ideologies of blue-collar experiences, and are not fully accepted in "white-collar spaces," and thus in their careers they experience **Black-collar professionalism**: the conduct, aims, or qualities that characterize a Black person's experience in American traditionally identified professional, and often white-collar, work environments, alongside their work ethics often aligned with traditionally defined blue-collar ideologies.

Black-collar television showcases the realities of African Americans via their characterizations through scripted roles, in careers that are neither easily defined as blue-collar or white-collar but are indeed their occupations, and these series define African American interaction realities within U.S. society, and thus showcases their professionalisms. This volume has a total of 17 essays, each focusing on one or several television series spanning from the 1990s until today. These series are highlighted because they portray the multilayers of what it means to be Black and working in the U.S. These series especially focus on Black characters with careers that are most likely salaried with benefits, and a more structured work schedule. However, these series also showcase Black characters whose careers are their calling, and often means they are entrepreneurs, and a well-defined schedule is not possible. Most importantly, these essays reveal the intricacies of being both Black and a professional, as can only be defined by the histories of African Americans in the U.S. which creates a Black-collar worker who can never deny their skin color in occupations where their skin means they are not dominant in defining what that occupation must look like. These essays break down what is real for Black characters and Black viewers who strive to love to go to work, but often do not—they are working while Black.

The first essay of this volume was written by me, LaToya T. Brackett. Entitled "Battling Impostor Syndrome: Authenticity, Urban Realities and the Black Bourgeoisie in *The Fresh Prince of Bel-Air*," this essay explores the battle of two Black realities on a popular 1990s series. *The Fresh Prince of Bel-Air* (1990–1996) was an NBC family sitcom that showcased the reconnection of Will (Will Smith) with his aunt, uncle, and cousins in Bel-Air, California. Will's mother forced him to go live with the Bankses to ensure his safety after an altercation in his West Philadelphia neighborhood. The plot line of the series is nicely summed up in the theme song. What is not summed up in the theme song is the showcase of a mash up between urban Black folks, Will, and the Black bourgeoisie, the Bankses. It is clear, particularly to Black audiences, that Will brings a forgotten reality of being from the streets to the Banks' household, while the Bankses perform a glimpse at blending into a predominantly white and wealthy neighborhood as a Black upper-class family. The idea of impostor syndrome relates to one feeling inadequate in their ability to meet the requirements of the high-level environment they are maneuvering, despite the ability to do so. I posit that in *The Fresh Prince* there were two issues of impostor syndrome happening in this series, one that Will was managing and another that the Bankses were managing. This essay focuses on analyzing the ways that impostor syndrome manifests primarily for Will and Uncle Phil (James Avery). In discussing their struggles, I first give foundational understandings of impostor syndrome, the Black bourgeoisie, African American language, code-switching, selling-out, and acting white. The essay concludes with a discussion of how Blackness unites, because despite Will and Phil's differences they both have a consistent battle of being Black in America.

In "ABC's *Black-ish*: A Critical Analysis of the Black Professional Parent," Mia L. Anderson focuses on the narratives of Black parents with successful careers. Through the years, the Black professional has been exhibited to mass audiences through the television sitcom. These portrayals, whether accurate or false, can contribute to audience beliefs about particular races or groups of people. As Cranmer and Harris (2015) asserted, "media has long been regarded as influential in shaping and altering individuals' perceptions of race and interracial interactions" (p. 153). Anderson's essay seeks to share insight into the image of Black parents with flourishing careers on *Black-ish*. The essay illuminates the evolution of the Black working couple on primetime television. Through analysis of four seasons of *Black-ish*, Anderson delves into the presentation of characters Andre (Anthony Anderson) and Rainbow (Tracee Ellis Ross) Johnson as they navigate work-life balance in a largely non–Black environment.

In "Black Brotherhood, Professionalism and Entrepreneurship as Depicted in *Martin*, *The Wayans Bros.* and *Malcolm & Eddie*," David

Stamps reflects on what it means to be brothers, even if not by blood. He explores both fictive kin relationships and familial relationships of Black men who are entrepreneurs or owners of their work in three sitcoms. Stamps' essay analyzes media characterizations of professional Black men and their male-centered friendships in three '90s situational comedies (sitcoms). These portrayals illustrate a range of media depictions of Black men as entrepreneurs, as well as representations of affection across generations, siblings, friends, and roommates. These scripted programs acknowledge Black men as working professionals and business owners, and the narratives presented here counter the overwhelming stereotypical media depictions of Black men as deviant, out of work, and as societal threats. Considering these overwhelming negative stereotypes, the acknowledgment of positive media representations of Black men in entertainment television is crucial. This recognition is even more imperative, considering the pervasive and numerous social stigmas and negative stereotypes that Black men face in society.

In the next essay, "'I'm glad I got my girls': Black Women, Working, Friending and Seeking Love in Fox's *Living Single*," I provide another analysis of a popular sitcom. When that memorable theme song kicked into gear, it hit many Black women like it was their personal anthem, for them and their crew. It spoke to the lives they may have already had, desired to have, or were trying to return to—Black women and men working, friending, and seeking positive romantic relationships. A sitcom of the 1990s, *Living Single* was ground-breaking for Black women narratives on prime-time television, and for laying a foundation for numerous television series to follow. *Living Single* showed Black people working across all levels of professions, but what was especially ground-breaking were the careers of Khadijah James (Queen Latifah), entrepreneur, editor, and publisher of an urban community focused magazine; Maxine "Max" Shaw (Erika Alexander), attorney at a major law firm and later the public defender's office; and Kyle Barker (T.C. Carson), a stock broker who continually grew in his career to the peak of an international job offer and acceptance. This essay explores these three main characters and discusses major moments in their careers and how such moments interacted with their Black, professional and single lives. Between these three, viewers saw the costs and benefits of their successful careers. Additionally, there is discussion of how *Living Single* did a particularly solid job at revealing the multiple layers to the decisions made by the characters, and how they engaged with these major moments in relation to their Black pride, professional exceptionalism, and desire for love.

In "Tackling Stereotypes: Portrayals of Black NFL Athletes on The CW's *The Game* and HBO's *Ballers*," Darnel Degand focuses on the world of professional athletes, from behind the scenes to on screen portrayals. Black NFL players are simultaneously stereotyped as dumb jocks (i.e., unintelligent athletes) and Black bucks (i.e., violent, unintelligent, over-sexed Black men who lust after white women). Degand's essay examines the source of these prejudicial assumptions. The first half uses cultivation theory to explain society's influences on media messages about Black men and football. The second half discusses how the first seasons of *The Game* (2006–2015) and *Ballers* (2015–2019) push back on extreme stereotypes by representing Black NFL players as multidimensional professionals who engage in both positive and negative behaviors.

In "#IamMaryJane: Blackness, Womanhood and Professionalism in BET's *Being Mary Jane*," Malika T. Butler and Kristal Moore Clemons share how a series focused on a Black career woman created real world interaction between Black viewers. The hashtag in their title reflects the ways in which this particular series engaged audiences so much so that a Twitter reference was created. *Being Mary Jane* was a popular television series not only for the Black Entertainment Television (BET) network, but for African American women who saw their lives mirrored in Mary Jane (Gabrielle Union), her family, friends and coworkers. *Being Mary Jane* was centered around the home and romantic life of a network television news anchor. The show invoked captivating storytelling, richly complex characters, and a kind of social and political commentary that mirrored the contemporary social and political landscape of the time. Butler and Clemons' essay provides an analysis of the show and more specifically insight into its main character, Mary Jane Paul. By using Black feminist theory (BFT), the authors describe how the show highlighted a successful Black woman maneuvering the critical intersections of her identity in the new millennium. Additionally, Butler and Clemons seek to use BFT as a lens to understand how the show oscillates between being a space of entertainment and a source of knowledge production and representation.

In "Capital Codes and Money Moves: The Ironies of Professionalism in *Empire*," Natalie J. Graham explores the ruthless world of a music mogul Black family, with dreams of Black ownership within an industry that flourishes off of the cultural creations of their own people. Co-creators Lee Daniels and Danny Strong sent shockwaves through the television industry with their megahit *Empire* (2015–2020). In this world of heightened drama, violence, and romance, characters grapple with an ever-shifting landscape of professional expectations in a music industry context where savagery is often imagined as a brutal and necessary pathway to Black freedom and power. This "get rich or die trying" ethos reinforces and normalizes brutalization of Black people. Like capitalism in the U.S., legacies of violence and threat are necessary to maintain the precarious professional systems of exploitation and oppression. Further, "professional" behavior and spaces are coded as white, where ironically, oppressive, racist and sexist violence is often understated or ignored. This definition of corporate professionalism stands in opposition to the show's figuring of violence as a central element of Black identity (i.e., hood, street, or real). Artists are not spared in this conception of authenticity. To maintain authenticity as an artist, musicians often must tap into a well of past and present pain. Thus, especially in the show's first three seasons, Black trauma is tied to Black authenticity and Black authenticity is tied to unprofessionalism.

In "Shonda Rhimes' *Grey's Anatomy* and *My Year of Saying Yes to Everything*," Adelina Mbinjama-Gamatham reveals the work of a Black female television series creator and how it influences one of her most prominent Black female characters on her first show to gain extensive recognition for its ability to showcase complex diverse roles. Mbinjama-Gamatham's essay is an interpretation of Shonda Rhimes' transformational work through her television series, *Grey's Anatomy* (2005–present) and how it challenges negative and stereotypical portrayals of Black women in the media. Rhimes does this by representing African American women as professionals. The aim of Mbinjama-Gamatham's essay is to discuss how *Grey's Anatomy* portrays African American women within the context of their profession as medical doctors. The essay reflects on Rhimes as the producer of the television series and why it is of importance to showcase Black female characters in a professional context. *Grey's Anatomy* suggests many politics of representation of Black women through the characterization of Dr. Miranda Bailey (Chandra Wilson), who is the focus of this essay. This essay reads Bailey as a symbolic echo of Rhimes' own professional work and personal life, by referring to Rhimes' TED X Talk *My Year of Saying Yes to Everything* (2016) based on her book, *Year of Yes* (2015). The main discussion points include conformity and Rhimes' ridding of the fear that haunts her throughout her professional career; a brief discussion on Black feminism, the significance of "the Hum" and the concept of belonging. Through the lens of the African Philosophy of "Ubuntu," it is evident that remaining true to oneself is a pivotal part of Rhimes' transformational work, which resonates with most Black professional women. Through an analysis of the character Bailey, Mbinjama-Gamatham's essay also explores the challenges that Black women experience in the workplace, particularly those related to professional conduct and sexuality. The essay concludes by emphasizing the global importance of Rhimes' television series, particularly for Africans in the Global South, with a personal vignette from Mbinjama-Gamatham herself—a Black South African woman who recognizes that Rhimes' *Grey's Anatomy*, as well as her professional work and personal life, serve to validate Black women as capable and hard-working professionals.

In "Sapphires with Stethoscopes: Black Women Practicing Medicine on Television," Phokeng Motsoasele Dailey reminds readers of the intricacies of stereotypes of Black women that have prevailed even into contemporary television. Mass communication scholars overwhelmingly agree that our experience with media is a major way that we acquire knowledge about the world and that television is a dominant societal storyteller. This mediated acquisition of knowledge has attitudinal and behavioral consequences. One area of focus has been on ways TV shows influence our social reality perception of occupational roles. In this essay, depictions of Black female medical professionals are examined from this perspective. The essay begins with a focus on individual characteristics of medical professionals on TV (how things are) and how those characteristics function in a fictional medical setting (how things work). This is contrasted with historical and contemporary media portrayals of Black female characters generally and Black women medical professional characters specifically. To do this, the discussion centers on three successful medical entertainment TV shows: *ER*, *Private Practice*, and *Hawthorne*, all of which feature Black women medical professional characters of varying professional rank and medical specialty. The characters also differ in terms of how central they are to the overall plot of each TV series. Dailey describes how things are and how things work for female Black medical professionals on TV and concludes by suggesting ways in which these two types of stories inform how Black women navigate professional spaces and real-life expectations of audience members (and what to do about them).

In "The Curious Case of the Black Male Doctor: Character Actualization and Moderate Blackness of *ER*'s Peter Benton," I discuss how the identity of the writer impacts how developed a Black character is on a series, especially in white dominated careers. Dr. Peter Benton (Eriq La Salle) on the NBC series *ER* (1994–2009), was a curious character, because no matter the various attempts throughout the series to unveil what defined his realities, so much about why he was the way he was, was never actualized. Benton was underdeveloped, and often oversimplified, and I posit it was due to the lens from which his character was written—a white lens. Without intricate details of Black experiences, writing a complex Black character often entails stereotypes and white understandings of Blackness, or simply placing a Black actor into a role written for a white doctor. This essay discusses this curious case of Dr. Benton through the lens of a concept known as moderate Blackness, coined by scholar Amy Wilkins in 2012, and the concept of character actualization. In assessing moments in the series when Benton fulfilled aspects of moderate Blackness, and storylines that were meant to make his character more actualized, it is shown how, despite later attempts to better actualize Benton, the white lens of the writers and producers were unable to do so due to the assumption that most of their understanding of Black professional men is aligned with moderate Blackness. This essay explores what is required to write Black stories, and the struggle of Black Americans to hide their truths behind a veil, especially in professional settings.

In "Anti-Blackness and Colorblindness in Post-Cosby Sitcoms: Likeable Black Teachers, Exceptional Black Students but/and *Everybody Hates Chris*," Amir Asim Gilmore digs deep in his use of Black critical race theory to deconstruct the portrayal of education in sitcoms in juxtaposition to one of the most prominent series. While television shows might be entertaining to some, Black audiences lack television shows that represent the plurality of their lived experiences. Gilmore's essay examines how the devaluation and stereotyping of Black people is not just a phenomenon of the past, but an enduring mark of the present by analyzing Black education-based sitcoms. In United States' popular culture, Black sitcoms like *The Cosby Show* are significant social and cultural influencers that have been widely criticized for their representations of Black people because their representations have the potential to shape racist public perceptions, attitudes, and stereotypes that can be potentially detrimental to Black people. By utilizing Black critical race theory (BlackCrit), Gilmore's essay interrogates instances and notions of anti–Blackness and color-blindness in post–Cosby sitcoms such as *The Steve Harvey Show*, *Hanging with Mr. Cooper*, *Smart Guy*, and *Everybody Hates Chris*. Through a BlackCrit analysis, his essay also shows how these Black education-based sitcoms embody anti–Black representations of Black male media-teachers and students but also shaped the public perception of Black children and the profession of Black education.

In "'*Dear White People*: It truly is *A Different World*': Representations of Black Male Faculty in Television Series," Dominick N. Quinney connects the realities of Black faculty in higher education with the representations of such on three series that focus solely on the college experience. What is unique about his essay is the time distance across these shows, the platforms they were/are on, the demographic of the colleges, and yet the ways in which representation is similar. The timeline for representations of Black men in their respective roles within higher education has grown and evolved over time. The same can be said for Black men's representations in professional roles on television, with a particular evolution of their roles and duties in higher education narratives. Quinney's essay explores the roles of three Black men in TV series focused on higher education: Colonel Bradford Taylor (Glenn Turman) from NBC's *A Different World*, Dean Walter Fairbanks (Obba Babatunde) from Netflix's *Dear White People*, and Professor Charlie Telphy (Deon Cole) from Freeform's *Grown-ish*. Quinney discusses student development through mentorship, drawing upon scenes and examples from each show, the campus experiences, and the relationships Black male faculty and staff had with students. For these Black characters, both faculty, staff and students, being Black on campus means it truly is a different world.

In "Not So Black and White: Race, Police and Double Standards in *The Shield*," Saravanan Mani grapples with the representations of Black law enforcement officers as both ethical and those pushed to be unethical in the fight for justice. *The Shield* (FX, 2002–2008) features a violent world where corrupt cops use unethical policing methods in the face of overwhelming law and order problems in the city of Los Angeles. The show focuses on an all-white Strike Team's brutal method in their pursuit of "justice" at whatever cost. The team's corrupt leader, Vic Mackey (Michael Chiklis) does not operate within the limits of police procedure and he justifies his underhanded methods by his effective results. The thrilling narration and the fast-paced action align viewers to enjoy the illegal actions of the Strike Team. Initially, the show's two prominently featured African American characters—the Internal Affairs Lieutenant Jon Kavanaugh (Forest Whitaker) and detective Claudette Wyms (CCH Pounder)—seem to be recycled versions of popular Black stereotypes, who simply reaffirm the power given to the white characters. However, by positioning Kavanaugh and Wyms against the Strike Team, the show questions viewers' alignment with unlawful police methods. Kavanaugh demonstrates the underlying problems with Mackey's actions by adopting them in his attempts to bring down the Strike Team. The contrasting images of morally compromised police officers reveal the double standards of ethics enforced for African American police officers. Wyms on the other hand, rises above the shady practices in day-to-day policing and pursues the course of justice without compromising her integrity. In this way, the professional ethics of these two characters allow them to overcome simplistic and stereotypical portrayals that have long since plagued African American police officers in popular culture.

In the next essay, "Mammies, Jemimas, Jezebels and Sapphires: Deconstructing Representations of Black Women Coroners on Crime Dramas," Tammie Jenkins takes us back into the continued prevalence of Black women stereotypes on the small screen. Focusing in on crime dramas reveals a consistent set of narratives for what Black women medical examiners must portray when it comes to this set of television representations. Medical examiners on popular television shows such as *Quincy*

(1976–1983), *CSI* (2000–2015), and *Psych* (2006–2014) were typically portrayed by white men working with law enforcement officers to solve crimes. The twenty-first century saw a change in these narratives as Black women characters on *Bones, Law & Order: Special Victims Unit*, and *CSI: Miami* began entering spaces once occupied by white men and women. These characters Dr. Camille "Cam" Saroyan (Tamara Taylor) of *Bones*, Dr. Melinda Warner (Tamara Tunie) of *Law & Order: SVU*, and Dr. Alexx Woods (Khandi Alexander) of *CSI: Miami*, respectively, were perceived by peers as professional in reference to their job performance. However, they were only humanized when their family life (e.g., marriage, motherhood, intimate relationships) were included in their show's plot. Jenkins' essay examines how the complex role of medical examiner on crime dramas, with a focus on Fox's *Bones*, is complicated by stereotypical representations derived from larger societal discourses of Black womanhood. Relevant examples from *Bones, Law & Order: Special Victims Unit*, and *CSI: Miami* are used to compare how Black women medical examiners are portrayed professionally and humanely. Jenkins uses intersectionality theory to demonstrate how the relationship between popular stereotypical representations are used to create Black female medical examiners in the twenty-first century. Additionally, she uses narrative analysis to trace the underpinning stereotypes that are embedded and rejected throughout the series by these Black female characters. In Jenkins' essay, the following guiding questions are employed: What stereotypical representations are used to portray Black women as medical examiners? How is Dr. Saroyan's character marginalized in the show's storylines? In what ways is this character progressive or regressive in comparison to similar characters on other crime dramas?

In "Black Woman: High-Powered but Not Balanced in Shondaland," Adelina Mbinjama-Gamatham and Eleda Mbinjama focus in on a Black female lawyer and professor who is working hard to help those hurt by the law and yet at times also breaks the law herself. These authors analyze the woman behind the career and the vulnerability her high-powered outside unveils to the audience as a not so put together woman. Mbinjama-Gamatham and Mbinjama's essay explores Black women lead characters, and representations of their high-powered careers and unbalanced lives in two television series produced by Shonda Rhimes. The discussion focuses primarily on Annalise Keating (Viola Davis) in *How to Get Away with Murder* (2014–2020) and makes reference to Olivia Pope (Kerry Washington) in *Scandal* (2012–2018). Both women are used to tell stories of Black womanhood and the personal journey they undergo in unraveling and unmasking parts of themselves in order to balance their professional and personal lives. It also discusses how the lead actresses, as Black women professionals, helped generate trending topics via Black

Twitter as episodes aired on American television, in order to build a community of active consumers. The support from its audience reinforces the significant contribution Rhimes has made to popular culture by allowing audiences to engage with, and to critique, how Black women characters are represented on television shows.

In "Awkward and Black: Redefining Representations of Black Women on *The Misadventures of Awkward Black Girl* and *Insecure*," Regina M. Duthely delivers a narrative that shares situations within the scripted television series, but also aspects of the Black woman creator and her journey to tell such stories. Duthely's essay examines the ways that Issa Rae's *The Misadventures of Awkward Black Girl* and *Insecure* present alternative representations of Black professional womanhood. Both series have created room for a Black woman professional that is flawed and nuanced in ways that are not always seen in mainstream media. Using Gwendolyn Pough's theory of wreck, Duthely argues that Rae's work brings wreck to the public sphere and disrupts representations of Black professional womanhood in the media landscape both through her presence as a television executive, as well as through the characters she creates on her shows.

Finalizing this volume is "Behind Their Masks: Complex Black Superheroes on the Small Screen," in which Christopher Alanye Covington explores the world of comic books and superheroes and the ways in which this make-believe space provided narratives of highly educated and gifted Black characters when others did not. In almost any family, group of friends, set of coworkers, or team, each person has a role. When it comes to the superhero genre of television, this is no different for Black characters. In Covington's essay you will learn of the ways Black characters can also fall into four categories: the STEM, Moral Compass, Conflicted Hero, or Renaissance Man. His essay reviews the beginnings of Black superheroes, from when they were a rarity only to be seen in comic books in the late 1960s to how far they have come today. Through the years, these characters have evolved as their adaptations extend across mediums such as television, film, and now streaming platforms. With these adaptations Black superheroes and characters are now being seen more often as recurring supporting roles and even as leading roles. Covington's essay reviews several shows that had Black superhero characters, with a focus on analyzing two shows more closely in relation to character roles and Black representation in the superhero genre: *Luke Cage* and *Black Lightning*.

This edited volume shares only a selection of the representation of how Black characters on television have showcased what being Black and professional can look like. This is not all of it: this is some of it, with the purpose of bringing to the viewers' attention that even if the career of a character is not central to the plot line, their profession defines their inter-actions. And such ways in which Black people manage their professional lives on TV is Black-collar television.

NOTES

1. Throughout this volume the editor and contributors capitalize Black and lowercase white in the tradition of the Black press, with the intent of centering truths of Black people. Additionally, in recognizing the ethnic group it references.

2. Throughout this volume the editor and contributing authors speak of African Americans and Blacks interchangeably. With the various series being discussed, they all focus on the narratives of African Americans, those descendants of enslaved Africans brought to the Americas against their will. When referencing Black culture or Black experiences this reflects African American realities. If non–African American Black narratives are to be shared, they would be discussed specifically.

3. The word "American" throughout this volume directly refers to the United States of America, aligning with the African American focus of the text.

REFERENCES

American Bar Association. (2020, May 8). *ABA National Lawyer Population Survey*. Retrieved from American Bar Association: https://www.americanbar.org/content/dam/aba/administrative/market_research/national-lawyer-population-demographics-2009-2019.pdf.

Association of American Medical Colleges. (2020, May 8). *Diversity in Medicine: Facts and Figures 2019*. Retrieved from Association of American Medical Colleges: https://www.aamc.org/data-reports/workforce/interactive-data/figure-18-percentage-all-active-physicians-race/ethnicity-2018.

Crain Communications, Inc. (1991). *Blacks Reveal TV Loyalty, Advertising Age, November 18, 1991*. Retrieved from https://library.uoregon.edu/sites/default/files/data/guides/english/nielsen_ratings.pdf.

DuBois, W. (1994). *The Souls of Black Folk*. New York: Dobbler Publications, Inc.

Greenberg, B. S., & Collette, L. (1997). The Changing Faces on TV: A Demographic Analysis of Network Television's New Seasons, 1966–1992. *Journal of Broadcasting & Electronic Media*, 1.

Heery, E., & Noon, M. (2017). *A Dictionary of Human Resource Management (3 ed.)*. Oxford University Press. Retrieved from https://www-oxfordreference-com.ezproxy.ups.edu:2443/view/10.1093/acref/9780191827822.001.0001/acref-9780191827822.

Lee, S. (Director). (1992). *Malcolm X* [Motion Picture].

Merriam-Webster, Inc. (2020, May 20). Retrieved from Merriam-Webster: https://www.merriam-webster.com/.

Mosharafa, E. (2015). All You Need to Know About: The Cultivation Theory. *Global Journal of Human-Social Science*, 23–37.

National Center for Educational Statistics. (2020, May 8). *Teacher Trends*. Retrieved from National Center for Educational Statistics: https://nces.ed.gov/fastfacts/display.asp?id=28.

The Nielsen Company. (2018). *THE NIELSEN TOTAL AUDIENCE REPORT Q1 2018*. The Nielsen Company. Retrieved from https://www.nielsen.com/wp-content/uploads/sites/3/2019/04/q1-2018-total-audience-report.pdf.

X, M., & Haley, A. (1965). *The Autobiography of Malcolm X*. New York: Grove Press.

PART I

Black Love: Families and Friendships

Battling Impostor Syndrome

Authenticity, Urban Realities and the Black Bourgeoisie in The Fresh Prince of Bel-Air

LaToya T. Brackett

The Fresh Prince of Bel-Air (1990–1996) was an NBC family sitcom that showcased the reconnection of Will (Will Smith) with his aunt, uncle, and cousins in Bel-Air, California. Will's mother forced him to move in with her sister, Vivian Banks (Janet Hubert-Whitten and later Daphne Maxwell Reid) and her husband Philip Banks (James Avery), to ensure Will's safety after an altercation in his West Philadelphia neighborhood. The plot line of the series is nicely summed up in the theme song written and performed by rapper-actor Will Smith. What is not summed up in the theme song is the showcase of a mash up between urban Black folks, Will, and the Black bourgeoisie, the Bankses. Beginning in the pilot episode it is clear, particularly to Black audiences, that Will brings a forgotten reality of being from the streets to the Banks' household, while the Bankses perform a glimpse at blending into a predominantly white and wealthy neighborhood as a Black upper-class family. The idea of impostor syndrome relates to one feeling inadequate in their ability to meet the requirements of the high-level environment they are maneuvering, despite the ability to do so. I posit that in *Fresh Prince* there were two issues of impostor syndrome happening in this series, one that Will was managing and another that the Bankses were managing.

Will's relocation into a lifestyle of the Black bourgeoisie—via the Banks' home—revealed the complications of reconciling being both Black and wealthy through the lenses of the high-class neighborhood of Bel-Air and urban Black experience. The Bankses, particularly Vivian and Philip, are attempting to fulfill the requirements of being upper-class, defined mostly by white upper-class Americans, which includes what they, as the dominant voice in the upper-class, define as the appropriate lifestyle. For both Vivian and Philip this lifestyle is not one they grew up with but is one they work to be accepted into. This is their impostor syndrome struggle; one that is more often demonstrated in media representations of Black people going from rags to riches and their struggle to maintain their status as accepted.

On the other hand, Will's presence in the home of the Bankses has left him with a major decision: leave behind his authentic self to gain acceptance, or remain authentic no matter the costs? Will refuses to be unauthentic, and in his refusal he fights to maintain his status as urban born and raised. In the series it is very clear that Will desires to showcase his "Blackness" by remaining true to his upbringing in an urban and predominantly Black space. The main way in which he does this is with his language. Commonly referred to as African American Language (AAL), Will refuses to change his language in his new Bel-Air communities, whether at home, school, or any outside spaces. For Will it is his struggle to maintain his "Blackness" that aligns with the struggles of impostor syndrome. These juxtaposed impostor syndromes are most commonly showcased when Uncle Phil and Will disagree in how they should present themselves in front of others and in public spaces.

Opposing Realities of Impostor Syndrome in The Fresh Prince

The concept of impostor syndrome originated in relations to high-achieving women in research from 1978, stating that this phenomenon is "used to designate an internal experience of intellectual phoniness" (Clance & Imes, 1978). In using the impostor syndrome, within the present essay, it mostly falls within the scope of phoniness as defined by the community the person wishes to be accepted into. Impostor syndrome often relates to the work environments people must manage. The reality is that for people of color especially, there are more spaces than work that can create internal struggle about one's abilities and thus acceptance. *The Fresh Prince of Bel-Air* centered around the family spaces primarily, but the careers of Phil and Vivian both provided a glimpse into the child-rearing of Black professionals and the ways in which they raised their children to promote certain career and lifestyle expectations. From private school, to extra-curriculars, the goal of Philip and Vivian was to raise children who would have unlimited opportunities. Philip does not so much believe himself to be phony but worries that the social society he is a part of and wishes to continue to be accepted in might see him as phony based on his own upbringing and if his children, including his nephew, showcase any type of behavior not associated with a higher class lifestyle. Will on the other hand cares little about fitting into the higher class, and more about *remembering where he comes from* and not *selling out*.

The Black Bourgeoisie

Aspects of the lifestyles of the Black bourgeoisie align with raising children who have opportunities often unheard of for a majority of Black folks in the United States. The Black bourgeoisie has roots in the era of emancipation when some free Blacks were able to gain economic hold and opportunities in a post slavery U.S. despite continued degradation of African Americans.[1] Aspects of defining the bourgeoisie altered over the generations, from fairer skin being more definitive of status to the more contemporary role of higher education in establishing someone's ability to be a part of this status. Throughout these generations the role of white society has always had a major influence on how Black bourgeoisie is defined (Benjamin, 2008). Today, within African American communities, the characterization of a Black person acting "bougie" often alludes to their attempt to act in a way in which they prioritize things or finances, often aligned with upper-class whiteness.

In *The Fresh Prince,* Will himself calls out the bourgeoisie of the Bankses within the lyrics of the original theme song (the theme song that opens the show is an edited, and abbreviated, version of this original) stating "But wait I hear they're prissy, bourgeois, all that…" (Jones & Smith, 1992). For his definition, calling someone bougie aligns with a type of uppity-ness and pretentiousness, and forgetfulness of their upbringing, and thus this is how I will use this term in this essay. In episode 3, of season 2, "Will Gets a Job" Will is upset that Uncle Phil told him he was just like Carlton (Alfonso Ribeiro) after asking for money for Homecoming. In speaking with the Banks' butler, Geoffrey (Joseph Marcell) who is making Will a sandwich, Will states:

> See man look, I know where I come from man, I'm coming straight out of Philly, and I'm proud of that … could you put that on croissant for me? … look man I haven't changed I'm not gonna change, I'm not down with this Bougie stuff.… Oh my God Uncle Phil is right G, I'm turning into Carlton … aight that's it no more of these sissy sandwiches, no more valet parking, no more of these preppy parties.

Will decides to pay for homecoming on his own by getting a job. He refuses to be seen as "elitist, uppity-acting … [someone] who identif[ies] with European American culture and reject[s] Blacks and Black culture" (Smitherman, 2006, p. 24). In other words, he refuses to be bougie.

African American Language and Code Switching

African American Language is prevalent throughout *The Fresh Prince* because Will maintains his linguistic style despite continual desire by his uncle to alter it. African American scholar, Geneva Smitherman has cultivated major aspects of AAL, and it is her definition that I utilize for this essay.

> Black or African American Language (BL or AAL) is a style of speaking English words with Black flava—with Africanized semantic, grammatical, pronunciation, and rhetorical patterns. AAL comes out of the experience of U.S. slave descendants. This shared experience has resulted in common speaking styles, systematic patterns of grammar, and common language practices in the Black community. Language is a tie that binds. It provides solidarity with your community and gives you a sense of personal identity [Smitherman, 2006, p. 3].

Because AAL is a major part of the cultural experience of African Americans, it is often required to be stifled in spaces with dominant white ideologies. The ways in which African Americans have spoken communally has consistently been dismissed and insulted by linguists, referring to it as "broken English" or "slang" denying the structures and consistencies at work (Smitherman, 2006). To speak AAL is, in the eyes of the white majority, improper English and is to be looked down upon. Many African Americans who have mitigated white spaces throughout their lives, particularly academic spaces, are capable of altering their verbal interactions to fit the desires of their surroundings. This is code switching. In her 2014 article, Jennifer M. Morton defines code switching as the following:

> Code-switching could be characterized as the ability to adapt one's behavior as a response to a change in social context much like bilingual speakers switch languages in response to a change in linguistic context. However, this statement of the ability is too general—every agent has to adapt her behavior in response to the different norms governing the various dimensions of her work, home, and social life. The case of upwardly mobile minorities is interesting because they exhibit an ability to switch between comprehensive and potentially conflicting value systems. Code-switchers appear able to navigate two (or more) distinct communities and reap the benefits of belonging to both [Morton, 2014, p. 259].

African American Language and code switching are realities for the Bankses and for Will in the series. Language is often a tool used to assess someone's abilities when first interacting with them; even Uncle Phil assumes so much about Will because of how Will speaks (Koch, Gross, & Kolts, 2001). Yet, an underrated commentary about *The Fresh Prince of Bel-Air* is the lack of centering Will's intelligence. He is intelligent—if he were not he would not be able to maintain his attendance at private schools. Unfortunately, within parts of the African American community, being smart is not always seen as a wonderful thing but more so as "selling out."

Selling Out and Acting White

When discussing the goals of being educated within the Black community it can often be associated with "selling out," or as Smitherman defines it, someone "who acts on behalf of Whites and compromises the Black community's principles, usually for personal gain" (2006, p. 42). Unfortunately, it often boils down to this: to be smart is not to be Black. In their 1986 article, "Black Students' School Success: Coping with the 'Burden of 'Acting White,'" Signithia Fordham and John Ogbu expressed the theory that Black students underachieve in fear of being seen as acting white. Since this article was published there has been questioning of their theory. Nevertheless, an association between being educated, which in turn often means speaking in Standard White American English, which is not AAL, and "acting white," remains. Whether Black kids specifically underachieve because of potentially being called "white" is not clear. The process of education as an entry into the Black bourgeoisie, often requires leaving one's roots and community behind—selling out. Selling out is something Will has always battled within himself even back in Philadelphia, and showcasing this internal battle revealed to viewers the multilayered experiences within the Black community.

These preceding terms and concepts lay a foundation for a better understanding of the dynamics and the push and pull between bougie and urban African Americans in the series. The remainder of this essay will analyze interactions on the show that reveal components of these concepts to lead to a better understanding of the ways in which this series revealed the multidimensional experiences of African Americans.

To Be Bougie and Black or Urban and Black

Throughout *The Fresh Prince of Bel-Air*, the Bankses are constantly trying to maintain a type of appearance that they see to be befitting of the crowd they are a part of: more wealthy, high-powered folks, who are predominantly white. When Will arrives, the series showcases a consistent back and forth, particularly between he and Uncle Phil to tame Will's behavior to ensure the image of the Banks' family. This is especially seen in the first season as Will's adjustment to the family, space, and customs continually show conflict for himself and the patriarch of the family, Uncle Phil.

It is a battle of impostor syndromes. Phil refuses to have Will or anyone in his family to represent him in a way that aligns with stereotypical associations of African Americans. This means wearing the right clothing, speaking the right way, and behaving appropriately. All of these things are not defined by the way that even Phil was raised but by the upper-class white society he has joined as a high-powered attorney, and he must fit in to maintain his success. Part of fitting into this group is having a family structure and behavior that resembles upper-class white society as well, and Will Smith from West Philadelphia is everything but that. Thus, Phil attempts to support Will in adjusting to his new environment.

On the other side, Will refuses to *sell out* because of his new upper-class environment and his bougie extended family. For Will he never wanted to go to Bel-Air but his mother forced him to with the desire to ensure he was safe. In juxtaposition to Phil, Will is not actively trying to defy anyone but rather refuses to deny his own identity. He however does impose upon his cousins, particularly Ashley (Tatyana Ali), and later little Nicky (Ross Bagley), his urban Black culture of language, dress, and mannerisms. Often, Will outwardly expresses a desire to save his cousins from being far removed from their roots, by introducing them to their culture which has in his view been absent. Unlike his uncle and aunt, Will was not inducted into this higher-class life style over time, and he also was not born into it like his cousins, he was dropped into it. Will must find a middle ground between sinking or swimming, and he manages this by maintaining his style, his language, and his intelligence. There are episodes in which the audience sees that Will is very capable of code switching. The reality is, throughout the series the audience mostly sees his refusal to code switch, to sell out, or to be bougie. And in doing so he is able to maintain his much-desired connection to his community and the mother who raised him.

Uncle Phil's Struggle with Where He Comes From

In episode 4, of season 1, "Not with My Pig, You Don't," Uncle Phil receives an award for his services to Black communities. He announced it to the family with a question: "What is the highest recognition a self-made Black professional can receive? … The Urban Spirit Award." In this moment Phil recounts three major civil rights demonstrations that he was a part of. Additionally, Vivian outlines the scholarships Phil started and the slum lords he fought in the courts. In recognition of this award Phil is the guest of honor at a ceremony and the center of a newspaper article. Phil flies his parents out from North Carolina to attend the event. The internal fight with his identity probably would not have been an issue if it weren't for Will meeting Phil's parents for the first time. Will wanted to know all about his uncle, because his uncle's story was never told to him. But also, Will connected with Phil's mother Hattie (Virginia Capers) more than anyone, because she was authentic in her Blackness as well—she was not urban and Black but country and Black. Granny gushed on her son's accomplishments to Will, stating: "We are real proud of Zeke," but also sharing narratives Phil would have rather remained unheard. Granny's return in future episodes continued her and Will's unique connection of non-bougie culture.

In preparation for the newspaper article, Phil orchestrates what his own children and wife were supposed to say—he does not trust them. He somehow believes that there is only one side of him, not his authentic self, that should be publicly shared. In fact, in hiding behind his professional accolades, the reporter becomes uninterested in writing the article at all. To save the article Will shares with the reporter all the details of Phil's childhood, the details Phil wants no one to know, and at times he perhaps wants to deny. When the article is published Phil is furious, and Will remains proud. When Uncle Phil confronts Will about the article and accuses Will of destroying Phil's image, Will is confused. Granny becomes insulted.

> **PHIL:** Of course you did. (Yelling at Will) Look at that story. I've got to walk into that banquet room tonight, filled with people who are gonna think I'm nothing but a hog-handling hick from Yamicraw. (Granny enters the room)
> **GRANNY:** But that is where you come from, Zeke. (Phil tries to interrupt) What have you got to be ashamed of? We always put food on the table and clothes on your back.
> **PHIL:** Mama, I'm not ashamed. There are just certain aspects of my life I don't wish emphasized.
> **GRANNY:** Where I come from they call that being ashamed…. Mr. Big Shot! (Granny begins to cry and walks out)

At the banquet the familial energy is harsh. Phil attempts to get his mother to forgive him and to enjoy the event, but she is not having it. She outwardly states a desire to fade into the background, and she pushes the envelope by bringing out of her purse home cooked food—food that Phil's colleague and colleague's wife begin to enjoy at this posh event out of a Tupperware container, with no criticism, but rather delight. This kind of juxtaposition of whiteness accepting Black culture is found throughout the series in comedic ways, but often it is upsetting to Philip. This moment is no different. Phil excuses himself and takes a break to the restroom.

In the restroom Will comes to check on his uncle. And in this moment Phil showcases a battle within himself of hiding his past in order to meet the expectations of his current self. Somehow, he sees his humble Black beginnings as unfitting with his current lifestyle and somehow would mean he does not belong. He is battling the feelings of being an impostor, or phony, despite very much being capable. In the moment of a major award he doubts that he is worthy of it, because based on where he comes from it cannot happen. In a moment of reflection with Will, Phil states as he looks at himself in the mirror:

> **PHIL:** I must be kidding myself. I had it all planned out. There was my family all lined up to meet the press. There I was with my perfect image. Philip Banks—pulled himself up from the streets with his own bootstraps. The only problem

was I didn't have it that hard. I had two parents who loved me and were always there for me. Worked hard to make sure I'd have everything they never had.
WILL: Why you worried so much about your image? The truth sounds real good to me.

Phil returns to the banquet and when receiving his award he shifts to his authentic narrative. In this moment, at a high achievement event, Phil pushes back on his belief that the same past that got him there, could somehow demote him. This episode closes with a Black-and-white image of actor James Avery, as a child, and closes with the voice of Granny singing "Wade in the Water," an old Negro spiritual. The closure of the episode alludes to the reminder for Black folks to remember where they came from.

Will's Struggle with Where He Is Going

Despite automatic assumptions that Will would want to fulfill the role of being upper class, and thus bougie, he does not. Rather, he down right refuses to change his language to please a more white upper-class lifestyle. In doing so, he does not attempt to affirm whiteness, but attempts to maintain his "Blackness." In his refusal to code switch into Standard White American English, Will attempts to hold onto his identity from Philadelphia. There are instances within the show that breaks down this desire, one being when he is visited by his friend Ice Tray (Don Cheadle), in which it is revealed that back in Philly, Will was attempting to hide any association to whiteness he may have been perceived as having. In this case it was his academic ability.

In episode 5, of season 1, "Homeboy, Sweet Homeboy," Will gets homesick and his aunt and uncle fly out one of his closest friends from Philly, Ice Tray. This is one of the first times in the series that Will's life in Philly is unpacked further. But it also showcases the fears of Phil and Vivian about their expectations of their children and nephew in regard to who they should be and who they should be with. Upon Tray's arrival Will becomes more animated and louder than he's ever been, and in this moment his family looks on at him and Tray as if they'd never seen such interaction. The most impactful aspect of Tray's visit is the discussion of education—the fact that the Bankses praise it and Tray dismisses it. The discussion begins with Carlton implying "So you're also a disadvantaged, inner-city youth, I hear." Tray responds with dismissal asking Will: "Hey man what's with him?" Will remarks on the lack of Black culture he always critiques of Carlton with, "It's a tan." The conversation switches to discussing the school Will and Tray went to. Tray shares that he "doesn't bother school and it doesn't bother him," also sharing that he has repeated the 10th grade 3 times. Carlton expresses how important school is and Tray asks, "like, who cares?"

As Tray and Will spend time just the two of them their brotherhood is revealed most intimately with the audience. It begins with them remembering the old days and utilizing a nuanced version of a common activity within Black culture—The Dozens.

The Dozens is defined by Smitherman as a "verbal game of talking about someone's mother, using outlandish, highly exaggerated, sometimes sexually loaded, humorous ritualized 'insults'" (Smitherman, 2006, p. 28). Tray and Will swap insults about ladies they had dated, with a PG rating of course, but completely overexaggerated and definitely inaccurate, which is another requirement of playin' The Dozens. As Tray ventures to investigate Will's new bougie environment he tells Will how dope it is. Tray then names expensive decorative items as he picks them up. The last item he picks up is the book *Crime and Punishment* at which point Will speaks up and says:

> **WILL:** They trying to force us to read that at school. I ain't goin' to read it.
>
> **TRAY:** Wait, wait. This is your handwriting. "Intriguing duality"? (Will snatches the book from Tray's hand and throws it on the table) Same old Prince, man. You know when I first met you, you was carrying your books in a pizza box so nobody would know you was studying. (Will attempts to divert the attention from his intelligence, by joking about being bullied for it.) You got a good deal here, homey. Don't blow it.

The simple statement of "don't blow it" was a moment of validation for Will and yet a quick moment, but ever so powerful to be showcased on television. The support of a loved one who has no opportunities but still cheers for someone else. Unfortunately, Will's validation and joy from Tray's visit was short-lived after Aunt Viv finds out that her daughter, Hilary (Karyn Parsons) falls for Tray romantically.

Vivian is highly upset, and out of character, as she is usually the one that supports Will and his friends, when Uncle Phil does not. But she yells at Hilary about ruining her life after she and Tray joke that they got married. Will is not amused, but rather especially hurt. Vivian tries to make up with Will but reiterates that Tray is not someone she'd want her daughter to be with, nor her nephew to respect.

> **VIVIAN:** No, you listen to me. Now, I can see why you like Ice Tray. He's a lot of fun. Everything's a joke to him—school, work, people. He doesn't care about anything.
>
> **WILL:** Yeah, well he always managed to care about me. (Vivian reiterates Tray's lack of caring) You weren't there.... When I was in 7th grade every time I'd try to bring books home from school, the kids would jump me, so Tray started

walking me home and if he hadn't been there to throw those punches and help me jump those fences, then maybe I wouldn't be here.

Once again Will stands up for himself, and remains authentic to his story, and has to push one of his relatives to reexamine their assumptions about those who don't live like them, sound like them, or dress like them. In telling his story to Aunt Viv Will reveals how without Tray, Will wouldn't be able to manage academically in the educational spaces deemed appropriate for the Bankses. And in Tray's extreme care for Will, Tray received no care from others for himself. Instead of blaming Tray for not caring for his own education and future professions, Will reminds Aunt Viv that it could happen to anyone. For Will education was something he desired back in Philly but literally had to fight for. Being in Bel-Air means education is not simply an accessible option but a requirement. Will hides his education from Tray, but also knows that Tray would push Will to succeed rather than to suppress his abilities. The same as what his aunt and uncle would do for him.

Nevertheless, Will hid from being associated with education back in Philly and in Bel-Air he also does not flaunt his abilities. His cousin Carlton wants nothing more than to be extremely smart, and the highest marked, even competing with Will and flaunting his success in Will's face. In episode 4, of season 2, "PSAT Pstory" when Will gets a higher score on the PSAT test than Carlton, Carlton doesn't know what to do with himself, yet Will tries to support his cousin and even downplay his own accomplishments. To Will education is important but not a tool to divide folks; he had seen that too much in his own community. Will refuses to sell out, he refuses to be defined as bougie, he rejects the idea that wanting education is "acting White" and thus he simply desires to be Black, educated, and his authentic self.

Concluding Thoughts: When Black Is Black, and Money Doesn't Matter

Despite this back and forth between the Black and bougie and the Black and urban, *The Fresh Prince of Bel-Air* is not centered on that. It is centered on family and the ways all families look different, and have members with different viewpoints and ideologies, but they are family. And in the series there are multiple times in which bougie and urban are reminded that their struggle is the same. Uncle Phil consistently wants to be seen as capable by his white colleagues and friends, but he continually reminds his family of where he came from, and thus where they came from. He has not forgotten, even if Will wishes to tell him so. Will too knows his uncle has not forgotten, perhaps Phil is just determined to ensure the opportunities for his children—including his nephew. Uncle Phil protects his children as any father would and that is made most clear in episode 6, of season 1, "Mistaken Identity," when Carlton and Will are arrested.

The most powerful moment of the "Mistaken Identity" episode, I postulate, is not when Phil and Vivian receive power over the police officers that arrested the boys, but when Carlton and Will are discussing the incident and Carlton is oblivious that the main reason it happened is because they are Black. It is a very powerful moment as Will, who often banters with Carlton all day, simply walks away. Uncle Phil catches Carlton distraught and inquires, and even shares his own interactions with police, and still Carlton is not aware. As much as Phil and Vivian attempt to provide their children with opportunities, they also shelter them from the way the world works. Will often is the one to remind them.

The Fresh Prince of Bel-Air is a series that showcases intimate moments within extended African American families: families layered with economic status differences, behavioral differences, different priorities, and different ways of navigating the U.S. while Black. But no matter the differences showcased, the series comes back to family is family, and no matter one's social status their Blackness will always bind them. So, no matter what impostor syndrome looks like for the Bankses or for Will, they are fighting the reality of being Black in the U.S. where there is no path guaranteed to be the "best" one. And it is this battle of the Black and bougie and the Black and urban, that makes *Fresh Prince* a storyline with narratives in which Black viewers can see aspects of their own lives reflected back at them.

Notes

1. In this essay I use African American and Black interchangeably. The concepts used align with the realities of the African American experience, those who are descendants of enslaved Africans who were brought to the United States by force. And within the U.S., Black people as a racial definition does extend to those Black people who have migrated voluntarily to the states, but most Black cultural references, like African American Language and the Black bourgeoisie, reflect the histories and ideologies of Black people descended from those who were enslaved. These are the Black people being referenced.

References

Benjamin, L. (2008). Black Bourgeoisie. In R. T. Schaefer, *Encyclopedia of Race, Ethnicity, and Society*. Thousand Oaks: SAGE Publications.

Clance, P. R., & Imes, S. A. (1978). The Impostor Phenomenon in High Achieving Women: Dynamics and Therapeutic Intervention. *Psychotherapy: Theory, Research and Practice, 15*(3), 241–247.

Doggett, J. A. (2019, October 10). *Imposter Syndrome Hits Harder When You're Black.* Retrieved from Huffington Post: https://www.huffpost.com/entry/imposter-syndrome-racism-discrimination_l_5d9f2c00e4b06ddfc514ec5c.

Fordham, S., & Ogbu, J. U. (1986). Black Students' School Success: Coping with the "Burden of 'Acting White.'" *The Urban Review,* 176–206.

Jones, Q., & Smith, W. (1992). The Fresh Prince of Bel-Air [Recorded by W. S. Prince & J. T. Jeff].

Koch, L. M., Gross, A. M., & Kolts, R. (2001). Attitudes Toward Black English and Code Switching. *Journal of Black Psychology,* 29–42.

Morton, J. M. (2014). Cultural Code-Switching: Straddling the Achievement Gap. *The Journal of Political Philosophy, 22*(3), 259–281.

Smitherman, G. (2006). *Word from the Mother: Language and Afrian Americans.* New York: Routledge.

ABC's *Black-ish*

A Critical Analysis of the
Black Professional Parent

Mia L. Anderson

In February 2017, Nielsen Media Research offered insight on the "mainstream appeal" of popular television shows with predominantly Black casts (Nielsen, 2017). Among the shows listed was ABC's *Black-ish* (2014–present), a show featuring an affluent, dual-income Black couple raising five children. The show boasts 79 percent non–Black viewership, second only to NBC's *This Is Us*, which boasts 89 percent non–Black viewership. While the number itself may be surprising to some, what is perhaps more important is the image of the Black family presented to a largely non–Black audience. Nearly 25 years after the premiere of *The Cosby Show* (1984–1992), Americans are once again offered a show about a thriving Black couple putting to rest "the myth that Black people couldn't be successful, well-educated, upper-middle-class families" (Cheers, 2018, p. 44).

As Cranmer and Harris (2015) asserted, "media has long been regarded as influential in shaping and altering individuals' perceptions of race and interracial interactions" (p. 153). *Black-ish* presents a unique series for study of this assertion, as both parents are seen working in White male-dominated careers (i.e., advertising and medicine). Further, Ford (1997) stated that stereotypes presented in the media can have a negative influence on the audience's daily interaction with others. Likewise, the positive portrayal of Blacks can create a positive image in the mind of viewers. With *Black-ish*'s largely non–Black audience, the series has the opportunity to not only rebuff longstanding racial stereotypes, but also to educate its audience on the nuances of upper middle-class Black lives and the historical foundations influencing such nuances.

This essay seeks to share insight into the image of Black parents with flourishing careers on ABC's *Black-ish*. The essay first illuminates the evolution of the Black family on primetime television. Utilizing three other Black television series as a foundation, the majority of the essay analyzes four seasons of *Black-ish,* delving into the presentation of characters Andre (Anthony Anderson) and Rainbow Johnson (Tracee Ellis Ross) as they navigate work-life balance in a largely non–Black environment. The central underlying components to their representation revolve around three assumptions of critical race theory (CRT; Tate, 1997). Overall, this essay points out ways in which *Black-ish,* like CRT, demonstrates that: (1) racism is normative rather than anomalous (i.e., placing Whites as "normal" and everyone else as "other" establishes racism as a normal part of everyday life, rather than an oddity or deviation emitted and experienced by only a few); (2) race is at the core of social institutions; and (3) people of color share a unique "voice" that stems from a shared experience of oppression and marginalization (Delgado & Stefancic, 2001; Bimper, 2015). Further, *Black-ish* and CRT assert that these shared experiences "are important and should be recognized and examined when considering larger societal structures" (Cranmer & Harris, 2015, p. 157).

Television Portrayals of Professional Black Couples

Among the 10 highest rated Black sitcoms, you will find *Black-ish* (no. 8), *The Cosby Show* (no. 3), *The Jeffersons* (no. 2), and *The Fresh Prince of Bel-Air* (no. 1; Grant, 2018), all shows centered on upward mobility and the Black family. On these shows, you find a mix of single- and dual-income households, all undoubtedly falling within or beyond the status of upper-middle-class. In 1975, audiences were introduced to *The Jeffersons* (1975–1985), though keen viewers may have recognized the couple from appearances on *All in the Family* (1971–1979). George Jefferson (Sherman Hemsley), the patriarch of the family, ran a successful laundromat business, while matriarch Louise Jefferson (Isabel Sanford) volunteered her time to local causes.

When *The Cosby Show* (1984–1992) premiered in the '80s, it opened the eyes of many Black viewers to the power of an education (Matabane & Merritt, 2014). Unlike Jefferson, you didn't have to be an entrepreneur to be successful. You could get an education and become a doctor, lawyer, or anything else you set your mind to. Set in New York City, the show focused on the lives of obstetrician Heathcliff Huxtable (Bill Cosby), his wife Clair (Phylicia Rashad), an attorney, and their five children. Though the show is criticized for failing to address racial issues (Gates, 1989; Inniss & Feagin, 1995), it cannot be denied that the show "changed the face of American television and set a new standard for representing African American families in non-stereotypical roles" (Havens, 2000, p. 371).

The Fresh Prince of Bel-Air (1990–1996) debuted in 1990 and tells the story of an upper-class Black family living in the Los Angeles suburb of Bel-Air. Philip (James Avery) and Vivian Banks (Janet Hubert [1990–1993]; Daphne Maxwell Reid [1993–1996]), a lawyer and stay-at-home mom, respectively, live with their children and their nephew, Will (the Fresh Prince; Will Smith). The Banks family also has a butler, Geoffrey (Joseph Marcell), in their mansion situated in a neighborhood they boast is home to a former president and other elite neighbors. Where some aspects of *The Fresh Prince* may seem unattainable to viewers, those presented on *The Cosby Show* and *Black-ish* may seem more within reach.

As Stamps (2017) points out, *The Cosby Show* and *Black-ish* share many similarities, including dual-parent, dual-income households with five children. On the surface, both shows "present images that oppose stereotypes" (p. 412). However, a number of elements make the more recent *Black-ish* unique. Unlike *The Cosby Show*, *Black-ish* "took a direct approach to addressing race and social class" (p. 414). In addition, *Black-ish* "utilizes family conflict and workplace interaction as a tool to create richer dialogue from different perspectives" (p. 414).

Analysis of Black-ish

One of the major differences between *The Cosby Show* and *Black-ish* is the overt discussion of race, from episodes about Black holidays (Season 4, Episode 1: "Juneteenth" [2017]) to one on disproportionate Black incarceration rates (Season 4, Episode 7: "Please Don't Feed the Animals" [2017]). Viewers will find within these racial elements underlying themes that resonate throughout the daily lives of Andre (Dre) and Rainbow (Bow) Johnson, a Black professional couple raising five children in an upper-middle-class Los Angeles suburb. Television depictions—however true or false—of the Black family have the potential to become beliefs or perpetuate stereotypes that mirror or distort Black familial structure, family values, work ethic, and cultural/societal integration.

Black Familial Structure and Family Values

As Burton et al. (2010) point out, critical race theories assert the principle that "race is a central component of social organizations and systems, including families" (p. 442). The inclusion of Dre and Bow's parents on the show provides a more complete picture of Black familial structure across generations and race. Dre's parents, Ruby (Jenifer Lewis) and Pops (Laurence Fishburne), hold a place of prominence on the show, as they are featured on most episodes and live with the family. At times, Dre seeks the advice of his mother or father, usually finding his mother to be his biggest supporter. Though Ruby is sometimes helpful, like when she provides dinner for the family (Season 1, Episode 10: "Black Santa/White Christmas" [2014]) or babysits the children (Season 2, Episode 3: "Dr. Hell No" [2015]), her opposition to some of the ways Bow is raising the children often proves challenging for Bow. For example, Bow chooses to let her youngest daughter Diane (Marsai Martin) wear her hair straightened. Ruby, wearing her hair in an afro style, states, "I don't let anyone hot comb out my heritage" (Season 1, Episode 8: "Oedipal Triangle" [2014]). Ruby's argument alludes to the idea that Black women straightening their hair is in fact an effort to have their hair appear like that of White people, reinforcing a principle of CRT—that White is inherently seen as normal. Though Bow's parents play a lesser role on the show, Bow acknowledges how her upbringing as a child of an interracial hippie couple has impacted her life and thought process.

Black Work Ethic

The study of work ethic in Black families often focuses on the role of the Black man. From the post-slavery years when Black men continued their work in the field as sharecroppers to today's executive or doctor, the burden has ideologically been placed on the Black man to be the breadwinner for the family. To be sure, "the Black male's best efforts in preparing for the job market do not necessarily ensure him equal employment opportunities or the chance to live out the American dream" (Johnson & Staples, 2005, p. 76). However, that fact does not lessen the amount of criticism offered to Black men throughout history nor does it alter the projection of the stereotypes of laziness and mental inferiority largely attributed to Black men and perpetuated through mainstream media.

In line with previous research, the show focuses more on Dre's career as an advertising executive than Bow's, though Bow has the more prestigious occupation of an anesthesiologist. Within their respective roles, they long for recognition—be it within the workplace or social settings— of their hard work. When Dre expects a promotion to senior vice president at his agency, he is disappointed that he is made Senior VP of the Urban Division, initially seeing it as a slight rather than recognition of his hard work. In this way, *Black-ish*, like CRT, explores the relationship between race, racism and power. In a sense, Dre is disappointed that he is being limited to Senior VP of the Urban Division, bringing to light the CRT assertion that, "everyone within racialized social systems may contribute to the reproduction of these systems through social practices" (Burton et al., 2010, p. 442). CRT also "questions claims of neutrality, objectivity, or meritocracy in the American legal and social systems in a manner that disadvantages people of color" (Cranmer & Harris, 2015, p. 157). Perhaps by accepting the position in the name of blazing a trail for future Black employees at the company, Dre also helped sustain a racialized system of stratification.

Though seeing Bow in the workplace is a rarity, viewers are well aware that she is a doctor from the first episode (Season 1, Episode 1: "Pilot" [2014]). In fact, viewers learn of Bow's career before finding out Dre is an advertising executive. Bow's career as a doctor is reiterated in numerous episodes, as Bow often reminds everyone that she is a doctor (Season 1, Episode 3: "The Nod" [2014]; Season 2, Episode 3: "Dr. Hell No" [2015]). In the episode "The Gift of Hunger" (Season 1, Episode 7 [2014]), one of the Johnsons' neighbors thinks that the family has fallen on hard times. Bow goes to great lengths to prove to the neighbor that she is a doctor and the family is well-off, to the point of driving a high-end vehicle she does not own while wearing her most expensive jewelry. It can be argued that Bow goes to such great lengths in an effort to quell stereotypes of Black people or to assert her financial status and that she is of the same standing as her White neighbors. In "Jacked O'Lantern" (Season 2, Episode 6 [2015]), the Johnsons' neighbor Janine (Nicole Sullivan) doesn't believe Bow is a real doctor, but rather that both she and Bow have dressed up as doctors for Halloween. This instance implies that Bow's neighbor cannot believe that Bow is a doctor because she is Black, reflective of CRT's assertion that racism is institutionalized and reproduces itself in social practices (Burton et al., 2010).

Societal Integration and the Case for Community

As previously mentioned, socialization of children in Black families is largely dependent upon the attitudes of the parents in regard to the merging of two cultures: Black and American. Peters (1988) stated:

> For Black families in the United States, socialization occurs within the ambiguities of a cultural heritage that is both Afro-American and Euro-American and a social system that espouses both democratic equality for all citizens and caste-like status for its Black citizens [p. 228].

Due to this complex duality, Blacks are often held to a double standard within their own community. Those who hold tightly to their Black heritage are regarded as anti–American or even disseminators of racism by establishing those outside the Black community as "other" and subsequently marginalizing their inherent value as human beings. On the other hand, Black people who attempt to assimilate into Euro-American culture are condemned for betraying their own heritage.

As members of a higher socioeconomic status than their parents, Dre and Bow find it challenging to make sure their children are aware of their Black heritage and Black colloquialisms. For instance, Dre emphasizes the importance of the Black barbershop as a place where boys learn to become men (Season 2, Episode 8: "Chop Shop" [2015]). When Junior (Marcus Scribner) fails to give the head nod to a Black person at his school, Dre and Pops explain to him and Rainbow how the nod is a staple among Black people and provides a sense of community in the midst of their struggle (Season 1, Episode 3: "The Nod" [2014]). This example illuminates CRT's claim that people of color share a unique "voice" that stems from a shared experience of oppression and marginalization (Delgado & Setancic, 2001; Bimper, 2015). This principle is evidenced further in "Colored Commentary" (Season 1, Episode 9 [2014]) when Dre narrates that he wants his kids to understand they are "part of something greater than themselves." Finally, it can be inferred in the "Jacked O'Lantern" episode (Season 2, Episode 6 [2015]) when Dre is happy that his children's cousins bully them every Halloween, because he feels it will prepare them for the real world.

Throughout the series, Dre shows support for his childhood friends, reflecting devotion to the Black community, his community. In one instance, Dre allows his friend Sha (Faizon Love) to sleep on the sofa, as Sha awaits artistic inspiration. Though Bow is aggravated with his friend's habits—many of which do not reflect those of a responsible adult—Dre argues that Sha took care of him when he was a kid and you're supposed to take care of your own (Season 2, Episode 9: "Man at Work" [2015]). When Dre's godbrother Omar (never seen on camera) is released from prison, Bow and Dre find themselves with differing viewpoints on how to handle his release. While Bow doesn't want an ex-con living in her house around her children, Dre feels he has the emotional and financial support his godbrother will need upon his release (Season 4, Episode 7: "Please Don't Feed the Animals" [2017]), solidifying the CRT idea of the shared experience of people of color.

Dre's sense of community extends beyond his friends to his workplace as well. When Dre thinks he will receive the promotion to senior vice president, he remarks on the "us vs. them" mentality of Black employees at companies managed by Whites, also stating, "when one of us made it, it's like all of us did" (Season 1, Episode 1: "Pilot" [2014]). Dre and another Black co-worker, Charlie (Deon Cole), express excitement when the co-owner of the company is revealed to be Daphne Lido (Wanda Sykes), a Black woman (Season 2, Episode 9: "Man at Work" [2015]). When Daphne asks Dre to fire Charlie, Dre does everything in his power not to, expressing to Bow that saving Charlie's job is about community. When Charlie leaves the company of his own volition, he thanks Dre for standing up for him, stating, "we look out for our own," reinforcing the sense of community so vital to Dre.

Though *Black-ish* offers frequent discussions on race, along with lessons on the history of race in America, there is value placed on the opinions of people who are not of the same race or social status. Whenever he is faced with a family dilemma, Dre seeks the advice of his co-workers, most of whom are White. In the episode "Crime and Punishment" (Season 1, Episode 5 [2014]) when Dre questions his decision to spank his son Jack (Miles Brown), he seeks the advice of his co-workers. When Dre's eldest daughter, Zoey (Yara Shahidi), questions her belief in God (Season 3, Episode 2: "God" [2016]), Dre discusses his feelings with his co-workers, some of whom express disbelief themselves. In this way, *Black-ish* moves away from (though by no means contradicting) CRT, asserting the idea that people are more alike than they are different, regardless of race. By and large, parents want their children to have better lives than they did. People want their children to be disciplined, even though they approach the act of discipline in various ways. Where CRT draws a line is in the opportunities afforded to the children, arguing that these opportunities may be afforded to them based on a racialized system in many ways designed to oppress people of color.

Implications and Conclusion

If we reflect upon Bandura's (1977) social learning theory which implies that we impose the information we receive from television on the attitudes and behaviors we exert in our everyday lives, the effects of a television series like *Black-ish* serve as edutainment (education-based entertainment) in a sense, educating audiences on upper-middle-class Black life and struggles, while providing humor within the everyday issues of marriage and the interracial work environment. In many ways, the show demonstrates how Black people and other racial and ethnic groups can learn from each other. Hunt (2005) asserted that "criticism of Black images has typically been leveled on two fronts: either the images are denounced as *distorted*, or they are attacked for being *damaging* in some way" (p. 15). This fact raises the importance of realistic depictions of the Black family on shows like *Black-ish* that help put to rest ongoing myths of Black work and family life. It also highlights the values that are projected as important to the survival of the Black family unit within a White world—professionally and socially.

In line with the declarations of Billingsley and Caldwell (1991), Black family sitcoms show that the Black family still places great value in spirituality, high achievement aspirations, and commitment to family. These values are linked back to the highly proclaimed Black institutions of church, family, and school. As illustrated in the projection of community and family values on *Black-ish,* Black people do possess unique cultural qualities that may or may not prevent them from assimilation into American society. The portrayals do not always promote the reality of all Blacks. However, they do speak to the bond held together in Black households through the maintenance of values such as: connection to culture, education/career, finances/status, and familial support.

REFERENCES

Bandura, A. J. (1977). *Social Learning Theory.* Englewood Cliffs, NJ: Prentice Hall.

Bell, D. (1987). *And We Are Not Saved: The Elusive Quest for Racial Justice.* New York: Basic.

Billingsley, A. & Caldwell, C. H. (1991). The Church, the Family, and the School in the African American Community. *The Journal of Negro Education, 60*(3), 427–440.

Bimper, A. Y., Jr. (2015). Lifting the Veil: Exploring Colorblind Racism in Black Student Athlete Experiences. *Journal of Sport and Social Issues, 39*(3), 225–243.

Burton, L. M., Bonilla-Silva, E., Ray, V., Buckelew, R., & Freeman, E. H. (2010). Critical Race Theories, Colorism, and the Decade's Research on Families of Color. *Journal of Marriage and Family, 72,* 440–459.

Cheers, I. M. (2018). *The Evolution of Black Women in Television: Mammies, Matriarchs and Mistresses.* New York: Routledge.

Cranmer, G. A., & Harris, T. M. (2015). "White-Side, Strong-Side": A Critical Examination of Race and Leadership in *Remember the Titans. Howard Journal of Communications, 26,* 153–171.

Delgado, R., & Stefancic, J. (2001). *Critical Race Theory: An Introduction.* New York: NYU Press.

Ford, T. E. (1997). Effects of Stereotypical Television Portrayals of Blacks on Person Perception. *Social Psychology Quarterly, 60*(3), 266–275.

Franklin, C. W. (1984). Black Male-Black Female Conflict: Individually Caused and Culturally Nurtured. *Journal of Black Studies, 15,* 139–154.

Gates, H. L. (1989, November 12). TV's Black World Turns—but Stays Unreal. *New York Times,* 12.

Grant, T. (2018, May 25). These Are the 10 Highest Rated Black sitcoms. *Ebony.* Retrieved from https://www.ebony.com/entertainment-culture/these-are-the-10-highest-rated-Black-sitcoms.

Havens, T. (2000). "The biggest show in the world": Race and the Global Popularity of *The Cosby Show. Media, Culture & Society, 22,* 371–391.

Hunt, D. M. (2005). Making Sense of Blackness on Television. In D. M. Hunt (Ed.), *Channeling Blackness.* New York: Oxford University Press.

Inniss, L. B., & Feagin, J. R. (1995). *The Cosby Show*: The View from the Black Middle Class. *Journal of Black Studies, 25*(6), 692–711.

Johnson, L. B. & Staples, R. (2005). *Black Families at the Crossroads: Challenges and Prospects.* San Francisco: Jossey-Bass.

Matabane, P. W., & Merritt, B. D. (2014). Media Use, Gender, and Black College Attendance: The Cosby Effect. *Howard Journal of Communications, 25,* 452–471.

Nielsen. (2017). For Us by Us? The Mainstream Appeal of Black Content. Retrieved from http://www.nielsen.com/us/en/insights/news/2017/for-us-by-us-the-mainstream-appeal-of-Black-content.html.

Peters, M. F. (1988). Parenting in Black Families with Young Children: A Historical Perspective. In H. P. McAdoo (ed.), *Black Families (2nd ed.)*, Newbury Park, CA: Sage Publications.

Stamps, D. (2017). The Social Construction of the Black Family on Broadcast Television: A Comparative Analysis of *The Cosby Show* and *Blackish*. *Howard Journal of Communications, 28*(4), 405–420.

Tate, W. F. (1997). Critical Race Theory and Education. *Review of Research in Education, 22*(1), 195–247.

Black Brotherhood, Professionalism and Entrepreneurship as Depicted in *Martin, The Wayans Bros.* and *Malcolm & Eddie*

DAVID STAMPS

Introduction

The following essay examines Black male characters in the 1990s prime-time television situational comedies, *Martin* (1992–1997), *The Wayans Bros.* (1995–1999), and *Malcolm & Eddie* (1996–2000). These scripted series represent symbolic media imagery that counters the competing narrative of Black men in mass media as deviant, prone to criminality, and absent from professional working spaces (Castle Bell & Harris, 2017; Dixon, Azocar, & Casas, 2003; Jackson & Dangerfield, 2004; Orbe, 1998; Tyree, 2011). More importantly, each TV series offer Black audiences' exposure to positive Black television portrayals, which may result in increased self-esteem and positive group perceptions (Matabane & Merritt, 2014; Sanders & Ramasubramanian, 2012).

Previous research recognizes the positive influence of affirmative Black television programs and Black characters who intentionally engage in discussions of racism, classism, and societal issues aligned with the Black community (Stamps, 2017). Contributing to this narrative, the following essay, and arguably this book, celebrates Black television and Black characters who demonstrate a diverse spectrum of Black identities, including Black individuals in professional roles as entrepreneurs. *Martin, The Wayans Bros,* and *Malcolm & Eddie* equivalently represent Black men who have achieved middle-class success via their professional careers. Likewise each program showcases Black men engaging in healthy male kinship.

Black Men as Media Subject

Mass media's impact as a socializing agent is influential among Black audiences as media provides a source of social learning, which teaches and reinforces certain qualities about the Black community (Dixon, 2001). Considering this, there are benefits in viewing positive media depictions of Black men, including decreasing stereotype formation and supporting positive intergroup interactions (Mastro & Stamps, 2018).

Previous literature demonstrates that the majority of Black television characters, past and present, are located within situational comedies (Gray, 1986). This genre of programming has remained the most open to Black actors as lead characters having dominant storylines and authentic character development (Brooks & Hébert, 2006). Within this genre, a variety of Black leading figures exist, dating back as early as the 1970s (e.g., *The Jeffersons* [1975–1985]). Also, Herman Gray's (1986) influential work examining the cultural politics of Black television illustrates themes of Black men as successful and affluent in television programming. These characterizations carried over into the 1980s through the early 2000s. The shows referenced in this essay are not the first to emerge in the media landscape, demonstrating Black male television leads in professional roles (e.g., *Benson* [1979–1986]). Instead, each show contribute to a rich lineage of positive depictions of Black men in entertainment media.

The television series *Martin, The Wayans Bros.,* and *Malcolm & Eddie* illustrate varied depictions of Black men in a way that many mainstream audiences may consider unfamiliar territory. The Black male characters across all three series either have their occupation as a significant part of each series' storyline, or the central narrative of the series is situated around the main character(s) role as an entrepreneur. Likewise, each character engages in witty banter; they laugh, hug, cry, and participate in authentic male friendships. Collectively, these images demonstrate a narrative that Black men are capable of healthy relationships, including engaging in intimacy and vulnerability with one another. Likewise, witnessing these characters within various work environments illustrates the limitless boundaries that Black men have regarding their career aspirations. These depictions are not to be understated; research supports that television may demonstrate aspirational norms for Black audiences, specifically for audiences that might not encounter affirmative scenarios in their day-to-day lives (Matabane & Merritt, 2014). As the late, great American activist

Marian Wright Edelman states, "You can't be what you can't see," and seeing oneself in affirmative narratives matters; and may illustrate immeasurable possibilities for Black people. To situate the potential influence of these shows, a brief overview of each television program is offered.

Overview of the Series Martin, The Wayans Bros. and Malcolm & Eddie

Martin. *Martin,* one of Fox network's highest-rated shows during its five-year run, aired from August 27, 1992, until May 1, 1997. Set in Detroit, Michigan, the series follows Martin Payne (Martin Lawrence), his girlfriend and later wife, Regina "Gina" Waters (Tisha Campbell-Martin); and their close friends Tommy (Thomas Mikal Ford), Cole (Carl Anthony Payne II), and Pam (Tichina Arnold). One of the earlier trademarks of *Martin* is the reoccurring characters portrayed by Martin Lawrence. Each of these exaggerated, larger-than-life characters create comedic conflict among the main cast members and provide running gags and comedic relief throughout the series. The characters include Sheneneh Jenkins, Mama Payne, Ol' Otis, Roscoe, and Jerome, the latter character whose rhythmic sentences gave audiences the memorable catchphrase, "I say Jerome in the house … watch yo mouth!"

Martin Lawrence's reoccurring characters create a unique and fun-loving engagement among the cast and audiences alike. However, Martin's professional ambition and male kinship are notably interwoven throughout the series. Martin begins his career as a disc jockey for the fictional radio station WZUP and soon transitions to hosting his own local public television show in Detroit. Later in the series, Martin becomes the host of the talk show, *"Word on the Street,"* and by the end of the series, Martin prepares to relocate to Los Angeles to continue his nationally syndicated talk show. In addition to Martin's career trajectory, scenes between characters are set within the workplace, including the radio station's sound booth and the set of the syndicated talk show, *"Word on the Street."* Audiences witness Black men working, and more importantly, Black men navigating their career path.

Martin's work-life balance is as consistent within the series as is his male kinship with his best friends, Tommy and Cole. Tommy is Martin's charming, sharp, and levelheaded counterpart. Cole, on the other hand, is the happy-go-lucky, well-intentioned, but often dimwitted part of the trio. Collectively these three Black men display a rich, jovial, and distinctive friendship and are unapologetic in their displays of affection and physical contact. For example, throughout the series, one of Martin's signature proclamations is "Give Me Love," in which Martin engages in a dramatic physical embrace with his castmates when he faces a highly emotional circumstance. These comedic, yet endearing, displays of affection often happen among various characters, including Martin's male friends.

The Wayans Bros. *The Wayans Bros.* aired from January 11, 1995, until May 20, 1999, on the Warner Brothers Television Network (The WB). The series featured real-life brothers, Shawn and Marlon Wayans, portraying themselves, and John "Pops" Williams (John Witherspoon) as their father. Throughout the series, Shawn and Marlon work numerous jobs, and after season one, Shawn becomes the owner of a newsstand that employs Marlon. Shawn's newsstand is located near the diner that their father also owns and operates. *The Wayans Bros.* provided multi-generational Black entrepreneurship and demonstrated a lineage of Black men who own and operate businesses that, in turn, provide employment opportunities for other individuals (Rhodes & Butler, 2004).

In addition to the series' workplace setting and generations of Black men business owners, depictions of Black male friendship are shown by displays of physical affection between both brothers and within the father-son relationship. Marlon's signature exchange, exemplifying physical affection and closeness, is his trademark handshake. Marlon's handshake involves pulling an individual into a dramatic embrace, Marlon patting and petting the individual and the culmination of the encounter, often resulting in Marlon parting ways with a forehead or cheek kiss. While this display of affection within the series is characterized as comedic, this action demonstrates a level of comfort with physical touch, which is rarely exhibited among Black men in television (hooks, 2004; Jackson, 2006).

The affection and intimacy among characters in the series, as well as between men in Wayans' family, are documented among journalists and critical cultural scholars. Scholars and writers alike praise the displays of affection among the Wayans' men, acknowledging how these actions are healthy, affirming, and necessary in attenuating violence and increasing self-esteem among Black men (Ray, 2016). These demonstrations of friendship and intimacy acknowledge that Black men's intersecting identities, including class (e.g., business owners) and sexual orientation, are not barriers to companionship and closeness. Instead, each of these qualities highlights the multidimensional identities and nuanced existence of Black men.

Malcolm & Eddie. The television series *Malcolm & Eddie* featured actors Malcolm-Jamal Warner and Eddie Griffin. *Malcolm & Eddie* premiered on August 26, 1996, and aired until May 22, 2000, on the United Paramount Network (UPN). In the series, audiences encounter an interwoven display of Black male kinship as Malcolm and Eddie are friends, roommates, and business owners. Malcolm owns and operates the sports bar, Malcolm McGee's, and Eddie owns a one-person towing company. Malcolm is the sensible, reasonable roommate, and Eddie embodies fast-talking, outlandish energy. Malcolm and Eddie's friendship is replete with attentiveness and consideration for one another. Similar to *The Wayans Bros.*, the television characters Malcolm and Eddie are comedic opposites, but as roommates, friends, and owners of their respective companies, they both support one another and protect each other from mischief. Numerous examples of Malcolm and Eddie's friendship and supportive nature are interwoven throughout the series. These examples include Malcolm pretending to be Eddie during pitches to potential customers to secure clients for his towing company (Perzigian, 1997) and Eddie rousing Malcolm as he works multiple jobs in pursuit of his career ambitions (Brown & Devanney, 1997). Also, both men, on numerous occasions, join forces creatively to promote their business endeavors (Jackson, 1997). These characters, similar to the Black men in each of the previous series, demonstrate the quintessential prototype of Black brotherhood, professionalism, and entrepreneurship. Both Malcolm and Eddie display social support and encouragement, exemplify atypical forms of professionalism, and above all, are businesspersons, creating and sustaining careers based on their talents and interests.

Similarities Among Martin, The Wayans Bros., *and* Malcolm & Eddie

Within each series, friendship among Black men is front-and-center, and it is worth noting that displays of male camaraderie have resonated deep within Black communities for centuries (Jackson, 2006). Black men create community and fraternal bonds in various places, including barbershops, community centers, and athletic spaces (Hecht, Jackson, & Ribeau, 2003). Black men laugh, tease one another, and engage in social support in meaningful ways. Likewise, throughout history, these encounters by Black men have prevailed as part of a collectivist identity that is often absent in media depictions.

These television programs highlight the intimate engagement among Black men in addition to portraying each character as career-driven individuals. For example, in the series *Martin*, during episode two of season six, "Workin' Day & Night" (1993), Martin decides to work double shifts at the fictitious radio station, WZUP, hosting the late-night and morning radio program slots. Martin has a laser focus on utilizing his garnered exposure by appearing on both segments and the potential opportunity that may arise from the publicity. Gina, Martin's partner, is the proverbial devil's advocate, asking Martin if his decision might leave him overworked and underpaid. The dilemmas presented here offer audiences a space to view how individuals navigate their career choices and the cost and benefits associated with those decisions.

Also, a theme within the same episode is Martin's articulation of affirming his masculinity within his romantic relationship. During various scenes, Martin joins dozens of other men to proclaim their masculine identity and each male character through different comedic posturing (e.g., removing their shirts) bond as a collective whole in attempts to enact masculinity. The dynamics within the episode are two-fold. Martin's focus on his career aspirations are front-and-center, and his dialogue with his partner is noteworthy as their discussion illustrates how partners work together to navigate career choices and work-life balance (Bowman, 1993). Likewise, managing and evaluating one's masculine identity within interpersonal communication is challenging and deserving of attention (Stamps, 2018). Life choices, such as these, are not easily managed, and viewing the intricacies of addressing both on the small screen offers audiences a roadmap that may resemble their attempts to cope with these same challenges.

Aside from male kinship, the themes and storylines within episodes across all three series showcase issues facing the Black community. In an early scene in episode seven, season one, "Afro Cab" (1995) in *The Wayans Bros.,* Shawn and Marlon's dialogue and character interactions highlight the continued discrimination that Black people encounter in everyday activities, including using public transportation. In the opening scene, Shawn, dressed in professional work attire, is worried about arriving late to work. After multiple cabs ignore Shawn, a taxi finally stops, but only once his brother, Marlon lies down in the middle of the street, placing his body directly in front of oncoming traffic. Marlon's action is intended to be comedic but highlights a genuine issue of discrimination, targets communities of color in general, and the Black community, specifically. Within the same episode, Shawn and Marlon discuss the lack of respect within public spaces and from their employers. Due to this conversation, Marlon decides to quit his job and create "Afro Cab," a cab company dedicated to serving Black people. Marlon's action is in response to the discrimination that he and his brother encounter earlier, as well as the disrespect he endured in the workplace (Wyatt, 1995).

The business venture, "Afro Cab," is short-lived; however, the storyline brings to the forefront discrimination that many Black individuals often face and, more importantly, the response by Black people to create Black-owned businesses to counter these biases. Shawn's work attire, level of professionalism, and his social status did not exempt him from the prejudices that Black people often face in society. Television may show Black characters in professional roles; however, the issues related to fair and equitable treatment within the workplace and in social spaces continues to be an obstacle for many Black people (Punyanunt-Carter, 2008).

Across all three series, Black men manage their professional careers. Moreover, Black men take on multiple jobs, whether focused on addressing financial constraints, steering their career trajectory or embracing varied career aspirations. For example, Malcolm, in episode three, season one, "On the Radio" (1996), aspires to be a radio sportscaster. When offered the opportunity for a substitute on-air disc jockey position, Malcolm excitedly accepts the position. However, Malcolm must continue his day job and balance his current priorities with those of his dream job. This action shows audiences that Black men have career aspirations, the tenacity to go after their ambitions, and likewise, will sacrifice for their dreams (Brown & Devanney, 1996).

The narrative of Black men as professional, career-focused entrepreneurs is significant across these programs. Within specific episodes, Black men create small businesses, acknowledge the difficulties of discrimination, and demonstrate that Black men are resilient and career-driven.

Martin, The Wayans Bros., and *Malcolm & Eddie* contribute to the rewriting of representations of Black men in professional roles and demonstrate affirming, healthy kinship. However, there are other aspects of the series that deserve a particular level of responsiveness. Each of these programs delivers laughter and authentic displays of Blackness, which are essential, yet noteworthy issues that resonate and profoundly affect the Black community have gone unrecognized. For example, discrimination regarding class and gender identities within the workplace, systemic racism, and the racialized power dynamics, including white supremacy and white privilege, hinder Black individuals in corporate America and warrant critical investigation. Considering the significant and far-reaching media platform of each series, which reached millions of households, this was a missed opportunity.

Across each show, critical insights regarding diverse aspects of Black culture are at times contained or limited. Within these programs, audiences learn about significant issues related to the Black experience (e.g., Nelson Mandela's historic presidency and the considerable influence of Historically Black Colleges and Universities). However, many complex social problems facing Black audiences did not receive substantial critique and were left unexamined by this programming. Two significant concepts within these series that were dominant were displays of male chauvinism and various forms of homophobia demonstrated in language and character interaction. Each of these viewpoints merits interrogation as the absence of this much-needed conversation may reinforce the continued vilification of Black people of varying intersecting identities.

Addressing social and cultural aspects of Black life, including racism, social inequality, and intersectional identities, is a hefty task for a comedically driven television show. The television series discussed here cannot be all things to all people. However, the narrative structure and thematic approach of *Martin, The Wayans Bros.*, and *Malcolm & Eddie*, while not able to address every issue, successfully interrupted the "typical" and often white television experience for audiences. These shows collectively centered Black male characters, told stories that focused on Black life and demonstrated solidarity and friendship among Black men. Within the series *Martin*, audiences witness its main character engage in upward career trajectory, starting as a local disc jockey and transitioning to hosting a nationally syndicated talk show. Also, *Martin* delivered for audiences a glimpse into a fun and jovial intragroup dynamic among Black people with dialogue that continues to be quotable and remembered for years to come.

The Wayans' Bros. gave audiences generations of entrepreneurial Black men: father and sons, who created businesses and employment opportunities within their community. Moreover, a level of male intimacy that is necessary and needed among Black men was paramount within the series. Lastly, *Malcolm & Eddie* presented a roommate/friendship and dual working partnership that was centered in brotherhood.

Malcolm and Eddie demonstrate a collectivistic identity, showing that their career successes were intertwined, and both men functioned to create a space for each to thrive and build a mutual support system. The Black men portrayed in these programs were professional, corporate climbing entrepreneurial individuals, thus providing audiences with an experience of viewing positive media portrayals.

Concluding Thoughts

The depictions of successful, professional Black men in television programming date back as early as *The Jeffersons* (1975–1985) and *Benson* (1979–1986). Within television programming, Black men have occupied professional roles, including those of entrepreneurs, trailblazers within the political arena, and as blue and white-collar professionals. This essay extends the narratives that explore media depictions of Black men who are goal-driven and career-minded as these characterizations are positioned to influence audiences' self-perception and well-being (Mastro & Stamps, 2018; Matabane & Merritt, 2014).

Lastly, audiences should be aware of and demand Black programming that showcases positive portrayals of Black individuals. Likewise, there is a need for more varied Black narratives and Black content creators across entertainment media, including, but not limited to, television. This text highlights the richness of Black male friendship and professionalism in 1990s sitcom television. For over eight years and 300+ episodes, *Martin, The Wayans Bros.,* and *Malcolm & Eddie* have and continue (through re-runs in syndication) to deliver narratives of professional Black men in intimate kinship among one another. Moving forward, audiences should continue to expect meaningful and diverse media narratives that display the rich spectrum of Black identities, including depictions of Black men.

References

Bowman, J. (Writer). (1996, September 19). Baby, It's You [Television Series Episode] In T. Crotzer. (Producer), *Martin*. Universal City, CA: Fox Network

Brooks, D. E., & Hébert, L. P. (2006). Gender, Race, and Media Representation. *Handbook of Gender and Communication, 16*, 297–317.

Carew, T. (Writer), & Keith, G. (Director). (1993, September 26). Workin' Day & Night. [Television Series Episode]. In J. Bowman. (Producer). *Martin*. Los Angeles: Universal Pictures.

Castle Bell, G., & Harris, T. M. (2017). Exploring Representations of Black Masculinity and Emasculation on NBC's *Parenthood. Journal of International and Intercultural Communication, 10*, 135–152.

Dixon, T. L. (2001). Social Cognition and Racial Stereotyping in Television: Consequences for Transculturalism. *Transcultural Realities: Interdisciplinary Perspectives on Cross-Cultural Relations*, 215–224.

Dixon, T. L., Azocar, C., & Casas, M. (2003). The Portrayal of Race and Crime on Television Network News. *Journal of Broadcasting & Electronic Media, 47*, 495–520.

Duclon, D. (1975). *The Jeffersons* [Television Series]. Hollywood: CBS Television.

Gray, H. (1986). Television and the New Black Man: Black Male Images in Prime-Time Situation Comedy. *Media, Culture & Society, 8*, 223–242.

Hecht, M. L., Jackson, R. L., & Ribeau, S. A. (2003). *African American Communication: Exploring Identity and Culture*. Routledge.

hooks, B. (2004). *We Real Cool: Black Men and Masculinity*. Psychology Press.

Jackson, J. (Writer). (1997, February 24). The Commercial. [Television Series Episode]. In J. Franklin. (Producer). *Malcolm & Eddie*. Los Angeles: United Paramount Network

Jackson, R. L. (2006). *Scripting the Black Masculine Body: Identity, Discourse, and Racial Politics in Popular Media*. SUNY Press.

Jackson, R L., & Dangerfield, C. L. (2004). Defining Black Masculinity as Cultural Property. *African American Communication and Identities: Essential Readings*, 197. Thousand Oaks, CA: SAGE Publications.

Madison, J. (Writer), & Smith, A. (Director). (1996, September 9). On the Radio. [Television Series Episode]. In C. Brown and T. Devanney (Producer). *Malcolm & Eddie*. Los Angeles: United Paramount Network.

Mastro, D., & Stamps, D. (2018). An Examination of Racial/Ethnic Inclusion in the Media and the Implications of Exposure on Audiences. In P. Napoli (Ed.), *Mediated Communication*. De Gruyter Mouton Publications.

Matabane, P. W., & Merritt, B. D. (2014). Media Use, Gender, and African American College Attendance: The Cosby Effect. *Howard Journal of Communications, 25*, 452–471.

Orbe, M. P. (1998). Constructions of Reality on MTV's "The Real World": An Analysis of the Restrictive Coding of Black Masculinity. *Southern Journal of Communication, 64*, 32–47.

Perzigian, J. (Writer), & Whittingham, K. (Director). (1997, February 17). Everynight Fever.

[Television Series Episode]. In J. Franklin. (Producer). *Malcolm & Eddie*. Los Angeles: United Paramount Network.

Punyanunt-Carter, N. M. (2008). The Perceived Realism of African American Portrayals on Television. *The Howard Journal of Communications, 19*, 241–257.

Ray, K. (2016, August 8). PDA: You Won't Believe the Controversy Behind This Wayans Family Photo. *Everythinggirlislove.com* [website]. Retrieved from: http://everythinggirlslove.com/marlon-wayans-kiss/.

Rhodes, C., & Butler, J. S. (2004). Understanding Self-Perceptions of Business Performance: An Examination of Black American Entrepreneurs. *Journal of Developmental Entrepreneurship, 9*, 55.

Sanders, M. S., & Ramasubramanian, S. (2012). An Examination of African Americans' Stereotyped Perceptions of Fictional Media Characters. *Howard Journal of Communications, 23*, 17–39.

Stamps, D. (2017). The Social Construction of the African American Family on Broadcast Television: A Comparative Analysis of *The Cosby Show* and *Blackish*. *Howard Journal of Communications, 28*, 405–420.

Stamps, D. (2018). Will Boys Be Boys: An Exploration of Social Support, Affection, and Masculinities within Non-Romantic Male Relationships. *Kentucky Journal of Communication, 37*, 56–75.

Tyree, T. (2011). African American Stereotypes in Reality Television. *Howard Journal of Communications, 22*, 394–413.

Witt, P. (1979). Benson [Television Series]. Los Angeles, CA: Columbia Pictures Television.

Wyatt, D. (Writer). (1995, February 22). Afro Cab. [Television Series Episode]. In M. Ember. (Producer), *The Wayans Bros*. Burbank, CA: Warner Brothers.

"I'm glad I got my girls"

Black Women, Working, Friending and
Seeking Love in Fox's Living Single

LaToya T. Brackett

When that memorable theme song kicked into gear, it hit many Black women like it was their personal anthem, for them and their crew. It spoke to the lives they may have already had, desired to have, or were trying to return to—Black women working, friending, and seeking positive romantic relationships. The television series *Living Single* aired from 1993 to 1998. Queen Latifah wrote the lyrics to the theme song, performed the rap portion of the song, and starred in the series for all 5 seasons as Khadijah James. A sitcom of the 1990s, *Living Single* was ground-breaking for Black women narratives on primetime television, and it would lay a foundation for numerous television series to follow. The series centered around the lives of four African American women, living with and near each other in New York City, it also made central the lives of two African American men, which additionally showcased new narratives of Black men. One major aspect of this series resides in the undertone of all the characters' experiences in their professions. *Living Single* showed Black people working across all levels of professions, but what was especially ground breaking were the careers of Khadijah James entrepreneur, editor, and publisher of an urban community focused magazine; Maxine "Max" Shaw (Erika Alexander) attorney at a major law firm and later the public defender's office; and, Kyle Barker (T.C. Carson) a stock broker who continually grew in his career to the peak of an international job offer and acceptance. Their careers fluctuate throughout the series, particularly with major alterations for Max and Kyle, and moments of reassessment for Khadijah.

Living Single promotes Black pride. It showcases the triumphs and tribulations of being Black and exceptional. It unveils the struggles among Black women, from friends, to mothers and daughters. It elevates the power of Black love. And it is a reminder of our roots as African Americans, and the kinships we are born with and the kinships we create. So how does having a high demanding career support or hinder the lives of African American women and men? There is no clear-cut answer, yet the series *Living Single* shared with its audience for 5 years the realities of being Black, professional, single, and familial. This essay will explore three of the main characters from the series and discuss major moments in their careers and how such moments interacted with their Black, professional, and single lives. Between Khadijah, Max, and Kyle viewers saw the costs and benefits of their successful careers, and *Living Single* did a particularly solid job at revealing the multiple layers to decisions made by the characters, and how they engaged with these major moments in relation to their Black pride, professional exceptionalism, and desire for love.

A Series Empowering Its Audience: "Keep your head up, what? Keep your head up, that's right"

There are so many beautiful aspects in the series *Living Single* in regards to Black pride and positivity from sisterly moments in the bathroom with the three roommates, and sometimes neighbor Max, getting ready for the day or even ready for bed. The showcase of Black women with bodies of all shapes, with hair of various textures and styles, with personalities that span from bubbly, sassy, determined to passionate, there was a mirror for many Black women watching this show back in the '90s and even today as it resurfaced on the streaming platform Hulu in 2019. These were definitely moments of pride for Black folks watching this series, it was for Black people, not always spelling out the nuances in African American Language, and communication style. There were moments where just the Black folks laughed, and laughed just a bit louder in recognizing that moment was just for them.

The show may be focused on four Black women but the two additional leads of Kyle and Overton (John Henton) are an essential part of this story. As Black men, they added the male narratives of understandings and ideologies to whatever dilemma the women may be faced with in each episode. Their presence was an important one in regards to Black women and Black men sharing positive friendships and romances. A core plotline centered the collaboration between the women and Kyle to make sure Overton and Synclaire (Kim Coles) reconnect after missed romantic opportunities, promoting community and fictive kinship. *Living Single* attempted to reflect Black experiences and yet go beyond. It shared realities, the more common ones and the ones often unspoken. No wonder Black women might find connection to the show's theme song and portrayal of sisterhood, "In a nineties kind of world, I'm glad I got my girls,"—Khadijah, Synclaire, Regine, and Max.

Black Professionals with Difficult Decisions: "Whenever this life get tough, you gotta fight"

Khadijah James: Superwoman Seeks Psychiatrist

Khadijah, editor and publisher of *Flavor*, a Black owned, urban focused magazine, is not a one woman show. However, her magazine is the main show in her life, and often without choice. Her dedication to having her magazine succeed is showcased especially in episode 19, of season 3 "Shrink to Fit," in which she gets diagnosed with anxiety and depression by a psychiatrist.

The myth of the superwoman pervades Khadijah's storyline throughout the show. Aligned with the idea of the strong Black woman, the superwoman narrative is one that stemmed from the desire of Black women to defeat and counter the negative stereotypes often assigned to them, such as the Mammy, welfare queen and Jezebel (Woods-Giscombe, 2). In attempting to prove their self-worth to a white audience and appraiser, Black women created an unattainable reality of perfection in everything they do, particularly in career and family- so much so that even without a white audience, Black women expect perfection no matter who is watching. This is Khadijah.

In the episode "Shrink to Fit" Khadijah is especially anxious due to a new magazine being launched called *Savor*—a magazine run by a big corporation that Khadijah says stole her own idea for content focus. Throughout the series *Flavor* goes through times of financial difficulty, prompting Khadijah to take a second job as a nightshift security guard. In this episode, Khadijah's friends call out her curious behavior, of excessive energy, and lack of rest.

After stealing *Savor* flyers and a bus billboard Khadijah is confronted by her friends and her own fears, at which point she calls her mother who tells her to see a therapist. This particular episode focuses on the stigma surrounding mental health issues, from Khadijah's issues of always being okay and figuring things out, to Overton's fear of clowns. It is not until she goes to a psychiatrist, Dr. Jessica Bryce (Jasmine Guy) that the realities and costs of always being on top of things is reflected back at Khadijah. Uncertain about her presence in the space, Dr. Bryce has to pull Khadijah into talking about herself and outlining her past days of no sleep and continued uncertainty with work and love.

The dialogue between these two African American women, Khadijah and Dr. Bryce, is yet another moment of the series where a barrier in Black culture was breached—the barrier of mental health in the Black community. One example of this happens when Khadijah looks for validation that she is indeed okay. Dr. Bryce does not agree:

> DR. BRYCE: There's more than one kind of depression, Khadijah. Bipolar depression can be the opposite from what you'd expect. You're on a high, you can't sleep, you have mood swings. Then eventually, you crash.
>
> KHADIJAH: Whatever. Look, the point is, I have my problems under control. Okay. I mean, what do I have to be depressed about? [sighs] I'm not depressed. [breathes hard] I'm happy. [begins to cry] I'm the happiest person I know. [continues to cry] What is this? I haven't cried since Mufasa dies in *Lion King*. Damn those hyenas.

Despite Khadijah's attempt to define her tears as superficial, Dr. Bryce insists that Khadijah's crying was about something deeper. Khadijah left the session still insisting that she had everything under control. Her friends find out she went to therapy and console her in each individual way that they do, from Max confiding that she had seen a therapist once and had thoughts she was unsure about, to Regine (Kim Fields) insisting that it's okay because the magazine *Essence* says therapy is in. Khadijah's anxiety reduces when the first *Savor* magazine is brought to her, and as she states, "this [magazine] is weak." To set her even more at ease, a top magazine media mogul dismissed *Savor* and told readers to go for *Flavor* "the leading edge magazine *Savor* tries to be." Khadijah's worries subside and in her calm she revisits Dr. Bryce to apologize for her behavior and to let her know she was feeling better—until she cries again.

> DR. BRYCE: You're an amazing person, Khadijah. You persevere, you achieve. You take care of so many people, but somewhere along the way you stopped taking care of yourself.
>
> KHADIJAH: Well I guess it would be kind of interesting to talk to you about that from time to time…. Damn, my friends are goin' wear me out over this one.
>
> DR. BRYCE: I know. Psychotherapy doesn't get much respect in our community.

Following this breakthrough, Dr. Bryce prescribes Khadijah with time off, a vacation with no work and no friends, and Khadijah in true superwoman fashion says she wouldn't know what to do with that. So, when being offered medication instead, Khadijah agrees to a vacation, and also to return for more therapy.

The series never again shows this counseling relationship, but the direct demand to continue coming, from a professional Black woman, to another Black woman who accepts the call to return is a major moment in reflecting for Black women watching. It tells viewers that self-care and mental health are too often put on the backburner and there is nothing wrong with seeking help.

Khadijah's mental health storyline reflects what researchers have found to be accurate about African American women, that they generally do not seek psychological services to deal with stress (Watson & Hunter, 2015, p. 604). Her superwoman characteristics hold her back from asking for help, and Watson and Hunter also found that such characteristics have been found as variables to the anxiety and depression some Black women experience (p. 604).

Additionally, it has been recognized in research that African Americans find stigma associated with mental health issues, and thus seeking help. It is barrier breaking that *Living Single* had Khadijah's mother tell her to see a therapist considering that African Americans hold "the cultural belief that sharing information outside of the family [is] strongly prohibited" (p. 605). When Khadijah first visits Dr. Bryce she is in full disguise, comically so due to the series being a sitcom, but it reflects a reality to the audience that African Americans are concerned about someone seeing them.

This stigma and fear also adds to the inability to seek mental health support, and adds to their anxiety, this episode aligns with the recommendations of Watson and Hunter that breaking that stigma could be the first step to having African Americans seek mental health support (p. 610). Khadijah's friends are an example of disrupting this stigma, as Max and Regine both validated therapy, and it was even Khadijah's mother who recommended therapy. This is where *Living Single* once again reflects back at African American viewers the often silent narrative, and perhaps pushes them to talk about it with their own friends and family.

Maxine Shaw: Choosing Integrity Over Opportunity and Career Over Love

Max, the college friend of Khadijah, and the unofficial roommate of the trio in the brownstone, is a powerful, quick-witted, determined, and passionate attorney. Max works for the law firm Evans & Bell, a firm named for and run by two Black male attorneys, and the firm where her eagerness caused a major blunder with a client and thus her career. In episode 27, season 1, Max is working on wedding contracts for Sheila Kelly (Anne-Marie Johnson) a talk show personality who Max encourages to think twice about not having a prenuptial agreement. In this scene Max reveals her own biases towards trusting men, due to her past experiences. Such a reflection perhaps pushes Max to be a strong woman informing another strong woman, in hopes to protect her. Sheila eagerly thanks Max for the advice, but later returns extremely angry accusing Max's advice of ending her engagement. Such a major blunder puts Max's law firm in a predicament to either get rid of Max or lose Sheila's business. Sheila protests: "As long as she's here, I can't work with you … you just don't know how old I am. It doesn't matter." Sheila storms out of the office, alluding to her struggle as a successful, post young, woman looking for love and having it taken from her. Max defends herself to the partners, by doubling down confidently on her decision to inform Sheila:

> I think I can see where this is going, but before we get there let me just say, our clients trust us to keep them fully advised. Anything less would be negligent, and with all due respect, you're not mad at me because you think I gave Sheila Kelly bad advice. You're mad at me because I was doing the job you should have, now … go ahead and fire me [Episode 27, Season 1].

In response to Max one of the partners stated: "Oh no, no, no, you're too sharp an attorney for us to just let you go." Max asserted her abilities and her ethical duties, and expected harsh repercussions, but she never expected the partners to require her to take an extended vacation. (Yet again, the series has supporting characters who either encourage or enforce hard-working Black women to take a break) Max would continue to refer to this forced vacation as a suspension.

Throughout Max's suspension she becomes almost unbearable to deal with, weeks of Max sitting in her friends' kitchen waiting for the call from Evans & Bell, and testing her hand at new hobbies showcases her lack of direction without an active career.

In episode 4 of season 2 "Working Nine to Nine-Fifteen," Max gets the call from Evans & Bell to return to work. Mr. Evans, on her first day back, reminds Max of how her overzealousness almost lost them their biggest client, then establishes her new work guidelines, before reiterating how valuable she is. Her value is stated in relation to Evans & Bell looking stupid if she were to go to another law firm. Again, Max is scolded on how impressive she really is, a catch-22 for her. Max quits the firm, with no job lined up, no future plans, except the plan to not belittle herself by being unofficially demoted, required to jump through hoops, removed from her office with a view, and no longer in charge of her own cases. In the words of herself, "a good lawyer never settles," and when asked by her friends how she could quit, she said "I had to … they'd never stop punishing me for what I did." Joblessness harms African Americans more than other demographics, and sharing a narrative of a Black person quitting a job with no future job lined up, is a definite imitation of real life. The question Khadijah asks of Max, "how could you quit?" not "why did you quit?" expresses the realities that *why* is not always essential, that ideologies of self-care, self-worth and wanting to love what you do for a profession, is not as essential as *how* will you manage? The reality is, throughout Max's unemployment the viewers are not privy to how she is affording to maintain her individual apartment, with no roommates. I would posit that the series breaks the mode of financial survival first for African Americans, but lacks in recognizing the ambiguity as to *how* survival is maintained, and focuses on the *why* to re-center self-care, self-worth and loving one's profession.

On episode 10, of season 2 "Double Indignity," Max finds herself offered the position of public defender. This job offer comes after Max was rejected multiple times from job inquiries via mail, and by a firm she interviewed for thinking she was sure to get the job. The moment she received the rejection call, she outwardly began to question her abilities, the direct opposite of her confident presence in her work and personal life. Max is suffering from Impostor Syndrome. The origin of Impostor Syndrome comes from the concept of impostor phenomenon defined as being "used to designate an internal experience of intellectual phoniness which appears to be particularly prevalent and intense among a select sample of high achieving women" (Clance & Imes, 1978).

Referring to herself as not qualified enough, Max was met with direct opposition from her friends who reminded her of her exceptionalism in her profession. And as she degraded her own personality Khadijah stepped in: "Max, you are arrogant. And hard-headed and overbearing and domineering. But that's what it takes to be a good attorney." Max continues to show disappointment, and almost asks for her job back at Evans & Bell, but ultimately held firm in her conviction despite uncertainty. Such uncertainty may not make sense to those other than Max, but impostor syndrome is like a "sinking sense that you are a fraud in your industry, role or position, regardless of your credibility, authority or accomplishments" (Wong, 2018). Despite the onset of these impostor feelings, Max holds onto the realities of her past as a very successful attorney, a potential push to viewers to stand strong in their convictions of their self-worth, even in uncertain times.

When a new supervisor, Preston August (Phil Morris), arrives at Max's public defender office the two are reminded of their romantic time together years prior and their admiration for each other as attorneys and the attraction they still feel.

Episode 19, Season 2, "Legal Briefs," displays yet another major decision in Max's career, between the potential of love and or stability of career. Max and Preston enter into a romantic relationship and find themselves debating and fighting the ethics of such a relationship in the workplace. Max's friends try their best to remind her of the trouble that comes with dating a coworker, but Max expresses how well she and Preston get along and connect, between their approaches to being attorneys to how simply being together makes anything more pleasant. It is their mutual jealously over the other's interactions with colleagues that makes them realize how much harder it is to work together, and for Preston to be Max's boss. Max and Preston express their inability to concentrate when around each other and how it interferes with their work, something both of them are passionate about. The two mutually decide to end the potential of continued romance in the name of their careers. Neither of them wanted to leave their current jobs, nor saw the relationship as potentially outweighing such a career opportunity. Could Max have passed up a very likely forever-relationship? Perhaps. This dilemma showcases the often more difficult realities of professional Black women not finding or being able to prioritize love.

Research has repeatedly shown that Black women in general are less likely to get married. Data from the 2006–10 National Survey of Family Growth, as referenced in the 2015 report "The Growing Racial and Ethnic Divide in U.S. Marriage Patterns," found that Black women have the highest rates of never being married by the age of 44, the lowest rates of stable marriages, and are least likely to be married more than once (Raley, Sweeney, & Wondra, 2015).

Black professional women are not necessarily less likely to have been married in comparison to non-professional Black women, being defined by number of years of education, but they remain double digit percentage points behind their white, and Hispanic counterparts by all levels of education (Raley, Sweeney, & Wondra, 2015). The issue is not simply that Max is a professional woman, it is the fact that she is a Black woman, which makes having a spouse less likely. And of course, Max's character has proven throughout the series to be "hard to love," and also harder for her to show her genuine feelings to the men she dates.

Kyle Barker: Black Hair Is Professional

Kyle Barker is a stock broker, and in the beginning of the series one may not have known this without the verbal statement of such. The reason for this is that he does not fit the American visual definition of a stock broker, he is a dark-skinned Black man, with short dread locked hair, who often wears Afrocentric attire, and speaks his mind. His presence in this series breaks so many stereotypes of what Black men are and can be. Kyle succeeds greatly in his career at his firm, but it was not without some trials and major decisions. It can be argued that in regards to professional investment versus personal identity that Kyle is the character that had the most racially charged decision between his identity and career.

In Kyle's move towards promotion, in episode 13, season 2 "A Hair-Razing Experience," Kyle proposes to establish and run an African Mutual Fund to the partners of his firm. For several days Kyle waits anxiously to hear the decision of the partners, worried that the partners were not impressed or only had bad news. Taking advice from his roommate and longtime friend, Overton, Kyle decides to reach out to another Black man in the firm Lawrence (Bobby Hosea), who had already reached such a level of promotion. Kyle only becomes discouraged by what Lawrence asked Kyle to do—change his hair. Lawrence informed Kyle in a very direct, unapologetic way that it was Kyle's hair that was hindering him from being promoted. Lawrence viewed Kyle's mutual fund proposal as impressive, but referenced his appearance as a stumbling block. Kyle, as he does often throughout the series, verbalized the high-end designers he was wearing, when Lawrence informed Kyle it was not his clothes but his hair that was the problem. Kyle inquired about the statement: "What does my hair have to do with becoming a Funds Manager?" To his question Lawrence stated the following before exiting the conference room:

> Well, we don't think it's corporate enough.... Kyle you don't get promoted around here by going against the grain. Look, if this Africa project goes through you'll be representing this company to a much higher level clientele. And then your appearance becomes much more important. So, take my advice … change the hair.

Following this encounter in the episode, Kyle is shown trying on wigs with Regine's help, seriously contemplating changing his hairstyle from dreadlocks to something more acceptable to Eurocentric corporate culture. Between Regine's insistence that wearing a wig would not be selling out because underneath it all he would still be Kyle, and Khadijah's direct rejection of ever changing her hair for a job and that's why she works for herself, Kyle remains conflicted. This conversation about hair speaks to the requirement to compromise as African Americans in professions that uphold a specific type of look.

> **KYLE:** But my dreads are an expression of my culture. If I change my hair wouldn't that be sellin' out?
> **REGINE:** Kyle, maybe you should try working within the system. Just till you get into a position of power. And then you can tell everyone else how they can wear their hair.
> **KYLE:** You know, I have worked too hard and come too far to let something like my hair hold me back now. Besides, maybe it is time for a change.

The show's audience is shown a very important but often unrealized reality of African Americans in corporate America, the dilemma of not looking too "Black," or too proud of one's Black heritage that does not align with the dominant culture of predominantly Eurocentric corporate professions.

After Kyle processes with his friends, he has a nightmare showing him as a jester, someone who plays the fool, for his partners in return for his promotion. In a follow up meeting Kyle requests with the partners, Kyle speaks up about his hair and that he would not be changing it, because he believed that the firm promoted ability over the superficial. He states that his hair is not just for fashion but a statement of pride. And similar to Max's stance at Evans & Bell, Kyle holds firm that whether promoted or not he will not change his hair. And in a simple statement one of the white partners simply says, "okay." Lawrence, Kyle's Black colleague sits in silence as the two white partners speak about their decision on Kyle's hair after Lawrence had brought it up to them. They asked Kyle how he even knew it was being discussed, in which Kyle pointed to Lawrence. Lawrence states, "You know I feel [his hair is] not in keeping with the company image." In which one white partner tells Lawrence he needs to loosen up, and further extends to Kyle that he was being promoted to Funds Manager. It is in this moment that both the audience and Kyle are made aware that it was a Black man who made Kyle's dreadlocks an issue in his promotion. And prior to closing out the scene a dialogue between these two Black male professionals revealed to a non–Black audience, and spoke more poignantly to the Black viewers about the complexities of being Black, professional, and trying to succeed in a white dominated system. Lawrence attempts to settle the entire issue by prescribing to Kyle that there should be no hard feelings, to which Kyle replies:

> KYLE: No feelings at all, man.
> LAWRENCE: Look, I was just trying to help.
> KYLE: You see, that's the sad part. You actually believe that. [Kyle exits the conference room.]
> LAWRENCE: Yeah. I do. [Spoken in an empty room to himself.]

Again, *Living Single* was ground breaking to have this conversation, and also to allow Kyle's choice to fall along his true desires of being himself and confronting his white bosses, alongside his Black boss Lawrence, only to be informed by his white bosses that his hair never mattered. Again the series revealed another nuanced experience of African Americans in professions where to be accepted often means conforming to the "white" norm; that the African American colleague who puts their career before their culture, their experience as a Black person, is seen from many as selling out. Contemporarily the concept of Respectability Politics is also used in referencing the assimilation type behaviors of African Americans in the workplace to survive and perhaps thrive.

Originating as a term in Evelyn Brooks Higginbotham's 1994 book about Black Baptist Church women, she used it to describe their social justice tactics and approaches.

> …the politics of respectability constituted a deliberate, highly self-conscious concession to hegemonic values. While deferring to segregation in practice, adherents of respectability never deferred to it in principle. The Baptist women's emphasis on manners and morals served to reinforce their sense of moral superiority over whites [Higginbotham, 1994, p. 193].

In Higginbotham's analysis and definition of Respectability Politics, it relates to a form of survival in a segregated time. Today, the term is utilized across marginalized groups in reference to attempts made by their own members (and selves) to police behaviors in order to demonstrate their social values as being compatible with dominant values, rather than challenging the mainstream for what they see as its failure to accept difference. Lawrence appears not to understand that he plays into respectability politics as an active tool of survival in the workplace. Thus, Lawrence expects his own people to survive similarly. Kyle, however, pushes back against the Eurocentric corporate image specifically in regards to his hair. Kyle utilizes this tactic to survive and thrive in his work as a stock broker; for him having his hair in a prideful style that showcases his heritage is a part of his identity and if he had to hide part of himself he would not survive.

In Kyle's hair dilemma, he does not retreat in this 1994 episode. It was only in 2019 that individual states began making hair discrimination against the law in the hiring process. This law has been prompted due to the ruling in the court case of Chasity Jones in 2010; Jones was offered a job and then the offer was rescinded after she refused to change her hair style from dreadlocks (Griffin, 2019). The judge stated that dreadlocks were not a discrimination based on race because all people's hair could be locked, and thus it is not only of African American culture. Issues of Black hair discrimination have been brought to legal questions for over forty years, and in July 2019 California became the first state to legally protect against hair discrimination. The law states:

> The history of our nation is riddled with laws and societal norms that equated "Blackness," and the associated physical traits, for example, dark skin, kinky and curly hair to a badge of inferiority, sometimes subject to separate and unequal treatment.... Professionalism was, and still is, closely linked to European features and mannerisms, which entails that those who do not naturally fall into Eurocentric norms must alter their appearances, sometimes drastically and permanently, in order to be deemed professional [Nasheed, 2019].

Once again, *Living Single* shares narratives African Americans often do not wish to showcase, dilemmas between our own, within ourselves. Yet such an action allows the audience to utilize the episode and series as a whole to initiate such conversations with friends and family in an approachable and relatable way.

Conclusion: "Check, check, check it out...."

Living Single was a ground breaking series showcasing the narratives of African Americans, with a major focus on balancing professional careers, family, friends, and love. It revealed narratives many African Americans experience and openly share, yet it also broke barriers by introducing hidden narratives that African Americans prefer to leave untouched and unspoken. It was a sitcom, so yes it was comedic, but it was also art imitating life, bringing in all emotions and types of experiences within the Black community. It was a series that led the way for sitcoms of the future like *Girlfriends* (2000–2008), and it remains a series that transcends time. No matter the generation of viewers, *Living Single* can connect, so check it out.

REFERENCES

Agada, E. (2015, January 11). *Sidney Poitier, Mike Brown, and the Myth of Black Exceptionalism.* Retrieved from Celluloid in Black and White: http://celluloidinBlackandwhite. blogspot.com/2015/01/sidney-poitier-mike-brown-and-myth-of.html.

Clance, P. R., & Imes, S. A. (1978). The Impostor Phenomenon in High Achieving Women: Dynamics and Therapeutic Intervention. *Psychotherapy: Theory, Research and Practice, 15*(3), 241–247.

Doggett, J. A. (2019, October 10). Impostor Syndrome Hits Harder When You're Black. Retrieved from *Huffington Post*: https://www.huffpost.com/entry/imposter-syndrome-racism-discrimination_l_5d9f2c00e4b06ddfc514ec5c.

Griffin, C. (2019, July 3). How Natural Black Hair at Work Became a Civil Rights Issue. Retrieved from JSTOR Daily: https://daily.jstor.org/how-natural-Black-hair-at-work-became-a-civil-rights-issue/.

Hamilton, K. (2005, April 21). The Dialect Dilemma. *Black Issues in Higher Education, 22*(5), 34.

Higginbotham, E. B. (1994). *Righteous Discontent: The Women's Movement in the Black Baptist Church, 1880–1920.* Boston: Harvard University Press.

Jackson, B. A. (1994, September 19). "Fresh Prince of Bel-Air" Begins Fifth Season. *Cover Story*, p. 56.

Koch, L. M., Gross, A. M., & Kolts, R. (2001, February). Attitudes Toward Black English and Code Switching. *Journal of Black Pyschology, 27*(1), 29–42.

Morton, J. M. (2014). Cultural Code-Switching: Straddling the Achievement Gap. *The Journal of Political Philosophy, 22*(3), 259–281.

Nasheed, J. (2019, August 9). *A Brief History of Black Hair, Politics, and Discrimination.* Retrieved from Teen Vogue: https://www.teenvogue.com/story/a-brief-history-of-Black-hair-politics-and-discrimination.

Raley, R. K., Sweeney, M. M., & Wondra, D. (2015). *The Growing Racial and Ethnic Divide in U.S. Marriage Patterns.* Department of Health and Human Services.

Ressner, J., & Moss, G. (1990). Raps to Riches. *Rolling Stone*, p. 45.

Washington, M. (2012). Interracial Intimacy: Hegemonic Construction of Asian American and Black Relationships on TV Medical Dramas. *The Howard Journal of Communications, 23*, 253–271.

Watson, N. N., & Hunter, C. D. (2015). Anxiety and Depression Among African American Women: The Costs of Strength and Negative Attitudes Toward Psychological Help-Seeking. *American Psychological Association, 21*(4), 604–612.

Wong, K. (2018, June 12). *Dealing with Impostor Syndrome When You're Treated as an Impostor.* Retrieved from New York Times: https://www.nytimes.com/2018/06/12/smarter-living/dealing-with-impostor-syndrome-when-youre-treated-as-an-impostor.html.

PART II
Publicly Figured Characters

Tackling Stereotypes

Portrayals of Black NFL Athletes on *The CW's* The Game *and HBO's* Ballers

DARNEL DEGAND

Black National Football League (NFL) players are simultaneously stereotyped as *dumb jocks* (i.e., unintelligent athletes) and *Black bucks* (i.e., violent, unintelligent, oversexed Black men who lust after White women). Athletes have been referred to as dumb jocks since, at least, the ancient Olympic Games when "[Greek athletes] concentrated so much on athletic training that they ignored intellectual development. This evoked widespread criticism from Greek philosophers, who saw the games as brutal and dehumanizing and the athletes as useless and ignorant beings" (Coakley, 2007, p. 59). NFL athletes face similar criticism because they engage in legitimized forms of violence, i.e., *brutal body contact* (Smith, 1983), and many hours of physical training. Yet, Black men have been historically viewed as threatening, regardless of their profession. The Black buck stereotype was born out of racist social beliefs. Its cinematic introduction occurred in the 1915 film, *The Birth of a Nation*, in which several Black men were shown wreaking havoc and lusting after White women (Bogle, 2016). This stereotype exists in contemporary media because these negative perceptions of Black men persist. These racist visuals train viewers to "suspiciously regard and viscerally react to African American men's physical features and patterns of interaction" (Page, 1997, p. 106). It is a cycle that feeds itself because some aspiring media producers regard the existing negative depictions of Black men as support for the creation of more media that reinforces these problematic beliefs.

This essay examines several prejudicial assumptions about athletes and Black men that negatively influence social opinions and media depictions of Black NFL players. The first half uses cultivation theory to explain society's influences on media messages about Black men and football. The second half examines how the first seasons of *The Game* (2006–2015) and *Ballers* (2015–2019) push back on extreme stereotypes by representing Black NFL players as multidimensional professionals who engage in both positive and negative behaviors.

First Half: American Football Culture

Cultivation Theory

Gerbner (1967) introduced *cultivation theory* to explain how society's influences on mass media messages can affect citizen's social beliefs and experiences. He wrote:

> A culture is that system of messages which cultivates the images of a society. The dominant communication agencies produce the message systems which cultivate dominant image patterns. They cultivate the broadest common notions of what is, what is important and what is right. They structure the public agenda of existence, priorities and values. People use this agenda—some more selectively than others—to support their ideas, actions or both… [Gerbner, 1967, p. 434].

American society positions upper middle class White American cultures as the broadest common notions of importance and righteousness. Black American cultures are devalued and seen as peripheral or deviant. This contributes to the persistence of opportunity gaps between racial groups. Many White Americans rationalize the persistence of social inequalities and inequities with explanations that are influenced by their negative beliefs about Black Americans (DiTomaso, 2013). Mainstream media producers often share these negative views and the content they produce reflects these biases (Bogle, 2016). As a result, Black Americans and Americans who might not practice heterosexual White American Christian cultures have historically been less visible and poorly portrayed in mass media.

Cultivation theory helps us understand how White America's long-held place at the center of American society has influenced media and helped it popularize the dumb jock and Black buck stereotypes applied to Black NFL players. Historically, the team rosters for the NFL and other mainstream professional sports leagues that are considered culturally "American" (e.g., baseball's American League) were predominantly White. Coaches argued that the athletic superiority of Anglo-Saxon men was the reasoning behind this exclusivity (Oriard, 1998). I argue that it was motivated by racism and a belief that White Americans were "American," by default. Nonwhite athletes were viewed as individuals from outside cultures and essentially banned from joining the "American" professional sports leagues. "Until 1933 the NFL usually included a couple of African American players and sometimes as many as half a dozen. From 1933 until 1946, however, African Americans were prohibited from playing in the league" (Finkelman, 2009, p. 235). Instead, many played for All-Black teams such as the New York Brown Bombers and the Chicago Black Hawks (Ross, 2005; Smith, 1988).

Once the NFL ban against Black athletes ended, they proceeded to dominate the sport which "spurred the evolution of specific stereotypes and myths in an attempt to explain their success and subsequent attack on the 'white status quo.' These stereotypes elevated the physical prowess of the African American athlete, but attacked his intellectual capabilities" (Sailes, 2017, p. 186). White athletes were stereotyped as dumb jocks who focused on physical exercise and neglected education. The Black buck stereotype automatically caused Black athletes to be viewed as unintelligent and unfairly strong, regardless of their education goals and physical training.

The influences of these social stereotypes on media are evident when we analyze the dominant image patterns of Black athletes. Sportscasters overemphasize the physical athleticism of Black players while praising the intelligence of White players (Rada, 1996). Movies and television shows often portray athletes as dumb jocks (Sailes, 2017) but also depict Black athletes as threats to White sports traditions (e.g., 2000's *Remember the Titans,* 1999's *Any Given Sunday*). Moreover, Black NFL athletes' celebrity status and race inspire news media outlets to misrepresent them as the faces of violence, especially against White women (Enck-Wanzer, 2009).

America, Football and Manhood

Football's popularity is largely due to its association with American cultural beliefs about manhood. The sport is so popular that (depending on age and ability) players can join youth, intramural, eSports, wheelchair, college, semi-professional, or professional leagues. Some parents use traditionally all-male youth football leagues as opportunities to teach their sons about manhood. Hartmann (2003) writes, "single mothers bring their boys to the teams I coach out of concern that their sons are insufficiently tough or physical because they lack a male influence" (p. 16). Unfortunately, lessons about accountability and responsibility (Steinfeldt et al., 2011) are paired with homophobic slurs and misogynistic speech (Adams, Anderson, & McCormack, 2010). Research suggests that adolescent boys are aware of the problematic aspects of these practices and often justify them as "just part of what it means to be a guy" (Pascoe, 2005, p. 335). There is a long history of complaints that have been made about these negative aspects of football culture but football continues to serve as America's most popular sport (Oates, 2017).

Football Culture and NFL Power

Mass media plays an important role in football culture. Many spectators attend live games but the majority watch the televised matches. College games attract a solid number of viewers but its viewership pales in comparison to NFL television ratings. The NFL is a powerful institution that profits (financially and culturally) from football's association with manhood and from its own control over multiple sports media outlets who want to broadcast NFL games. It often ignores critics (e.g., Queer activists, cheerleaders, Black and Indigenous groups) that characterize its "racialized hypermasculinity as problematic and outdated" (Oates, 2017, p. 6) but sometimes it takes action against attacks on its branding. For example, the NFL forced the cancellation of ESPN's *Playmakers* (2003), a successful television drama that examined negative aspects of NFL culture (e.g., homophobia, racism, drugs). NFL management described the show as a "gross mischaracterization of our sport." ESPN cancelled it to ensure that their multibillion dollar, multiyear contract with the NFL would be renewed (Sandomir, cited in Oates, 2017, p. 44). Moreover, the NFL leverages its influences by contributing to conversations about children's physical health through its "Play 60" marketing campaign. However, Rugg (2019) cautions that:

> …despite assertions from the NFL that Play 60 is not football-centric, an analysis of these materials illustrates that the program operates as a Trojan horse for familiarizing students with the league, its players, and the verbiage of the game as well as training them in the physical skills required to perform the sport [p. 82].

The NFL season's schedule broadcasts multiple games throughout the week and during holidays (e.g., Thanksgiving, Christmas, and New Year's). The season concludes with the highest viewed and most financially lucrative event in America, Super Bowl Sunday. This can only persist through the nurturing of tomorrow's players and viewers which suggests that this is one of the motivations behind the football content included in the "Play 60" campaign.

Second Half: Tackling Stereotypes

Historically, White men have held the majority of writers, producers, and directors' positions in Hollywood (Smith, Choueiti, & Pieper, 2016). As a result, media depictions of Black people have largely been constructed from their limited understandings of Black lives. DuBois' (1994) description of Black people's "double-consciousness" concerning their "second-sight in this American world" (p. 2) is reproduced through this media. Black viewers literally have "this sense of always looking at one's self through the eyes of others" (DuBois, 1994, p.2) when Whites create television that shows Black viewers a White person's conceptualization of Black experiences.

Fortunately the mediascape increasingly provides viewers with depictions of multidimensional Black characters who challenge the stereotypes that have been historically offered. I provide *The Game* and *Ballers* as examples. These television series are the focus of the second half of this essay where I conduct a comparative analysis of their attempts to push back on stereotypes of Black NFL players.

The Game

In February 2007, Indianapolis Colts' Tony Dungy and Chicago Bears' Lovie Smith simultaneously became the first Black head coaches to lead their teams to the Super Bowl. That game capped the end of the 2006 NFL season and it challenged the long-held stereotype that Black NFL athletes did not have the intelligence needed to become successful head coaches. The first season of *The Game* was released during that NFL season. I argue that it also pushed back against Black NFL player stereotypes with honest portrayals of their positive and negative behaviors. Its plots revolved around the struggles experienced by a Black live-in couple, rookie NFL athlete Derwin Davis (Pooch Hall) and medical school student Melanie Barnett (Tia Mowry-Hardrict).

Behind-the-Scenes

The Game premiered on The CW network in 2006 and its first season consisted of 22 episodes. Mara Brock Akil, a Black woman, created the show as a spin-off from her successful series, *Girlfriends* (1999–2008). Her writing staff was equally split between Black and non–Black writers (Henderson, 2011). Akil stated:

> In my writers' room, you will typically find an even split between male and female writers ... various religious beliefs ... diversity in sexual orientation ... different class backgrounds.... Honestly, we're all living in this world together, so how can only one of those experiences come to dominate the writers' room? [Curtin & Sanson, 2017, p. 25]

The benefits of her diverse staff are evident in my analysis below.

Contrasting Characters

The Game critiques past depictions of Black NFL athletes by contrasting stereotypes with multidimensional characters. The motivations behind the Black players' actions are gradually revealed within the context of their professional experiences, personalities, and backgrounds. For example, Black quarterback Malik Wright (Hosea Chanchez) is a financially irresponsible, womanizer. His teammate Jason Pitts (Coby Bell) is a frugal Black man married to a White woman, Kelly Pitts (Brittany Daniel). *The Game*'s writers make these details explicit during a heated argument between the players. Malik says: "you like everything white … your music, your clothes, your wife," and Jason's responses include: "I'm really sorry I don't drive nine cars at once, MC stereotype." Their teammates laugh at both players but some also agree with Jason's comments. Malik is oversexed. He is shown with multiple women (often half-naked), before and after sex, in several episodes. However, Malik's dialogues throughout the season reveal that his actions are inspired by his need to maintain the alpha male status on his team. He spends money on teammates to boost team morale because he is co-captain. We also learn that some of his extravagant parties are scheduled opportunities for him to network with professional entertainment industry collaborators. Lastly, there are several instances where he reveals his desire (albeit shallow) to eventually commit to a mature relationship.

Team co-captain Jason is not an exaggerated stereotype. He has a loving relationship with Kelly. He is the highest-paid player on the team but he despises the idea of overspending. He chooses to boost team morale by making donations in each teammates' names to Hurricane Katrina victims instead of giving them extravagant gifts. Later in the season we also learn that Jason's financial insecurities are due to his experiences as the son of a former NFL player who wasted his fortunes. Jason's financial decisions are similar to those of several former and current NFL athletes who choose not to waste their salaries (Kutz, 2017).

Multidimensional Characters

The Game's writers often contrast Derwin with Malik because they are opposites. Derwin prays regularly, keeps a journal, and often expresses his love for Melanie. He even physically places himself between Malik and Jason to stop their fight. However, Derwin's flaws are often on display, especially when Melanie's independent spirit clashes with the NFL's chauvinistic culture. This culture requires football to be Derwin's priority. Even his proposal to Melanie is a televised NFL halftime commercial. As the season progresses, Derwin increasingly exhibits questionable behaviors and Malik joins Jason in repeatedly warning him that he is sabotaging his relationship with Melanie. Nevertheless, Derwin resents Melanie's constant refusals to submit to football culture and he eventually cheats on her. These Black NFL athletes are depicted as multidimensional characters. Like the rest of society, they are constantly evolving, complex individuals. The players are often told to "act professionally" but professionalism is an implicitly defined term used to describe their skills and behaviors. They must practice, compete in games, maintain elite physical health, study playbooks, and behave appropriately during interviews and public appearances. However, they must also represent manhood off the field and engage in violent performances on the field. *The Game* depicts these experiences and reveals the contrasting motivations behind Black NFL athletes' "positive" and "negative" behaviors.

Ballers

In February 2015, a Super Bowl commercial addressed domestic violence for the first time. A voiceover of a woman on a 911 call accompanied footage of a house in disarray. This woman disguised her call for help (from her abuser) by pretending to order pizza. The commercial did not show the perpetrator and victim, which allowed for speculation. The culprit could have been an NFL player or one of the millions of viewers watching the game. The first season of *Ballers* debuted four months after this commercial aired. *Ballers* also addresses the violence that is often associated with NFL athletes. This series follows retired, half-Black, half-Samoan, NFL athlete Spencer Strasmore (Dwayne Johnson) as he simultaneously attempts to succeed in a white-collar profession and navigate stereotypes that typecast him as a violent man.

Behind-the-Scenes

Ballers premiered on the HBO network in 2015. Its first season consisted of 10 episodes. Stephen Levinson, a White man, created the show. His writing room was not as diverse as that of *The Game* but it included retired Black NFL athlete and Super Bowl champion, Rashard Mendenhall (IMDb, n.d.). Mendenhall had been contacted by HBO after he published an essay announcing his retirement from the NFL and his desire to become a writer (Mendenhall, 2014; Wiedeman, 2015). He was initially wary of the idea of *Ballers* but he eventually concluded that HBO wanted to create an authentic show. Mendenhall stated: "As a player, when you see these shows about football, it feels so outside-in—just one big party without the real stories" (Wiedeman, 2015, para. 9). He was a staff writer during the first season and was promoted to editor and producer in later seasons (IMDb, n.d.).

Violence: Motivations and Consequences

Ballers' shows Black NFL athletes behaving violently and reveals the motivations and consequences of those actions. The first scene of the pilot episode alternates between shots of now-retired Spencer in pain as he struggles to get out of bed and past footage of Spencer violently tackling another NFL player. The scene ends with the tackled player lying motionless on the field and cuts back to Spencer swallowing a pill. The consequences of football violence are demonstrated through Spencer's multiple doctors' visits, the painkillers he swallows each episode, and his guilt over the career-ending hit on the previously mentioned player. The motivations behind these hits are seen in episodes where professional coaches insult and scream at players to hit harder. Spencer eventually tracks down the injured player from his flashbacks and apologizes: "I meant to hurt you that day … it's the type of player I was back then." *Ballers* also shows Black NFL player Ricky Jerret (John David Washington) punching a White man after he insults Ricky for having public bathroom sex. The stranger says, "I guess the rules, they don't apply to you, huh? You guys with your fucking self-entitlement. Y'all ain't nothing but a bunch of selfish, womanizing assholes." As Ricky leaves, the man yells, "Get ready to break out that checkbook!" This encounter reveals this stranger's beliefs about NFL players, his excitement over catching Ricky in the act, and his plans to sue Ricky. In a later episode, we see Ricky engage in similar behavior when he fights with a teammate after sleeping with that teammates' mother.

Spencer is a financial consultant and his ability to walk away from circumstances where he might wish to respond violently is valuable and necessary, but he still makes mistakes. Football is the focal point of an NFL athlete's life until they exit the league. The lifestyle change can be jarring when they begin to consider options for their next professional career. Their skills do not automatically translate into other professions and the "dumb jock" stereotype persists because of the many years they have spent focusing on athletics. Nevertheless, Spencer uses his past financial mistakes (e.g., failed investments) as motivation to recruit and advise current players. His role as a trusted, level-headed NFL mentor assists him with recruiting his mentees as clients. He cautions Ricky about financial opportunist who instigate fights and he helps another Black NFL player, Vernon Littlefield (Donovan W. Carter), with financial decisions. Unlike Ricky, Vernon is selfless, family-oriented, and peaceful. He loves bird-watching and photography. We even see Vernon reprimand his friend, Reggie (London Brown), for disrespecting women. However, Reggie is also Vernon's money handler and he views Spencer as a threat to his livelihood. During one of many arguments between Spencer and Reggie, we see Spencer lose his temper. He forgets his own advice to Ricky and shoves Reggie to the ground.

MULTIDIMENSIONAL CHARACTERS

The contrasting of various multidimensional characters in *Ballers* provides viewers with a range of personalities that challenge the Black buck and dumb jock stereotypes. Ricky exhibits some of these stereotypical traits but he is also a loyal friend. He ruined his own relationship by cheating on his ex-partner but he still chooses to offer the following heartfelt advice to his friend, retired Black NFL player Charles Greane (Omar Benson Miller): "You've got a special thing with your wife. A thing I'm far too selfish and immature to have for myself. You need to go home." Like Vernon, Charles is friendly, non-violent, and family-oriented but he is also flawed. There are several episodes where we observe him entertaining sexts and sexual invitations from a woman he met at a party. His wife confronts him after she sees a sext from the woman and Charles chooses to move out. I argue that Ricky's ability to listen, sympathize, and advise Charles to return home reinforces the message that Black athletes should be allowed to be seen as constantly evolving, complex, and multidimensional individuals. The ambiguity concerning what professionalism means for NFL players is visible in *Ballers*. Viewers see players in practice, games, gyms, interviews, and clubs. We see their attempts to represent manhood in public and we see their efforts to meet the violent expectations of the game. *Ballers* also reveals how conversations between Black NFL athletes are not limited to their professional performance on the field. Other topics include racism, manhood, families, intimate relationships, home communities, post–NFL careers, financial health, physical health, and many other life concerns and interests.

Conclusion

The NFL is an influential professional organization that encourages behaviors that are generalized, misunderstood, and stigmatized. The first half of this essay uses cultivation theory to explain how social influences on media impact stereotypes about athletes, Black men, and their behaviors. The NFL's power over how mass media depicts its organization and its athletes is also discussed. In the second half of this essay, *The Game* and *Ballers* are provided as examples of series that push back against stereotypes by depicting both the positive and negative behaviors that professional Black athletes engage in. The motivations behind their actions are examined within the context of their professional experiences, personalities, and backgrounds while also accounting for the unspoken expectation that NFL athletes continue to serve as representations of American manhood.

REFERENCES

Adams, A., Anderson, E., & McCormack, M. (2010). Establishing and Challenging Masculinity: The Influence of Gendered Discourses in Organized Sport. *Journal of Language and Social Psychology, 29*(3), 278–300.

Bogle, D. (2016). *Toms, Coons, Mulattoes, Mammies, and Bucks: An Interpretive History of Blacks in American Films*. New York: Bloomsbury Publishing.

Coakley, J.J. (2007). *Sport in Society: Issues and Controversies* (9th ed.). Boston: McGraw-Hill.

Curtin, M. & Sanson, K. (2017). *Voices of Labor: Creativity, Craft, and Conflict*. University of California Press.

DiTomaso, N. (2013). *The American Non-Dilemma: Racial Inequality Without Racism*. New York: Russell Sage Foundation.

DuBois, W.E.B. (1994). *The Souls of Black Folk*. New York: Dover Publications, Inc.

Enck-Wanzer, S. M. (2009). All's Fair in Love and Sport: Black Masculinity and Domestic Violence in the News. *Communication and Critical/Cultural Studies, 6*(1), 1–18.

Finkelman, P. (Ed.). (2009). *Encyclopedia of African American History, 1896 to the Present: From the Age of Segregation to the Twenty-first Century Five-volume Set* (Vol. 1). Oxford University Press.

Gerbner, G. (1967). An Institutional Approach to Mass Communications Research. In L. Thayer (Ed.), *Communication Theory and Research: Proceedings of the First International Symposium* (pp. 429–445). Springfield, IL: Charles C. Thomas.

Hartmann, D. (2003). The Sanctity of Sunday Football: Why Men Love Sports. *Contexts, 2*(4), 13–21.

Henderson, F. D. (2011). The Culture Behind Closed Doors: Issues of Gender and Race in the Writers' Room. *Cinema Journal, 50*(2), 145–152.

IMDb. (n.d.). *Rashard Mendenhall*. Retrieved from https://www.imdb.com/name/nm3135260/?ref_=ttfc_fc_wr2.

Kutz, S. (2017, April 29). NFL Players and Veterans Advise Rookies on How to Invest Their Newfound Wealth. Retrieved from https://www.marketwatch.com/story/nfl-players-and-advisers-offer-financial-advice-to-incoming-rookies-2017-04-25.

Mendenhall, R. (2014). Why I Retired at 26. *The Huffington Post*.

Oates, T. P. (2017). *Football and Manliness: An Unauthorized Feminist Account of the NFL*. University of Illinois Press.

Oriard, M. (1998). *Reading Football: How the Popular Press Created an American Spectacle*. University of North Carolina Press.

Page, H. E. (1997). "Black Male" Imagery and Media Containment of African American Men. *American Anthropologist, 99*(1), 99–111.

Pascoe, C. J. (2005). "Dude, you're a fag": Adolescent Masculinity and the Fag Discourse. *Sexualities, 8*(3), 329–346.

Rada, J. A. (1996). Color Blind-sided: Racial Bias in Network Television's Coverage of Professional Football Games. *Howard Journal of Communications, 7*(3), 231–239.

Ross, C. K. (Ed.). (2005). *Race and Sport: The Struggle for Equality On and Off the Field*. University Press of Mississippi.

Rugg, A. (2019). Working Out Their Future: The NFL's Play 60 Campaign and the Production of Adolescent Fans and Players. *Journal of Sport and Social Issues, 43*(1), 69–88.

Sailes, G. A. (2017). *African Americans in Sports*. Routledge.

Smith, M. D. (1983). *Violence and Sport*. Toronto: Butterworths

Smith, S. Choueiti, M., & Pieper, K. (2016). *Inclusion & Invisibility? Gender, Media, Diversity & Social Change Initiative*. Los Angeles: Annenberg School for Communication Media Diversity and Social Change Initiative.

Smith, T. G. (1988). Outside the Pale: The Exclusion of Blacks from the National Football League, 1934–1946. Journal of Sport History, 15(3), 255–281.

Steinfeldt, J. A., Foltz, B. D., Mungro, J., Speight, Q. L., Wong, Y. J., & Blumberg, J. (2011). Masculinity Socialization in Sports: Influence of College Football Coaches. *Psychology of Men & Masculinity, 12*(3), 247.

Wiedeman, R. (2015, July 01). Rashard Mendenhall: The Real Player Behind "Ballers." Retrieved from https://www.mensjournal.com/adventure/rashard-mendenhall-the-real-player-behind-ballers-20150701/.

#IamMaryJane

Blackness, Womanhood and
Professionalism in BET's Being Mary Jane

MALIKA T. BUTLER *and*
KRISTAL MOORE CLEMONS

Introduction

Being Mary Jane (2013–2019) was the Black Entertainment Television (BET) network's first hour long scripted drama. The show first aired July 2, 2013, and was created by African American screenwriter, Mara Brock Akil. Prior to the debut of *Being Mary Jane* Brock Akil and her husband, Salim Akil had found success with *Girlfriends* (2000–2008) and *The Game* (2006–2015), two highly popular shows for the United Paramount Network (UPN). The couple's work has been considered groundbreaking for their ability to bring Black voices to network television. *Being Mary Jane* became another success for the team by introducing the world to Mary Jane Paul (Gabrielle Union), a successful Black woman cable news' anchor with a flair for critical discourse, fashion, and the acquisition of the "finer things in life." The character's birth name is Paulette Patterson, however Mary Jane Paul is her professional moniker. Mary Jane Paul, portrayed by actress Gabrielle Union, is a fiercely independent woman navigating the world of love, work, and family in a society that has been impacted by globalization, social media, and the election of Barack Obama, the first Black president of the United States of America. Paul is considered a very relatable Black female lead in a drama series because her drama-filled story-line included a string of undeniably attractive love interests, a family who depends on her to help them emotionally, mentally, and sometimes financially because she is the "responsible" one, and a professional ambition that catapults her career into the famous and wealthy realm.

Mary Jane also represents a television persona influenced by the world around her and is unapologetic about speaking out against racial bias, gender discrimination, and other forms of bigotry. Much of her commentary appears to be influenced by the tenets of Black feminist thought. Mary Jane's experiences in both her professional and personal worlds problematizes what it means to be both Black and woman in American society.

Being Mary Jane: *Understanding Black Women and Television*

Being Mary Jane served as a response to Black women's desire for adequate representation on television. Over the last sixty years television programming has been and continues to be an integral part of American life. Cable networks and streaming services like Netflix and Hulu have invested millions of dollars to create their own special programming television viewers have a number of viewing options that range from sci-fi, romantic comedies, and medical dramas. Historically, the array of television programming has not been comprised of a healthy number of programs that broadcast a strong Black female lead. Much like the past, television like other industries, still struggle with adequate representation. Compounding this issue is the often stereotypical and caricatured portrayals of Black women on television. These depictions have often been used as a mode of information by mainstream society to interrogate, critique, and assume the lived experiences of Black women (Jewell, 1992).

While Black women have been represented in television and film their representation as lead characters has been disappointing. For instance, the American Broadcasting Company (ABC) introduced its first Black female lead with the show *Beulah* (1950–1953). Although Beulah (Ethel Waters) was the lead character she played a stereotypical role of the maid who "fixed" her White family's problems. Eighteen years later Diahann Carroll was given the role of *Julia* (1968–1971). This was a momentous occasion because *Julia* was the first sitcom that had a leading Black woman playing a non-stereotypical role. Even with Julia being given the role of a nurse, the T.V. show which aired in 1968 rarely discussed issues around racial oppression. *Julia* was ahead of its time, but it would take forty-four years before another show existed that had a Black woman lead.

The history of Black women in television has been marred with erasure, stereotypes, and caricatures and unfortunately little has changed to improve these circumstances. With the popularity of Shonda Rhimes' *Scandal* (2012–2018) starring Kerry Washington and other major networks debuting shows with Black female leads; National Broadcasting Company's

(NBC) *Deception* (2013) starring Meagan Good and Columbia Broadcasting System's (CBS) *Extant* (2014–2015) starring Halle Berry; the introduction of *Being Mary Jane* came at an optimal time. Although both Good and Berry's shows were not renewed for future seasons, it was evident that networks recognized the significance and popularity of Black female lead characters. Since the premiere of *Being Mary Jane* there has been an increase in these roles including Rhimes' *How to Get Away with Murder* (2014–2020), Issa Rae's *Insecure* (2016–present), Ava DuVernay's *Queen Sugar* (2016–present), and the comic book series *Black Lightning* (2019–present) and *Watchmen* (2019). All of these shows bring a contrast that allow television viewers to recognize that Black women are not a monolith and these shows nuance the ideas of how Black womanhood has been defined historically and presently.

As stated earlier, the show's creator, Mara Brock Akil had much success centering the lived experiences of Black women with her shows *Girlfriends* and *The Game*. Both shows highlighted the lives of young professional Black women as they juggle their professional lives and love lives. This premise was also seen in *Being Mary Jane*.

Mary Jane Paul: Familiar and Stereotypical Depictions of Black Womanhood

The Presence of Black Feminist Theory in *Being Mary Jane*

Black feminist theory offers insight into a complex history of Black women's work and activism. It also provides a tool of analysis when discussing Black women authors and characters in texts, films, artwork, and music. Historically, Black women have been actively engaged in fighting against gender and race disparities. Black women offer a unique outlook rooted in lived experience and critical consciousness. What follows is a brief overview of Black feminist thought and an articulation of how the show *Being Mary Jane* and the main character Mary Jane oscillate between familiar and stereotypical depictions of Black womanhood.

In *Black Feminist Thought: Knowledge, Consciousness, and the Politics of Empowerment*, Collins (2000) describes the importance of an Afrocentric feminist understanding. Collins writes,

> I knew that when an individual Black woman's consciousness concerning how she understands her everyday life undergoes change, she can become empowered. Such consciousness may stimulate her to embark on a path of personal freedom, even if it exists primarily in her own mind. If she is lucky enough to meet others who are undergoing similar journeys, she and they can change the world around them [Collins, 2000, p. x].

Collins (2000) reminds us how the act of sharing one's story and drawing upon a connection to other Black women who have similar experiences is powerful and can aid the understanding of the many challenges people face. Collins describes the first tenet, "as a collectivity, U.S. Black women participate in a dialectical relationship linking African-American women's oppression and activism" (p. 22). The second tenet sets out to understand Black women's standpoint and it "emerges from tensions linking experiences and ideas" (p. 27). The third tenet of Black feminist thought recognizes there is an important relationship between linking or understanding oppression and activism. This dialogical relationship characterizes Black women's collective experiences and group knowledge (p. 30). The fourth tenet looks at the contributions of African American women intellectuals. Collins writes, "Black women intellectuals from all walks of life must aggressively push the theme of self-definition because speaking for oneself and crafting one's own agenda is essential to empowerment" (p. 36). In each episode of *Being Mary Jane*, the audience views the complex history of Black women's work, art, and activism.

Black Families in Black Spaces on Television

Being Mary Jane fills a void during a time where much of the market is oversaturated with reality TV stars and stereotypes. Gabrielle Union's character, Mary Jane Paul, is an unmarried news anchor and the primary breadwinner for her entire family. She also negotiates dating and the desire to be married and have children. Brock Akil depicts Mary Jane in situations where she navigates break ups, romantic love, and making critical choices about her reproductive health. Her parents are still married and both of her parents and siblings (two brothers) are very close. She also has a niece, the daughter of her eldest brother, with whom she has a very close relationship. Throughout the series, we see the dynamics of their relationships in the midst of challenges and triumphs.

Mary Jane's life is set in Atlanta, Georgia, where she grew up as upper middle class. Both Paul's parents are professional, middle class, African Americans. Her mother was a school principal and her father was an airline executive. What is interesting about Paul's story line in comparison to her Black female lead in a television series counterpart, Olivia Pope from ABC's *Scandal*, is that while both were surrounded by wealth and prestige it seems that many of Pope's circles were exclusively White. Paul's character was affiliated with social circles that included Black elite organizations such as Jack and Jill of America, the Links, and the Boule. This is a very important aspect to note since other television programs that consist of a Black character or family who are characterized as upper class are almost always insulated into a largely White existence. The narration of Black affluence unfortunately reinforces stereotypes that the only way Black people can be upwardly mobile is if they have proximity to whiteness. Historically Black people who arrived at their distinct social standings through inheritance, higher education, or hard work often represented a community from Black social organizations such as the three mentioned earlier (Wright, 2018). Much of what has been presented in terms of a Black family on television has portrayed Black children attending elite private White schools. Further, they work almost exclusively with White colleagues and much of their social circle largely comprise of White networks. Brock Akil situates the Pattersons' home base in Atlanta, which has a long lineage of elite Black families and highlight elite and historic Black social clubs and organizations is significantly divergent from the traditional narrative of Black upper-class families and characters in television.

Stereotypes in the Series

There are a number of ruptures and fragments in personal relationships between the three generations of Pattersons. The Pattersons' networks, professional careers, and ivy league educations affords them privileges of the elite however it did not come without challenges. For the purpose of this section we will investigate the intergenerational relationships between Mary Jane, her mother, Helen (Margaret Avery), and her niece, Niecy (Raven Goodwin) and the ways in which Black motherhood is represented on the show.

Wyatt (2000) has done extensive work on Black gender stereotypes by focusing on the Strong Black Woman role. She reviews Collins' (2000) critical work and provides a historical context for the role origins and development. In addition, Collins reminds us of the added psychological and emotional dimension of navigating spaces as a both Black and woman. We see this phenomenon in the storyline pertaining to Helen, Mary Jane, and Niecy's relationship. Through their characters the audience saw what it meant for everyday African American women to live up to the gender role requirements of a "Strong Black Woman." Strength is often a symbol associated with Black female television characters, especially Black mothers. From Florida Evans (Esther Rolle) on *Good Times* (1974–1979) being widowed, becoming the household's breadwinner and raising her three children as a single parent to Clair Huxtable's (Phylicia Rashad) portrayal as the career woman who has it all on *The Cosby Show* (1984–1992).

Black mothers on television are often defined by their ability to be resilient, strong, and keep their families together. Mary Jane's mother, Helen's persona is a bit divergent from the traditional portrayal of Black mothers. Helen is played by American actress, Margaret Avery. She maintained a regal disposition while battling the autoimmune disease Lupus. She dressed well, articulated every word and expected her daughter (Mary Jane) and granddaughter (Niecy) to follow the societal norms of womanhood (i.e., attend college, find a husband, get married, and have children— in that order). The relationship both Helen and Mary Jane have with Niecy was challenging. The show revealed that both Mary Jane and her mother acted as a kind of gatekeeper of respectability politics.[1] For example, in the show Niecy represented a complex juxtaposition; she was a curvy, plus size young woman, and she was a working-class, unmarried, teen mother with two children by two different men. Helen and Mary Jane passed judgment on Niecy by communicating to her that she was not living up to her full potential. In that moment, the viewer sees remnants of respectability politics at play as Helen and Mary Jane criticize Niecy from a dominant cultural lens. Further, their interactions and dialogue moved along the same lines of Collins' (2000) work, particularly her groundbreaking work on standpoint theory, toward a collective standpoint on the "Strong Black Woman" gender role and its psychic and emotional costs.

#IamMaryJane: Audience Reacts to Being Mary Jane *on Social Media*

Live tweeting during shows is a recent phenomenon that has become extremely popular. It allows viewers to create a community to discuss and analyze their favorite shows (Nielsen, 2015). *Being Mary Jane's* time slot recorded thousands of Black women live tweeting their reactions to Paul's sometimes erratic decisions around love, her trials with her family, and her continued pursuit of career success. Additionally, others would empathize with Mary Jane while also vocalizing how they experienced similar situations. Live tweeting during shows like *Being Mary Jane*, *Scandal*, and *How to Get Away with Murder* became another collective space and community that Black women carved out to speak candidly about their shared experiences and existence. This space was also used to air out grievances as well, including criticisms of Paul's casual sexual relationships and other character flaws that were deemed unacceptable because they fed into stereotypes of Black women.

Those criticisms led to a hashtag known as, #IamNotMaryJane which countered the show's hashtag of #IamMaryJane. The group highlighted that their frustrations grew out of the show suggesting that Mary Jane represented "every day" Black women. The group authored a statement that expressed their disdain for how the current generation's representation of Black women lacked morals and values because of their sexual exploits unlike previous generations who had Clair Huxtable, Esq. to aspire to (Tounsel, 2015). These reactions to Mary Jane's character and *Scandal's* Olivia Pope is a direct result of Black women's fear of how television and film create certain perceptions and cultural imagery that is used in mainstream society to denigrate, discriminate, and disrespect Black women. While the grievances are understandable many who take this position fail to see that regardless of how Black women and girls are portrayed on film or television, racial, gendered, and class systems will remain and continue to uphold the oppression that places Black women at the bottom. Further, by limiting Black women characters to perfection it creates a narrative that promotes the idea that Black women aren't human instead they are robots. These attitudes not only stifle the creative process but it limits whose narrative is acceptable to share in the public realm. It creates a hierarchy of which Black women's stories are deserving of being told and which aren't. Most importantly, it limits the humanity of Black women. No longer can Black women characters be nuanced, flawed or experience a range of emotions, instead these characters are forced into becoming monotonous imitations of a singular narrative used to combat racist and gendered stereotypes of Black women.

Conclusion: Becoming Pauletta and the Final Episodes of the Series

Earlier in this essay, we shared Mary Jane's birth name was Paulette Patterson and Mary Jane Paul was her professional moniker. The last episode of *Being Mary Jane* appropriately titled "Becoming Pauletta" aired on April 23, 2019, which brought full circle the story of our protagonist. This two-hour series finale opens with a proposal from Justin (Michael Ealy) and Mary Jane discovering she was expecting a baby. The pregnancy causes a strain on her relationship with fiancé, Justin. This discord in their relationship was brought on by Justin's personal challenges with raising a child that was not biologically related to him and Mary Jane not sharing with him prior to accepting the marriage proposal that she had been implanted with embryos from donor sperm. This is a critical crossroads for Mary Jane because throughout the series she had been searching for her "happy ending."

Due to her relationship with Justin ending abruptly, Mary Jane reconnects with a college sweetheart, Beau (Morris Chestnut). Beau supports Mary Jane during the birth of her son and their relationship grows deeper as he expresses an interest in marrying Mary Jane. Brock Akil places Mary Jane in a romantic dilemma that mainstream television has historically shied away from—positioning a Black female lead as the object of not one, but two men's desire. The episode fast forwards to her wedding day with Mary Jane having her happy ending with Justin. This sends the audience through a wave of emotions which Brock Akil is famous for. Much of her work is reflexive of real life which often complicates and nuances situations. This is highlighted when we see Justin as the groom. Although Justin broke off the engagement because of Mary Jane's personal decision to go through with the procedure of in vitro fertilization, similar to Mary Jane he also longed for a happy ending. The frenzy for this happy ending was also coupled with the fact that both knew they were constrained by time.

Both Mary Jane and Justin felt time was passing them by and that they needed to make critical decisions about their futures. This is particularly apparent in Mary Jane's decisions to undergo in vitro fertilization. We see firsthand Mary Jane articulating a dedication to career and "doing things in order." She felt she had no other options and thus decided to break the order and unfortunately then experienced rejection for being pregnant. While one could assume her out-of-wedlock pregnancy deemed her promiscuous, it was not. Invitro is an example of Mary Jane choosing herself. Throughout the entire series, the audience witnessed Mary Jane constantly choosing others whether it be her career, her family, or other male partners before herself. The idea of her having a child before time ran out was paramount to her.

Further, *Being Mary Jane* articulated the dynamics of intergenerational relationships with millennial women being the focus. Mary Jane's story appealed to a generation of millennial women and this was highlighted by how Mary Jane had to navigate the professional and personal world that looked nothing like the world of her parents and grandparents. We see Mary Jane as a Black woman having to make critical decisions about what it means to be Black, woman, professional and happy. As stated earlier, the Black female experience is not monolithic, however audiences could relate to Mary Jane in so many ways. Throughout her career, Brock Akil has specialized in presenting portraits of Black womanhood. *Being Mary Jane* nuanced the struggle of stretching oneself too thin to be there for family and friends. She used Mary Jane to articulate the often painful challenges of searching for love and a quality partner who wants to be married and have a family. She problematized what it meant to be the only Black woman in a professional space struggling to not be the "angry Black woman" stereotype while standing up against racism, sexism and prejudice in the workplace. Mary Jane showed us the vulnerability of wearing one's natural hair in the workplace and controversy Black women face over what is considered "professional." Brock Akil used *Being Mary Jane* to give us a popular culture example of the humanity of Black womanhood.

Notes

1. The politics of respectability are a set of "appropriate behaviors, manners, and social values" that members of the Black community and more specifically Black women should adhere to in order to be accepted by society. Though these "appropriate" behaviors were meant to combat racist and sexist stereotypes about Black women that made them more susceptible to violence, harassment, and other forms of marginalization it did little to counter those stereotypes. Instead it policies and reprimands Black women who refuse to follow these particular social norms. Historians Evelyn Brooks Higginbotham and Darlene Clark Hine and more recently Treva Lindsey and Brittany Cooper have problematized notions of Black women and the politics of respectability by stating this was actually a strategy for Black women to navigate hostile public spaces.

References

Collins, P. (2000). *Black Feminist Thought.* New York: Routledge.

Erigha, M. (2018) Black Women Having It All. *The Black Scholar,* 48:1, 20–30, DOI: 10.1080/00064246.2018.1402253.

Harris, F., & Coleman, L. (2018). Trending Topics: A Cultural Analysis of Being Mary Jane and Black Women's Engagement on Twitter. *The Black Scholar,* 48(1), 43–55.

Lundy, A. D. (2018) Caught Between a Thot and a Hard Place, The Black Scholar, 48:1, 56–70, DOI: 10.1080/00064246.2018.1402256.

Nielsen (2015) First Impressions: When and Why Social Program Engagement Matters. Retrieved from:https://www.nielsen.com/us/en/insights/news/2015/first-impressions-when-and-why-social-program-engagement-matters.html.

Tounsel, T. (2015). The Black Women That Media Built: Content Creation, Interpretation and the Making of the Black Female Self. (Unpublished doctoral dissertation). University of Michigan, Ann Arbor, Michigan.

Wright. J. (2019). *Empire and Black Images in Popular Culture.* Jefferson, NC: McFarland.

Wyatt, J. (2008) Patricia Hill Collins' *Black Sexual Politics* and the Genealogy of the Strong Black Woman, Studies in Gender and Sexuality, 9:1, 52–67, DOI: 10.1080/1524065 0701759516.

Capital Codes and Money Moves

The Ironies of Professionalism in Empire

Natalie J. Graham

In the world of *Empire* (2015–2020), Fox's supernova television series, characters grapple with an ever-shifting landscape of professional expectations in a music industry context where savagery is featured as a brutal and necessary pathway to professional freedom and power. At the helm of the series' corporate empire is antihero, Lucious Lyon (Terrance Howard), the pure hip-hop artist turned bloodless CEO of the record label and lifestyle brand, Empire Enterprises. The series centers on Lucious; his three sons, Jamal (Jussie Smollett), Hakeem (Bryshere Y. Gray), Andre (Trai Byers); and his ex-wife, Cookie (Taraji P. Henson). At the start of the series Jamal and Hakeem are music artists, Andre is Empire's CFO, and Cookie, returning from a seventeen-year prison sentence for drug trafficking, quickly becomes a music producer and Empire Enterprises' co-executive.

The series puts family, capitalistic enterprise, tragedy, and madness through the lens of a Black family that has risen to fame and notoriety. This dysfunctional family dynamic is the backdrop of Empire Enterprises' business acquisitions and corporate maneuvers. The decaying familial relationships fester throughout the unfolding of the series, and lead each member to desperate, often violent measures to protect the empire and their stake in it. Following well-established stereotypes of options and opportunities for Black young urban dwellers, Cookie and Lucious live hand-to-mouth at the inception of Empire Enterprises and resort to drug dealing to generate capital to produce Lucious' first album. Much like capitalism in the United States, the violence, threat, and trauma that are necessary to maintain a successful drug operation are the same methods both parents of the Lyon dynasty employ to remain within the precarious professional and social systems of exploitation and oppression of the boardroom milieu in the would-be publicly traded corporation. Overlaying this violent, precarious backdrop, throughout the series, corporate professional behaviors at Empire Enterprises are coded as white or white-privileging where white oppressive violence is often muted or ignored. Characters who are either unable, or refuse to, perform according to historical expectations of Black identity suffer in the name of good business and corporate capitalism. Even in a mostly Black boardroom, whiteness must be affirmed and aspired to by artists and executives alike. This definition of corporate professionalism stands alongside paternalist, corporate systems and in opposition to common codes for Black artists and people that figure trauma as a constitutive element of a core identity (i.e., hood, street, or real). This essay will highlight the way that Black authenticity is defined in opposition to corporate professionalism and is defined by ongoing trauma as a foundational element of the series.

What Is Corporate Professionalism in Empire?

Empire begins with a premise that heightens the consequences of demands on characters to perform in ways that align with the series' vision of corporate values or what could be considered corporate professionalism. Lucious' mission to take Empire Enterprises public is a recurrent theme in the first season that is used to comment on a character's behavior or a fact that is used by characters to manipulate each other. Going public requires the ultimate performance of mainstream, corporate values. Values which render the truth of their selves and pasts a liability to the desire to represent a flawless, corporate structure. In episode 1 of season 1, "Surprise Visit" (2015), in what could be considered the first of Cookie Lyon's many attempts to force Lucious to give her more creative control over Empire artists and the company, she threatens to expose the fact that her drug money initially financed the company. This strategic move was designed by Cookie to pressure Lucious into allowing her to manage Jamal Lyon. Lucious agrees out of fear that investors will back out if they discover the company's illicit beginnings. Corporate professionalism is shown to be a force that generally opposes individual authenticity and truth. To be professional and to claim corporate power, characters often cannot be fully honest for fear of white investors and industry professionals.

This perception of corporate professionalism and power as opposing or interrupting authentic expression of identity and relationship is used by Lucious to explain his rejection of Jamal. When Jamal racializes his father's homophobia as issuing from, and endemic to, the Black community, Lucious makes a point to remind him that he is concerned about the response of Empire's 75 percent white consumer base in episode 1 of season 1, "Surprise Visit" (2015). Lucious makes it clear that he is unwilling to understand or accept Jamal's sexuality and rejects him outright as a son throughout the series. As a character who represents the chilling and detrimental impact of corporate professional expectations on humanity, family, and artistry, Lucious also disingenuously blames his rejection of Jamal on the demands of the market. Yet, during the first episode, we see a recurring flashback that Jamal has often of a younger Lucious throwing him in the trash as a child when he finds Jamal playing dress up in Cookie's high heels. Here and throughout, Lucious, Cookie, and other characters that lead the board of directors, behave in and excuse inexcusable and inhumane behavior. Any threat or act of violence that is meted out to save the company is characterized as business as usual; the needs of the corporation are preeminent to the feelings or desires of any individual. To be professional one must not display human needs or desires. Such displays in the series are described as selfish, ungrateful, or dramatic.

As in the case with Jamal, definitions of professional behavior are used to both subjugate Cookie's individual desires and condemn personal expression. Lucious chides Cookie's characteristic ability to disrupt and interrupt as not being fit for the new corporate face of Empire. In episode 2 of season 1, "The Outspoken King" (2015), Lucious says, "You need to start acting more professional and stop acting like a hoodrat." Cookie's characterization by others as bossy and unruly recalls recent television shows with Black female leads. "Clearly, Bailey and Keating are conceptualized as 'bitchy Black women,' a persistent stereotype faced by many African American women in positions of leadership (Allen, 1998), despite commentary about a supposed postrace society" (Wilson-Brown & Szczur, 2016, p. 235). Cookie advocates strongly for keeping Empire icon, Elle Dallas (Courtney Love), acknowledging that women who have a voice in corporate spaces are often pushed out and labeled as difficult. Her advocacy backfires as she is sabotaged by Anika Calhoun (Grace Byers), Lucious' romantic interest in season 1. In this season, Anika secretly drugs Elle, an opioid addict in recovery. As she does throughout the season, Anika moves to marginalize Cookie and undermine her as a professional. Cookie's role as "bitchy" and "bossy," however is ratcheted up in the series as she has a sort of magical access to spaces and people which minimizes the type of restrictions that are placed on women deemed loud and aggressive. Cookie is not just an interrupter, she is a magical interrupter, appearing out of nowhere, floating upstairs, onto closed sets, through locked doors, secretaries, and security. Her power to pop up ignores the real threat that Black women in professional and public spaces face for behavior deemed "unruly."

As might be expected, corporate professional identity in the series is primarily racialized by Lucious as white. The record executive selecting talent and molding artists to be more palatable to a white audience is a phenomenon well documented in Berry Gordy's assembly-line approach to artist and music development. Like Gordy's professionalization of Motown artists by controlling their dress, speech, and public interactions, to make them marketable to white audiences, the series presents the corporate professional as one who must adhere to conservative norms of behavior and dress. Anika, with her debutante past, is the ideal figure of Black corporate power sees power as issuing from more connection to Lucious, elite networks, and strategic financial action from the beginning. In episode 2 of season 1, "The Outspoken King" (2015), when Cookie accuses Lucious of being fake to please white corporate expectation, he explains his behavior as necessary and specifically connects his professional image to speech practice as a performance for white audiences, "I've got to go on white TV and try and talk in a way that don't frighten these folks to death." Professional corporate expectations demand that Black characters sanitize and discipline their behavior for white consumption. Their efforts are often specifically rooted in the desire to protect themselves from the white fear. Protecting Black folks from the violence and oppression associated with white fear is no new motivation for corporate professionalism. Black hair, speech, and dress are common targets of supposedly race-neutral efforts to discipline Black people. The representation of Black people as unruly in need of domestication to be presentable for public and professional spaces is not a novel one in U.S. popular culture. The early representations of professional Black characters in minstrelsy culture in the U.S. were often shown as unable to speak clearly or dress appropriately for white public or professional space. They were audaciously and absurdly out of place. These characters made white Americans continue to feel superior, comfortable, entertained, and content.

Although race is often treated obliquely, *Empire*'s figuration of traditional corporate identity as racialized takes partial aim at the way imagined corporate neutrality obscures oppressive, racial inequity by making a world where white corporate professionalism is synonymous with hypocrisy, dishonesty, and inauthenticity. Lucious' dismissive treatment of Andre comes in part from Andre's ability to perform white professionalism too convincingly. Lucious says in episode 9 of season 1, "Unto the Breach" (2015), "They will never accept you. They will accept your money, Dre, but they will never accept your Black ass; and I don't give a damn how many white women you marry." Here, Lucious Lyon represents a traditional Black capitalist perspective that assumes the impossibility of racial acceptance and integration because of the durability of racial oppression.

Corporate Patriarchy and Family Values

> Empire *is family. I mean that's what we're selling, that's the whole showcase.*
>
> *—Lucious Lyon*

Professionalism doesn't exist in a vacuum. The professional businessperson is often rewarded or punished in corporate systems for their alignment with traditional corporate patriarchy. Patriarchy endures by functioning within established norms of male dominance over social and professional entities. While there have been some spectacular rifts in structural oppression, professional corporate norms, patriarchy and capitalism are inextricably linked. In *Empire* the coordination of patriarchy and capitalism is all the more resonant because of the overlapping definitions of corporation and family. Systemic oppression exploits emotional attachments to idealized organizations like family and nation and the coordinated expectation of loyal subjects. Lucious wields the word family like a talisman, a reason for Cookie and his sons to do his bidding.

In his quest for control and domination, it's clear through the series that Lucious intends for Empire Enterprises to model norms of capitalist patriarchy that place men at the head of groups that support their ruling authority. His vanity is expected, and other characters often support, actively or passively, this view of Lucious as the only possible authority. For instance, when Hakeem is beginning to reconcile his relationship with Cookie, a central reason for his disdain for her is her "bossiness." Importantly, he does not reject the idea of being bossed. He rejects her authority as the controller of the family. In episode 8 of season 1, "The Lyon's Roar" (2015), Hakeem says, "You don't run the show. Dad does." Furthermore, Cookie does not protest being placed beneath Lucious in the corporate or family hierarchy. Her role is the most consistent evidence of the continued power of patriarchy. It is Cookie that continually sacrifices under the banner of family and uses the ideal of family to draw her sons back to their abusive father. This same banner almost crushes her under its weight as in the last season she tries to escape the co-dependent relationship that binds her to Lucious in episode 8 of season 3, "Cold Cold Man" (2019).

The fact that family is a more constitutive element of Cookie's character than any of the other similar figures in the series is in line with the coverage of women in journalism that disproportionately represent women leaders as being "primarily family-oriented, therefore perpetuating the stereotype that these women compromise their commitment to and/or competence at their jobs in ways that male leaders do not" (French & Webster, 2016, p. 20). Cookie regularly wrangles brothers Hakeem and Jamal when they refuse to work with each other, her, or their father. Even though she was in prison for seventeen years, she and other characters make consistent reference to the fact that Lucious did not parent their children while she was gone. She immediately assumes the role of mother, even though Hakeem is initially very resistant to her role and her identity as mother. Cookie never questions this identity and is unflagging regardless of Hakeem's vicious rejection.

Even though Cookie claims later that she was motivated by money, she makes an emotional appeal to Hakeem and Jamal to work together for the sake of their father, while Lucious literally stands in the shadows only to emerge later to certify her appeal as their mother in episode 7 of season 1, "Our Dancing Days" (2015). Later in the same episode at an investor showcase Lucious asks Cookie to speak for him rather than his fiancé Anika or CFO Andre. Her role as the mother of the sons of the empire assigns her value that supports a vision of the corporation as a stable family that will be sustained for future generations. In this speech, Cookie describes Lucious as a "musical god," placing him as the ultimate and immortal creator of Empire's legacy. This image of Lucious as the father/god is a theme throughout the series. When he tries to bribe Hakeem's love interest to leave, in episode 10 season 1, "Sins of the Father" (2015), Lucious says, "You know how God made man in his own image? I'm making Hakeem in my image." In the figuration of a paternalistic enterprise, Lucious is the father, lord, and controller of others and they more often than not begrudgingly agree to the role or face his wrath, which often means eventual death or banishment.

As a partner to Lucious, Cookie often supports Lucious and his Empire as if there is no other way forward. Getting what is hers cannot be articulated outside of Empire and by extension Lucious, while clearly in the realm of the series, Empire can thrive without her presence. Her ambiguous lines early in episode 1 of season 1, "Surprise Visit" (2015), "Cookie's coming home" and "I'm coming to get what's mine" are functionally operative as her being Lucious' wife or partner in business. Her asking for half, never assumes the possibility of joint leadership. Violent and conniving acts *must* be done to preserve Empire Enterprises, and Empire Enterprises is for Cookie more often than for others synonymous with the family unit. As Andre says in episode 7 of season 1, "Our Dancing Days" (2015), "I cover for him even when I don't know what I'm covering."

Black Authenticity as Trauma

In contrast to the corporate professional, and both inside and outside of corporate and familial expectations, is the music professional. Although these identities are defined in opposition to each other as ideal forms, they often overlap in the main characters. As Lucious, Jamal, Hakeem, and Cookie each jockey for administrative power, control of their projects or the label, they also create iconic music. So, if corporate professionals must perform a muted identity that minimizes alignment with truth, poverty, or Blackness and produces hidden and indirect violence against the self and others; then, music professionals in the series must endure silencing, violence, and trauma to reveal a soulful self in their music.

In the first few moments of episode 1 of season 1 "Surprise Visit" (2015), Lucious Lyon uses both past trauma and the shadow of death to inspire one of his female music artists to improve her performance. He begins by saying in "I need you to sing like you are going to die tomorrow, like this is the last song you will ever sing." It is unclear precisely what musical elements need to improve, but Lucious senses that she is still holding something back, and therefore, has not yet fulfilled the song's true potential. After another inexplicably unsatisfactory take, Lucious goes into the recording booth with her, holds her near him, and asks her to remember the moment she learned her brother died and the feeling of being asked to identify the body. This scene provides a foundational defining characteristic of Black professional musicians employed by Empire that will be reinforced throughout the first seasons. In this scene, Lucious and the characters around him who don't reject his methods situate Black people's trauma as a mode of professional development that seasons an artist, giving them authenticity and a performance edge. In this scene Lucious explicitly ties the music artist's meditation on death and trauma to "soul," a long-time signifier of Black authenticity and an undefinable ideal for Black music.

This ideal of the revealed Black soul being one that must seek out and enter into a state of pain to be the most authentic and therefore the most profitable entertainer has its roots not only in the maudlin performances of the minstrel stage, but also in the earliest scholarship of Black professional music. In *Souls of Black Folk,* while DuBois attests to his limited knowledge of music in the chapter "Sorrow Songs," his claims about music are still central to the development of definitions of value in Black music history. He claims that "the *true* Negro folk-song lives in the hearts of those who have heard them *truly* sung and in the hearts of the Negro people." (DuBois, 1903, par 5, emphasis mine). What is the essential emotional core of this real music that Black people know bone and blood deep? According to DuBois it is "death and suffering and unvoiced longing." (DuBois, 1903, par 6). Of critical importance is the fact that DuBois is not referring to who we might typically consider to be "raw" folk musicians making music to accompany their work or as part of their faith practice. He is primarily referring to the Fisk Jubilee Singers as an authentic counterweight to the minstrel stage. This comparison is all the more curious given that the Jubilee Singers regularly sang crowd-pleasing, popular songs by minstrel composer Stephen Foster. (Lloyd, 2004, p.16) Even if the Foster songs are set apart, however, the Fisk Singers still sang traditionally arranged, a cappella choral music as an ensemble for the express purpose of fundraising for white audiences.

Like DuBois, *Empire*'s first scene aligns Black trauma with Black musical authenticity. This alignment is not surprising considering that it is a central formation of the Black professional identity in hip hop, R&B, and gospel. For example, after being described multiple times in terms of the unfathomable sadness of her eyes, award-winning *Rolling Stone* author, Mikal Gilmore writes "Aretha Franklin took her pain and transmuted it into something that moved the land with her voice." (2018, par 19) For the series, however, a character must not only have lived through past pain. Throughout *Empire* Black characters must remain in pain or return to painful places to rise to their best artistic selves. Threat of violence, indirect and direct, physical and emotional, is necessary and commonplace for maintaining authenticity. Lucious Lyon is dismissed throughout much of the first two seasons as the "true artist" who lost his way because of his comfort from and preoccupation with financial success. He is unwilling to travel through his pain to ascend to his previous heights. This trajectory begins in the episode 1 of season 1, "Surprise Visit" (2015) as well with Jamal Lyon saying Lucious is no longer a "true artist," because "now he's more concerned with selling t-shirts and watches and whatever." Similarly, in episode 3 of season 1, "The Devil Quotes Scripture" (2015) Cookie Lyon asks, "What has this money done to you?" In order to make a successful return to music, Lucious must return to the site of his childhood trauma. When he brings up music awards Cookie bristles, reminding him in episode 13 of season 2, "The Tameness of a Wolf" (2015), "If you don't put your whole truth into this video, then what's the damn point?" Although ultimately Hakeem is able to emerge as a triumphant pop star, *Empire* both positions money and privilege as antithetical to successful, authentic Black performance.

The stakes of this aligning pain with Black authenticity as entertainment are dramatized by Spike Lee's *Bamboozled* (2000) which shows the legacy of Black entertainment as a site for the reproduction and commodification of Black death, trauma, and violence. The increased marketability of movies like *When They See Us* (2019) and *12 Years a Slave* (2013) are examples of the way Black death is popular entertainment in part, because of the association between death of Black authenticity. To be "real" Black creative arts production must represent Black suffering often unto death. Lucious Lyon represents the evils of capitalism and hypocrisy but becomes a necessary evil ally as the embodiment of Empire Enterprises and the producer of pain, as he pushes "real" artists into their pain and creates and exacerbates the trauma in the lives of his family.

Conclusion

Even with the over-the-top, soap opera framing of the series, it's clear that many of the most curious and virulent stereotypes are not merely elements of drama. Alongside the show's many innovative and progressive triumphs, co-creators, Lee Daniels and Danny Strong, represent the results of corporate professionalism, reinforce white corporate norms, and create a foundation for a series in which Black characters must be traumatized to stay authentic. Aligning core values of the series, loyalty and family, for example, with Black trauma folds easily into traditional representations of Black life. "Thus, the intersection of racial representation and the representational convention of verisimilitude as true-to-life representation brings into stark relief the role of television as a repository of the accepted and common perceptions of African Americans in society" (Nama, 2003, p.25). Violence in *Empire* becomes a necessary vehicle, not just for dramatic effect, but to maintain expectations of professional behavior and Black identity. Each of the characters is violent, and in the end, that violence is excused. Since violence is a stereotyped behavior that is expected, the aggression of the white professional environment is not addressed because beside the blatant and hyperbolic behavior of the Lyon clan, that environment is portrayed as the one that makes sense. The corporation of Empire Enterprises is just a snapshot of the endemic issue of white-washing Black behavior in white professional spaces and the impossibility of participating productively in an inhumane white patriarchy.

References

Daniels, L., Strong, D. Grazer, B., Calfo, F., Hamri, S., Hammer, D., Pyken, M., & Mahoney, B. (Executive Producers). (2015–2020). *Empire* [TV series]. Imagine Television in association with 20th Century Fox Television.

Du Bois, W. E. B. (1903). "Chapter 14: Of the Sorrow Songs" etc.usf.edu. https://etc.usf.edu/lit2go/203/the-souls-ofBlackfolk/4458/chapter-14-of-the-sorrow-songs/.

French, S. L., & Webster, L.B. (2016). Who's the Girl? The (Mis)representation of Female Corporate Leaders in *Time*. In V. Stead, S. Mavin, J. Williams, & C. Elliot (Eds.), *Gender, Media, and Organization: Challenging Mis(s)representations of Women Leaders and Managers* (pp. 225–242). Information Age Publishing. Gilmore, M. (2018, September 27). *Inside Aretha Franklin's Epic Life. Rolling Stone*. https://www.rollingstone.com/music/music-features/aretha-franklin-tribute-cover-story-queen-729053/.

Lloyd, T. (2004). "Shout all over God's heaven!": How the African-American Spiritual Has Maintained Its Integrity in the Face of Social and Musical Challenges. *The Choral Journal, 45*(1), 9–25.

Nama, A. (2003). More Symbol Than Substance: African American Representation in Network Television Dramas. *Race and Society, 6*(1), 21–38.

Wilson-Brown, C. & Szczur, S. (2016). Working in Shondaland: Representations of African American Women in Leadership. In V. Stead, S. Mavin, J. Williams, & C. Elliot (Eds.), *Gender, Media, and Organization: Challenging Mis(s)representations of Women Leaders and Managers* (pp. 225–242). Information Age Publishing.

PART III

Medical Professionals

Shonda Rhimes' *Grey's Anatomy* and *My Year of Saying Yes to Everything*

Adelina Mbinjama-Gamatham

Introduction

There is rising interest in scholarly work allied to how Black women, in today's society, are represented in the media (see Faluyi, 2015; Kissell, 2016; Stoffel, 2016; Schug et al., 2017; West, 2018). From these works we learn of what Asare (2017, p. 343) deems "constant discrimination against Black females," as amplified in the media. Through her television series *Grey's Anatomy* (2005–present), Shonda Rhimes has pushed positive representations of Black professional women in the media to the forefront.

Rhimes, in her roles as writer, executive producer and creative producer, is known as the titan behind *Grey's Anatomy*. The continued success and popularity of Shonda Rhimes' shows highlight her dominance in the television space, and thus emphasize the significance of her work in subverting stereotypical representations of Black women and, in turn, individuals' perceptions of themselves (Bess, 2015). Rhimes' transformational work is momentous as she tastefully, and at times loosely, explores the Black professional woman through the character of Miranda Bailey (Chandra Wilson).

Year of Yes: *Conformity and Ridding of Fear*

While *Grey's Anatomy* first aired in March 2005, it is a little over a decade later, at a TED X Talk entitled *My Year of Saying Yes to Everything* (2016) based on her book, *Year of Yes* (2015), that one gains more insight into Rhimes' mind and work ethics, and begins to hear her characters from her television series expressed through her TED X narration. Rhimes discusses how saying 'Yes', and doing all the things that she was afraid of, for one year helped her undo her anxieties related to the fear of failure. She recounted that, even though she had a dream job, saying "Yes" and agreeing to play with her three children every time they asked her is likely to have saved her career.

With Rhimes' anecdote in mind, it is central to this essay to consider how the African American women characters of *Grey's Anatomy*, particularly Bailey, are portrayed within the context of the medical profession. Further, it is critical to reflect on Shonda Rhimes as the producer of the television series and why it is important to showcase Black female characters in a professional set-up.

In the first episode of the first season of *Grey's Anatomy*, viewers are introduced to the first Black female resident surgeon, Dr. Miranda Bailey, who is in charge of a group of interns. This group includes the series protagonist, Meredith Grey (Ellen Pompeo), who prior to meeting Bailey knew of her only as "the Nazi." On seeing her, the interns were surprised that Bailey appeared anything other than a Nazi, as she is a short, Black, young woman, and is generally pleasant looking—until she stares them down, greets them coldly and demands that they follow her and adhere to her rules and those of the hospital. Bailey is then immediately perceived as strong-willed, confrontational, hardworking, unfeeling and only interested in her professional work.

In analyzing Bailey's stance, it would be fair to call her a feminist, or she could be considered by viewers as "just another angry Black woman." Yet it could be possible that, like many other Black women, Bailey is concealing her "behavioural conformity" behind a mask, whilst also showing acts of resistance against forms of dominant force (Collins, 1990, p. 91). However, to be more objective, it should be noted that Bailey does not fit into the stereotypical representation of an 'angry Black woman.' Rather, as a Black woman who wants to get things done, she has to work harder than her white male and female counterparts. Bailey's character epitomizes the Black woman who refuses to take on the "mammy image"—a historical and common representation of a dark skinned, big, Black woman responsible for taking care of the master's children on the plantation (West, 2018). In this respect, Bailey constantly rejects performing emotional services as these rarely result in monetary rewards or respect in the workplace (Beaubouef-Lafontant, 2013).

Black Feminism

Bailey's professional stance was made evident when she refused to encourage or acknowledge the sexual relationship between Derek

"McDreamy" Shepherd (Patrick Dempsey) and Meredith Grey. Bailey emphasizes to Grey that having sexual relations with her boss would hamper her career trajectory as she would be seen to have slept her way to the top; thus, Bailey is shown to be acutely aware of the burden of "perception" placed upon women professionals, to which their male counterparts are not subjected. In this regard, she is shown to be even more aware of the deeper implications of this for the Black woman subject in the professional environment. Based on theory and narratives, Black women at the top of their professional institution's or company's structural hierarchy are often looked down upon with suspicion and are often considered to have received promotion through sexual or romantic relations with their male counterparts. This is complementary to bell hooks' (1990) assertions of gender politics and race and representation (hooks, 1992). An analysis of Meredith Grey, a white female intern, indicates that she is not concerned about the perceptions of her sexual liaison with her boss, presumably due to the privilege she experiences as a white woman. This interaction between the two women implies that Black Feminism is taken into account and is concerned with the sexual, racial and cultural ideologies that Black women have to navigate in the professional environment (hooks, 1993; hooks, 1994). The show exposes this unfortunate dichotomy of white versus Black women.

In their comparison between feminism and Black feminism, Lorde and Clarke (2007) warn that whilst the former is recognized as a more traditional or equality-focused form of feminism, it is important to understand that Black feminism is not "white feminism in Blackface" (p. 60). Young (2014) articulates that "white feminism is the feminism that doesn't understand western privilege, or cultural context. It is the feminism that doesn't consider race as a factor in the struggle for equality" (p. 1). Although Bailey does not explicitly raise the issue of race, the portrayal of her emotions in this scene—disapproval and repugnance—position her as a Black feminist cognizant of the impact of structural systems around her in their exercise of "power that generate[s] privilege and oppression" (Hankivsky, 2014). As a result, she is aware of but not concerned about others questioning the credibility of her work as a Black female surgeon.

Where Grey remains aloof or slightly disconcerted about the consequences of her affair with Shepherd, Bailey chooses to deal with her male colleagues in a direct and professional manner, leaving no room for any abstract thoughts or confusion. When a visiting doctor arrived during Thanksgiving, he only wanted to work with the doctor everyone referred to as "the Nazi." However, he had no idea that Bailey, with whom he had been interacting throughout his visit, was the person he had been looking for. Stereotypically, he thought she was "just another surgeon" and assumed "the Nazi" was a male doctor. What stands out in this episode is Bailey's ability to maintain composure despite the visitor's repetitively condescending behavior towards her. She continued to put in the necessary work and refused to focus on the politics of being victimized or stereotyped. When the visiting doctor finally learns that Bailey is "the Nazi" with whom he had hoped to meet, he is shocked and taken aback for not realizing who she was much earlier and regretted that his opportunity to work with her had passed. Bailey's determined decision to forego argument or be consumed with feelings of resentment for not being recognized as "the Nazi" makes her appear more professional and less petty than the white male visiting doctor who did not bother getting to know the real name of the person who medical staff referred to as "the Nazi."

The Hum

In season two of *Grey's Anatomy*, Bailey's all-strong and powerful role begins to take on a different form, in that despite fighting for recognition and working hard to excel, she is forced to take a back seat. In Rhimes' TED X talk, she reminds her audience of the need to be present in the now and to enjoy life. She describes her experience of work as follows:

> I love working. It is creative and mechanical, and exhausting, and exhilarating, and hilarious, and disturbing, and clinical, and maternal, and cruel, and judicious. And what makes it all so good is "the hum." There's some kind of shift inside me when the work gets good. A hum begins in my brain and it grows and grows. And that hum sounds like the open road and I can drive it forever. The hum is more than writing—the hum is action and activity. The hum is a drug; the hum is music; the hum is light and air. The hum is God's whisper right in my ear. And when you have a hum like that, you can't help but strive for greatness. That feeling … you can't help but strive for greatness at any cost. That's called the hum. Or maybe it's called being a workaholic. Maybe it's called genius. Maybe it's called ego. Maybe it's just fear of failure. I don't know.... I just know I am not built for failure and I just know that I love the hum [Rhimes, 2016].

Rhimes explains that she experienced a point in her professional career where she no longer enjoyed what she did. There was no "hum." She states that "Inside of me was silence." Despite her hum being broken, she was doing all the things she used to do—working through weekends and foregoing sleep. This is complementary to Bailey's character which epitomizes resilience despite the many challenges and opportunities she faces at the workplace.

When the Black male Chief of Surgery, Richard Webber (James Pickens, Jr.), learns that Bailey has been offered five resident fellowships from five different hospitals, he is concerned she will leave Seattle Grace Mercy West Hospital, until she reveals she is pregnant and will not be leaving. This follows a brief moment of silence and awkward reaction from Webber who, in later scenes, informs her that people are questioning her confidence as a surgeon. This scene is significant for viewers because we witness a quasi father-daughter relationship between Webber and Bailey. It also offers a less positive portrayal of Black male professionals who do not outwardly defend their Black female colleagues for fear of victimization or being accused of playing the race card.

As her mentor, Webber appears troubled about others' perceptions of Bailey. In contrast, she is largely not surprised that she is being undermined. Since Webber knows how competent Bailey is, his non-defense of Bailey could be interpreted as a positive portrayal. That Webber was fearful of losing Bailey to another hospital exemplifies the many instances in which Black females are persistently head-hunted and offered better packages outside of their current employment but choose to remain due to conflicting or unforeseen circumstances (McGirt, 2017).

When Bailey went on maternity leave, she announced: "I will return!" This declaration is symbolic and resonates with Rhimes' own claim of being committed to her work, and of the occurrence of certain life events that force a break from the hum and rhythm of work. Bailey worked throughout her pregnancy, as did Rhimes. When Bailey was on maternity leave and came to the hospital to give birth, instead of being concerned about preparing for the arrival of her baby, she gave instructions to her interns whenever she saw them. This demonstrates her addiction to her work and a sense of feeling lost without it. Black women are not represented in the media as hardworking or determined. It is often men that are portrayed as being over-committed to and driven within the workplace. This scene resonates with Rhimes' philosophy of work:

> The hum is more than the writer. The more expectations there are is when you are successful. Then the hum stops. Overworked, over-used, over-done, burned out, the hum stops.... What happens when the thing you do and the work you love starts to taste like dust? [Rhimes, 2016].

This relates to Rhimes' own admission that when she was forced to be still, after being exhausted and missing out on her children growing up, she began to feel a renewed energy after embarking on a commitment to give fifteen minutes of her time to her children whenever they requested it. She asked: "When the hum stops, who are you? ... I am still ... a hum creeps back. Not the hum ... a hum. It's love specific" (Rhimes, 2016).

Ubuntu and Being an Individual

Bailey's renewed love for her work and for her newborn is demonstrated when she takes her baby to work. This act could be something most Black women would need and appreciate at the workplace—especially those who work very long and tedious hours, and who often need to find time to see and take care of their children. What Rhimes does, in the scenes that follow, is place emphasis on the communal role of raising children, with Bailey's colleagues assisting with baby-sitting, changing diapers and feeding the new-born. These scenes reflect the spirit of "Ubuntu" that resonates with audiences from the Global South, particularly Africa. The principle of Ubuntu, an African philosophy, introduces the concept of belonging and caring (Nolte and Downing, 2019, p. 9–16). This philosophy is often used to analyze the collective contribution by members of a community, other than family, to rearing a child in order to free up time for the mother to perform other duties. The concept of collectivism can also be found in African American culture, as it has transformed over the years.

In season nine of *Grey's Anatomy*, some of the cast members are seen at a Christmas dinner table, with Bailey and her father seated next to each other. This scene is memorable because Bailey's father reprimands her by saying "Even if surgery is your whole life, you don't have to talk about bowels at the dinner table!" After a lengthy awkward silence, Bailey presents an emotional speech about how she and her son are happy, and that she has chosen not to settle into marriage. This pivotal moment exemplifies how Black women often have to defend themselves and justify the choices they make. The scene would not have been significant or meaningful if Bailey had kept quiet in response to her father's statement.

Rhimes knows that Bailey's character is extremely important in unearthing the many ways that Black female professionals succeed and fail (McGirt, 2017). The generational gap between Bailey and her colleagues, as well as her father, is exemplary of the many ways in which families fail to understand how work can infiltrate one's personal space. Bailey's intent in standing up to her father is not to be deviant but to assert that her life choices, and those that she made on behalf of her son, are ultimately for their happiness. Rhimes' statement that "The real hum is peace" is exactly what Bailey's character was agitatedly voicing in this scene, thus presenting a Black feminist ethos, along with individualism, in line with the emphasis on self-care.

When giving a colleague, Dr. Cristina Yang (Sandra Miju Oh), advice about having children, Bailey admitted that she loves working around them and considered a pediatrician fellowship. She also voiced how she thought about not having her son and had considered an abortion. She mentioned how she took a moment to "pause" and then realized that she could do it. She knew having a child would compromise her love for being a surgeon, her residency fellowship, her marriage and motherhood. She added: "I knew I could do this … you just have to know. And when you don't know then no one can fault you for it. You do what you can do, when you can, while you can. And when you can't, you can't." This scene was enlightening—almost rhetorical—for working women of color who can relate to these two womenfolk in terms of what it takes to go through being questioned about one's womanhood, and how to become successful and happy with the choices one makes.

Both Yang and Bailey have very high hopes and standards for their professional careers, but the pressure to have and build a family are internal and external factors that can drive Black women into states of anxiety, depression and feeling burdened. This scene connects with Rhimes' own personal narrative where she says "I don't like playing…. I love work more than being at home" (Rhimes, 2016). Although Rhimes' words here may appear selfish and individualistic, perhaps they speak quite pointedly to the dilemma of the modern, professional, Black woman.

Professionalism and Sexuality

Another dilemma faced by Bailey is her worry about going on a third date with an African American male intern, Ben Warren (Jason Winston George). For this date, she is advised by Dr. Callie Torres (Sara Ramirez) on how to sexually prepare her "surgical field" (referring to the vaginal area). Torres mockingly informs Bailey that a "third date is a sex date" which causes much anxiety for Bailey who has not dated for many years since her divorce. This scene is fundamental in exploring how the workplace is also a playground to meet people with whom one can form very close bonds and date, thus blurring the lines between what is considered public and private, that is, the realms of colleagues and friends.

It is noteworthy that Bailey had to seek advice from Torres, another woman of color. Unlike Torres (whose surname suggests that she is Spanish/Latina), Bailey represents the conservative, Black, professional woman who is afraid of showing emotion, dating, getting condoms for her third date and having someone look at her vagina. This became apparent in the first season of *Grey's Anatomy* when medical intern, George O'Malley (Theodore Raymond Knight) held Bailey and looked at her vagina while she gave birth. Bailey's experiences suggest that a professional Black woman must deny herself the right to embrace her sexuality or she will be considered a whore. This conservative viewpoint challenges Rhimes' own personal life story, in which she chose to be a single mother and not to get married, thereby pushing the limits of what is expected from a successful African American woman.

In later seasons of *Grey's Anatomy*, Bailey marries Warren, who is in the same medical profession. Thereafter, she experiences marital challenges with him because of her dedication and passion towards her work. Her journey symbolizes a deep-seated connection that Bailey—and others like her—has with her work as someone who is "married to her job" and struggling to find a balance between work and family life.

Conclusion

Grey's Anatomy is a unique television series if one looks closely at the short-storied characters represented through the Black women characters. Refreshingly, the series refuses to promote stereotypes surrounding African American communities and cultures; instead, it works to demystify and subliminally foreground the professional innuendos that Black women face and have to survive at the workplace. These relate to issues of workplace bullying, competitiveness, sacrificing the homestead for promotions and patient/client satisfaction—all of which the viewer is able to engage through the character of Dr. Miranda Bailey. The absence of, or rather limited focus on, colorism might also correspond to Rhimes' personal approach to her professional life.

One would assume that because she is an African American media mogul, Rhimes would be pushing a transformational agenda (by screening Black female professional characters) with "loud speakers." By this, one would then accept that narratives about Black females would conventionally emphasize their brokenness, lawlessness, sexualized bodies and stigmatic and failed relationships, which has become stereotypical of Hollywood's depictions of Black womanhood. Rhimes avoids this by casting African American women who are mostly dark-skinned, with natural African features, and their natural curly hair. Bailey, with short-ironed hair, represents a historical period where Black women had to conform to white standards in order to be perceived as professional. However, it is made implicit that in Bailey's case straight hair is a choice, rather than an indication that she not care or does not know how to deal with natural hair; this is evident when she chastises Grey and lets her know that people are judging her for not taking care of her adopted Black daughter's hair properly—in this moment Bailey goes out of her way to show Grey how to do it in the fashion in which Black mothers would care for their daughters' hair. Rhimes pointedly shows that Black women are aware of the assumptions that people make about Black women's appearances.

While we can appreciate Rhimes' attempt to build a "racially heterogenous ensemble in favour of promoting a more harmonious organic picture of the casting process" (Long, 2011, p. 1068), one has to refer to Rhimes' speech in which she claims that her mind is 'global.' Even though Rhimes does not question the racial institutional norms that subliminally impact upon the Black female characters, her decision to take a race-blind casting approach cannot be perceived as a complete failure, as her show's diversity is credited to this method (Long, 2011, p. 1067). By placing some pressure on casting agencies, Rhimes was able to find Black female actresses who best executed the personalities she wanted to depict (Long, 2011, p. 1080).

Rhimes' global approach in *Grey's Anatomy* is extremely powerful as, even though it is not intentional, audiences begin to form their own narratives around the Black female characters in her television series—specifically, why, how and when she uses them in specific scenes. By zooming in, one notices that there is a distinct connection amongst the Black female characters. They are mostly smart, hardworking, driven, strong and unemotional, yet compassionate. Equally, each has a uniqueness about them. More interesting is Rhimes' ability to present her characters as able to compete internationally and amongst other races.

This global mentality inspires African women, including me, a first-generation graduate degree holder, whose parents come from a lower income, working-class background. Although born in Mozambique, I grew up in South Africa with roots in various parts of the diaspora, and am pursuing a professional academic career. Aside from knowing a few professional Black women in the Global South who are the first in their families to obtain postgraduate let alone degree qualifications, the experiences and narratives of African professional women in the workplace are under-researched and under-represented in the media. There are a few African female professional characters in popular soap operas such as *Isidingo* (1998–present) and *Generations* (1994–2014), but much of South Africa's television shows focus on gangster families. Currently, there are very few medical shows, besides *Binnelanders* (2005–present) which is an Afrikaans soap opera. However, over a decade ago, *Jozi-H* (2006–2007), a hospital drama series set in Johannesburg, with Black women in professional roles was broadcast for less than four months (13 October 2006–2 February 2007). For these reasons Rhimes' show and her TED X Talk based on her book *Year of Yes* matters to me and other professional women on the African continent. It is not every day that you get to see Black women in professional roles as surgeons. To also learn that behind the show is a successful African American woman, who has made these representations possible, is even more satisfying and reassuring.

REFERENCES

Asare, R. (2017). "The Shonda Gaze": The Effects of Television and Black Female Identity. *UK. Journal of Promotional Communications*, 5(3), 342–361.

Beauboeuf-Lafontant, T. (2013). Our Plates Are Full: Black Women and the Weight of Being Strong. In A. Hayes-Conroy (Ed.), *Doing Nutrition Differently: Critical Approaches to Diet and Dietary Intervention* (pp. 41–58). Farnham, VT: Ashgate.

Bess, Y. (2015). *Representations of Black Women in Media: Identity Development of African American Adolescent Girls.* Academia.edu. Available from: https://www.academia.edu/15148387/Representations_of_Black_Women_in_Media_Identity_Development_of_African_American_Adolescent_Girls [Accessed 1 May 2017].

Collins, P, H. (2000). *Black Feminist Thought: Knowledge, Consciousness, and the Politics of Empowerment.* 2nd Edition. London: Routledge.

Faluyi, D. (2015). An Exploration into the Objectification of Self in Female Hip-Hop Culture as a Form of Misogyny or Empowerment in the Eyes of the Viewer. *Journal of Promotional Communications,* 3(3), 446–464.

Hankivsky, O. (2014). Intersectionality 101. *cal,* 64(1), 238.

hooks, b. (1990). *Yearning: Race, Gender and Cultural Politics.* Boston: South End Press.

hooks, b. (1992). *Black Looks: Race and Representation.* Boston: South End Press.

hooks, b. (1993). Male Heroes and Female Sex Objects: Sexism in Spike Lee's *Malcolm X.* Cineaste, 19(4), 13–15.

hooks, b. (1994). *Outlaw Culture: Resisting Representations.* New York: Routledge.

Kissell, R. (2016). Ratings: ABC's *Scandal, How to Get Away with Murder* Fade Further Thursday. *Variety.* Available from: http://variety.com/2016/tv/news/ratings-abcs-scandal-how-to-get-away-with-murder-fade-thursday-1201710499/ [Accessed 26 Apr. 2017].

Long, A. (2011). Diagnosing Drama: *Grey's Anatomy,* Blind Casting, and the Politics of Representation. *The Journal of Popular Culture,* 44,(5), 1068–1080.

Lorde, A. & Clarke, C. (2007). *Sister Outsider.* Berkeley: Crossing Press.

McGirt, E. (2017). The Black Ceiling: Why African American Women Aren't Making It to the Top in Corporate America. *Fortune.* Available from: http://fortune.com/go/careers/Black-female-ceos-fortune-500-companies/ [Accessed 3 March 2019].

Nolte, A. & Downing, C. (2019). Ubuntu—The Essence of Caring and Being: A Concept Analysis. *Holistic Nursing Practice,* 33(1), 9–16.

Rhimes, S. (2016). *My Year of Saying Yes to Everything* [Video file]. Available from https://www.ted.com/talks/shonda_rhimes_my_year_of_saying_yes_to_everything?language=en [Accessed 20 February 2019].

Schug, J., Alt, N., Lu, P., Gosin, M. & Fay, J. (2017). Gendered Race in Mass Media: Invisibility of Asian Men and Black Women in Popular Magazines. *Psychology of Popular Media Culture,* 6(3), 222–236.

Stoffel, A. (2016). Emerging Feminisms: Is Shonda Rhimes a Feminist? *The Feminist Wire.* Available from: http://www.thefeministwire.com/2016/03/emerging-feminisms-is-shondarhimes-a-feminist/ [Accessed 21 Apr. 2017].

West, C. M. (2018). Mammy, Sapphire, Jezebel, and the Bad Girls of reality television: Media representations of Black women. In J. Chrisler & C. Golden (Eds.), *Lectures on the Psychology of Women* (5th ed.) (pp. 139–158). Long Grove, IL: Waveland Press.

Young, C. (2014). This Is What I Mean When I Say "White Feminism." Battymamzelle.blogspot.co.uk. Available from: http://battymamzelle.blogspot.co.uk/2014/01/This-Is-What-I-Mean-When-I-Say-White-Feminism.html#.Vceh3LNViko [Accessed 19 Apr. 2017].

Sapphires with Stethoscopes

Black Women Practicing Medicine on Television

Phokeng Motsoasele Dailey

A cognitive approach to mass communication emphasizes how experiences with media play a critical role in shaping our mental reality about the world (Bandura, 2009; Sanborn, 2013; Shrum, 2002). Knowledge acquired through media shapes our attitudes and behavior (Slater, 2002). Most of what we know, think we know or believe is not a result of personal experience, but rather, a product of what we have heard in the form of stories. And television is a dominant societal storyteller. There are essentially three types of stories: stories about *how things are*, stories about *how things work*, and stories about *what to do about them* (Gerbner, Gross, Morgan, & Signorelli, 1986; Jhally, 1997). Television not only informs our perception of reality (*how things are* and *how things work*), but also provides a script for how to engage that reality (*what to do about them*). In this way, stories are primary modes of cultural transmission, which cultivate our values, beliefs and normative behaviors (Gerbner et al., 1986).

The basic premise of cultivation theory is that the symbolic world of TV is different from objective reality, and heavy exposure to the TV world alters our perceptions of the real one (Gerbner, Morgan, Gross, Signorelli, & Shanahan, 2002). TV functions as a tool for us to observe what we don't see, or interact with, on a daily basis, and we generalize those TV observations to our real-life environments (Tan, Fujioka, & Lucht, 1997). Those generalized transfers become real-life expectations. The more time we spend consuming TV the more likely we are to believe social reality aligns with the reality portrayed on TV (Gerbner & Gross, 1976). The cultivation effect is particularly pronounced for those with limited real-life exposure to what and whom they are viewing (Sigelman & Welch, 1993). In the original Cultural Indicators Project, an analysis of non-white characters found that minoritized racial-ethnic groups made up only 11 percent of characters in prime-time TV dramas (Gerbner & Signorielli, 1979). The number of Black characters would slightly increase over the next two decades; however, TV still does not accurately reflect the range of ethnic-racial groups in the United States. Non-white racial groups were as underrepresented in the early 2000s as they were twenty years before (Greenberg, Mastro, & Brand, 2002; Mastro & Greenberg, 2000). While this is important, cultivation theorists argue that our attitudes and beliefs are not only shaped by *who* is on TV, but also by *how* those groups are depicted (Punyanunt-Carter, 2008). Misrepresentation is equally as important as lack of representation.

Television is an important source of information about what it means to be Black and TV portrayals contribute to public perceptions of Black women (Wilson, Gutierrez, & Chao, 2003). For example, if someone watches a lot of television, the chances are high that if asked about their perception of Black women they would reflect a combination of long-standing TV depictions (Punyanunt-Carter, 2008). Black characters are often depicted as low-achieving and unemployed. When they are employed they are generally depicted in service roles or what is most associated with blue-collar occupations, e.g., house cleaner, or postal worker (Punyanunt-Carter, 2008). They are also disproportionately depicted in occupational roles such as a cook, entertainer, athlete, or musician. Black women, in particular, are rarely depicted as having highly recognizable professional or supervisory positions in comparison to white TV characters (Baptista-Fernandez, 1980; Punyanunt-Carter, 2008). Typical negative personality characteristics associated with Black women characters include them being violent, menacing, greedy, untidy, noisy and untrained (Dates, 1990). Positive attributes assigned to Black women characters are typically associated with maternal and/or caregiver attributes (Ladson-Billings, 2009).

Even when Black women characters are assigned positive characteristics there are consistent negative undertones. For example, the Black woman character who is presented as highly educated and financially successful is simultaneously depicted as narcissistic and overbearing (Springer, 2007). The *Amos 'n' Andy Show* (1951–1953) is credited with the creation of what is now considered a long-standing stereotypical portrayal of Black women on TV: the Sapphire. From 1951–1953, Sapphire Stevens (Ernestine Wade), a domineering, emasculating and aggressive woman draws laughs from the show's audience by consistently berating her lazy, con-artist husband. The show is eventually removed from broadcast due to complaints about the way in which African Americans are portrayed. Despite the removal of the character the idea of a humorous, aggressive Black woman persists. The contemporary version of the Sapphire is what is commonly referred to as the "Angry Black Woman" or "Sistas with

Attitude." She's bitchy, bossy, stubborn and generally unlikeable yet she commercially sells.

Cultivation theory (Gerbner et al., 2002) makes a case for the larger social implications of how TV depicts Black women medical professionals (BWMPs/Black WMPs). Depictions of BWMPs matter because they shape audience perceptions of what medical professionalism looks like when clothed in a Black female body, and our expectations of real-life communicative interactions with them; particularly for those with limited or non-existent real-life experiences with BWMPs. Our perception of *how things are* and *how things work* for BWMPs provides a script for how to engage them in real life. Medical drama shows, like other first-responder TV shows, are unique in the sense that the plot often centers around the daily activities central to the occupation or profession of its main characters. Because of this, audiences are afforded the opportunity to see Black women depicted in a way that emphasizes their occupation. This also means audiences are more likely to make comparisons with those depictions and the historically traditional depiction of medical professionals as either male or white. For example, there is an association with watching *Grey's Anatomy* and the perception that real-world doctors are courageous, and the greater this perception the more satisfied viewers are with their real-world doctors (Quick, 2009). Exposure to medical shows such as *Grey's Anatomy* and *ER* influence audience attitudes, knowledge and behavior regarding health related behaviors (Brodie & Foehr, 2001; Rideout, 2008).

In the concluding chapter of her book, *Black Women's Portrayals on Reality Television*, Allison (2016) poses two important questions. She asks whether "a series of 'positive' new roles for Black women on scripted television can undo the harm done by the stereotypical depictions of Black women on television?" and "whether these new images are 'positive' or just repackaged mammies, jezebels and sapphires" (p. 234). An examination of BWMPs on TV may partly answer those questions. In this essay, Black woman medical professionals featured in three contemporary TV medical dramas (*ER, Private Practice, & Hawthorne*) are compared to historic depictions of male, white medical professionals and the original iconic BWMP (Julia Baker, from the late '60s show *Julia*). Real-life implications of these depictions are also discussed.

Historical Depictions of Medical Professionals: The Original BWMP and the White Male Doctor

The World Health Organization (2013) defines medical or health professionals as individuals who maintain health in humans through the application of evidence-based medicine and caring. A medical professional studies, diagnoses, treats and prevents human illness, injury and other physical and mental impairments. Occupations within the medical profession are classified into several groups: Medical doctors (MD's)—both generalist and specialist, nursing professionals, midwifery professionals, dentists and pharmacists (World Health Organization, 2013). TV serves as a potential source of information regarding *who* medical professionals are, *what* they do, and what expectations we should have of them in real life.

In the 1960s to 1970s, medical professionals on TV were most often young or middle-aged white male doctors and white female nurses. Doctors (i.e., white males), more so than any other medical professional, were symbols of power and authority (Mclaughlin, 1975). The organizational structure, which cast nurses (i.e., white women) as subservient to doctors concentrated power in the male doctor, and Black medical professionals of all ranks were almost non-existent (Mclaughlin, 1975). Not only was the white male doctor a symbol of power and authority, he was also unrealistically successful in solving patient problems beyond the scope of his expertise. The TV doctor possessed the remarkable ability to exercise control over the lives of others (Mclaughlin, 1975). He was depicted as an "omnipotent healer" (Mclaughlin, 1975, p. 184), whose actions enabled patients to come to terms with the uncertainty inherent in medical treatment and forge stronger bonds with their friends and family. As a conclusion to his content analysis of 15 network shows featuring medical professionals, CBS researcher, James McLaughlin (1975) wrote "Television doctors may not cure their patients, but they can always solve their personal problems" (p. 182).

The Original Black Woman Medical Professional

In the late '60s writer-producer, Hal Kanter, creates the TV show *Julia* (1968–1971), which features a Black woman, in what was then, a non-stereotypical role. Julia Baker (Diahann Carroll) is a middle-class, widowed single mother and a nurse. The series is considered ground-breaking as Black women, up until then, had been primarily depicted in domestic servitude roles on TV. Because of its success the show garners critical attention. Early critiques are broad in scope and steeped in the political unrest of the late '60s: Numerous clashes between law enforcement officers and the militant Black Panther Party. Beloved civil rights leader, Martin Luther King Jr., is assassinated, and in response violent uprisings and protests break out across many Black communities. *Julia* is seen as being completely out of touch with the realities of Black life at that time, and even worse, silent on race issues (MacDonald, 1983).

Others have since argued that the show functioned as a "site of social tension" (Bodroghkozy, 1992, p. 414). The show became the site for dialogue (e.g., viewer response mail) between the audience, media critics and the show's writers and producers (Bodroghkozy, 1992). One critique centers on the curiously lavish, and consequently unrealistic lifestyle of Julia, who was a single mother surviving on a nurses salary (Morreale, 2003). In many ways critics of the show were articulating a dissatisfaction with the narrow and inaccurate representation of the life of a single Black mother, working a pink-collar job, in 1968 America. The show did little to accurately portray what Black woman professionalism looked like in a country marred by a history of enslaving, murdering, raping, and economically excluding Black women.

Contemporary Black Women Medical Professionals: The Sapphire

In the '80s and '90s TV portrayals of medical professionals begin to shift. Shows like *St. Elsewhere* (1982–1988) depicted doctors and the medical system as imperfect. Doctors made mistakes and the medical system did not always serve its patients adequately (Jiwa, 2012). By the early 21st century medical professionals are depicted as having numerous flaws. The TV show, *House* (2004–2012), provides a sharp departure from the traditional portrayal of doctors as empathetic, humane, personable and respectful to patients. The main character, a white male doctor, is addicted to pain killers, and unsympathetic to his patients—a virtue which allows him time to focus on the "real" work of doctors—solving medical problems. Another very important theme emerges during this period on TV: the unorthodox or rebellious medical professional. His often unorthodox, and in some cases illegal, approach to patient care is the source of constant conflict between Dr. Gregory House (Hugh Laurie) and his colleagues, yet he is ultimately celebrated for his revolutionary methods. Breaking the rules becomes a virtue of medical professionalism, and medical show plots spin on the axis of a doctor disobeying orders and taking initiative regardless of their qualifications. In House's case, a lack of compassion or care for patients seems to make him a better doctor.

The Black woman medical professional stands in direct contrast to the persistent characterization of Black characters as untrained, low achieving and/or lacking in recognizable professional or supervisory positions. By virtue of her role as a BWMP the Black woman is afforded some of the defining characteristics of the profession. Inherent in the title of medical professional is the understanding that the individual possesses a specialized knowledge acquired through long and intensive preparation. This knowledge is signaled to patients, and in the case of TV to the audience, by props and costume elements commonly associated with the medical profession (e.g., white coat, scrubs, stethoscope, etc.). While this may be viewed as progression, we see other ways in which the BWMPs specialized qualifications are undermined.

Black WMPs are penalized for behaviors white male doctors are celebrated for on TV. While the contemporary male doctor is awarded by his colleagues, and the audience, for his unorthodox and rebellious approach to treating his patients and the recommendations of his co-workers, those same behaviors are punished when exhibited by a BWMP. *ER* (1994–2009) senior nurse Connie Oligaro (Conni Marie Brazelton), whose character hails back to the very first episode of the show, is fired in season 10 as a result of a protest over the treatment of nurses during the reign of terror by ER chief Robert Romano (Paul McCrane). Oligaro and two other nurses are given a 90-day suspension and immediately replaced. Oligaro is never seen again in the ER, although in episode 4 of season 12, "Blame It on the Rain" (2005), another nurse mentions that she's covering for her.

Dr. Cleo Finch (Michael Michele) is introduced in the 6th season of *ER*. While Finch is portrayed as a generally competent doctor, like other BWMPs she is penalized for deviating from standard procedures in the ER. In episode 4 of season 6, "Sins of the Fathers" (1999), Finch, who is a pediatric fellow, performs an emergency thoracotomy to stabilize a patient until a surgeon can be found. There are no surgeons available to perform the laparotomy on the dying patient in the aftermath of a stabbing in the ER. Finch is reprimanded by her then boyfriend and senior colleague, Dr. Peter Benton (Eriq La Salle).

In episode 1 of season 2, "A Family Thing" (2008), *Private Practice's* (2007–2013) fertility specialist, Dr. Naomi Bennett (Audra McDonald), experiences similar collegial sanctions when she consents to an ethically questionable medical procedure. Bennett has agreed to help a family, with a leukemia-afflicted child, conceive a second child for the purposes of using the infants umbilical cord blood to save the older sibling. When things go awry with the pregnant mother, her best friend and colleague, Dr. Addison Montgomery (Kate Walsh) responds with a self-righteous anger and questions Bennett's professional and moral compass.

While the Black woman medical professional is implicitly assigned the specialized qualifications of her medical profession role, she is simultaneously stripped of some of the other individual characteristics associated with what is often termed white-collar professionalism. Cue the contemporary Sapphire. She's loud, aggressive, and angry and stands in direct violation of the social norms of the medical profession. The most explicit way in which BWMPs are assigned Sapphire characteristics is through the portrayal of them as lacking in collegial civility and/or courteousness. The BMWP asserts her authority by way of aggressive verbal interactions with co-workers. In the opening scene of the pilot episode of *Hawthorne* (2009–2011), the audience immediately understands why the Sapphire is also known as the Angry Black Woman. Not only is the central character, Chief Nursing Officer Christina Hawthorne (Jada Pinkett-Smith), loud she is also verbally and physically aggressive. Hawthorne, who shows up to the hospital in the middle of the night in sweats and looking disheveled, is denied entry into the hospital by a security guard who mocks her—even after she identifies herself. After a prolonged back and forth between the two, police officers are summoned, and she is arrested for breaking security protocol. The audiences first interaction with the central character of the series is watching her kick and scream as she fights to get out of the police officers' grip.

When she's not angry, the BMWP is at minimum seemingly annoyed. Her primary social currency within the medical profession is fear and intimidation of co-workers. Unlike her white male counterparts who gain authority by way of their specialized knowledge and role-specific medical feats, the BMWP establishes authority with co-workers and subordinates through negative interpersonal contact, regardless of her hierarchical status within the organization's structure. She is a Sapphire with a stethoscope who makes her mark on the medical organization by altering or destroying its structure. *ER* character, Dr. Catherine Banfield (Angela Bassett), first appears in episode 2 of season 15, "Another Thursday at County" (2008). Banfield is hired to become the permanent Chief of the Emergency Department, replacing a physician who was serving as acting chief. The board of directors decides to offer the permanent position to Banfield upon the death of their first choice. Though qualified, Banfield is still a second choice. Her entry into the ER and show is marked with a clear sense of disruption. She is a disruption to the organizational structure of the ER and to a beloved character, Doctor Abby Lockhart (Maura Tierney). On her first day as Chief, Banfield immediately puts the entire ER on edge with her tough attitude. She clashes with Lockhart who is finishing her last shift on her last day at County General—immediately putting her at odds with an audience that has a 15-year relationship with the Abby character. Her interactions with her co-workers are marked by the stereotypically angry and overbearing characteristics of the Sapphire.

Interestingly enough, the Black WMP is also punished for the absence of Sapphire characteristics, i.e., lack of emotion or sternness. In the same way that *Julia* became the site for dialogue between the audience and the show's writers and producers, contemporary medical shows that feature

Black WMPs who are perceived as dispassionate, also elicit audience feedback. *ER's* Dr. Cleo Finch is consistently criticized by the audience for lacking a personality. Her perceived lack-luster personality is often interpreted as the absence of patient sensitivity and a disregard for the personal trials of her colleagues. Audience commentaries include statements like "'Personality change? She needs personality, period,' 'The woman must use Bounce laundry detergent since her impeccable clothes show more life than she does,' 'You can count the times she smiled all season long on one hand,' and 'Cleo needs less of a personality change than a personality installation'" (Sims, 2014). Despite having a relatively central role in seasons 6–8, Finch is given the 41st spot in a ranking of the cast of *ER*. David Sims (2014) of *The Atlantic* describes her as "one of two disastrous additions to the cast … a pediatric fellow who was sadly never interesting. Not remotely, not once. She wasn't annoying either; there's really nothing to say about Finch except that she leaves the show with Benton, who she ends up with."

Dr. Naomi Bennett of *Private Practice* receives similar feedback due to what critics perceive as a bland personality. *The LA Times* (Caramanica, 2008) describes Bennett as "rigorously firm, almost dispassionate," and goes as far as to say that "she looked as if she might like to be on another show altogether—something on PBS maybe." This is in response to the fact that, unlike her colleagues who spend an inordinate amount of time bed-hopping and engaging in emotionally insubstantial sexual encounters, Bennett appears neither emotionally nor sexually moved by the young male office assistant, Dell (Chris Lowell), who pledges his undying love and loyalty to her or by her sultry ex-husband, Dr. Sam Bennett (Taye Diggs).

Implications

Workplace data provides a vivid picture of how society engages the "Angry Black Woman" stereotype. Black women are less likely than others to be promoted and/or receive support from their bosses largely due to the perception that they lack collegiality (Rosette & Livingston, 2012). Black women in leadership positions are more likely to be criticized or punished when they err on the job (Rosette & Livingston, 2012). White patients are more likely to interpret treatment recommendations of Black women physicians as communicatively aggressive than those of white women physicians (i.e., viewed as collaborative and supportive) (Stinson & Heischmidt, 2012). We also see ways in which Black women are forced to navigate the stereotype. Black women professionals describe a tendency to wait until everyone else has spoken before weighing in during professional discussions, smiling more so as not to appear aggressive, and downplaying Afrocentric militant characteristics in efforts to reduce the chance of being perceived as threatening or confrontational (Cheeks, 2018; Reynolds-Dobbs, Thomas, & Harrison, 2008). Much of the rhetoric concerning women in workspaces centers around them overcoming the glass ceiling; the invisible barrier that prevents them from career ascension and progression. For Black WMPs, this glass ceiling may seem even more impenetrable because they must also overcome the Sapphire stereotype. While many women of color may relate to the issue of racial stereotyping in the workplace, the Sapphire stereotype is only directed at Black women. At the beginning of this essay a case was made for how TV informs our perception of reality and provides a script for how we engage that reality. While the days of brazen caricatures of Black women dominating U.S. television appear to be trailing off, the fact that recent shows such as *ER*, *Private Practice*, and *Hawthorne* still portray decades-old stereotypes, remains troubling.

References

Allison, D. (Ed.). (2016). *Black Women's Portrayals on Reality Television: The New Sapphire*. Lanham, MA: Lexington Books.

Bandura, A. (2009). Social Cognitive Theory of Mass Communication. In J. Bryant & M. B. Oliver (Eds.), *Media Effects: Advances in Theory and Research* (2nd ed., pp. 94–124). Mahwah, NJ: Erlbaum.

Baptista-Fernandez, P. (1980). The Content, Characteristics, and Communication Behaviors of Blacks on Television. In B. S. Greenberg (Ed.), *Life on Television: Content Analysis of U.S. TV Drama* (pp. 13–21). Norwood, NJ: Albex.

Bodroghkozy, A. (1992). "Is this what you mean by color TV?": Race, Gender and Conflicted Meanings in NBC's *Julia*. In L. Spigel & D. Mann (Eds.), *Private Screenings: Television and the Female Consumer* (pp. 143–167). Minneapolis: University of Minnesota Press.

Brodie, M., & Foehr, U. (2001). Communicating Health Information Through the Entertainment Media. *Health Affairs, 20*(1), 192. Retrieved from bth.

Caramanica, J. (2008, September 28). Naomi's woes are good medicine. *Los Angeles Times*. Retrieved from https://webcache.googleusercontent.com/search?q=cache:zVtpWVD DtT8J:https://www.latimes.com/archives/la-xpm-2008-sep-28-ca-monitor28-story. html+&cd=1&hl=en&ct=clnk&gl=us.

Cheeks, M. (2018, March 26). How Black Women Describe Navigating Race and Gender in the Workplace. *Harvard Business Review*. Retrieved from https://hbr. org/2018/03/how-Black-women-describe-navigating-race-and-gender-in-the-workplace.

Dates, J. (1990). A War of Images. In J. Dates & W. Barlow (Eds.), *Split Images: African Americans in the Mass Media* (pp. 1–25). Washington, D.C.: Howard University Press.

Gerbner, G., & Gross, L. (1976). Living with Television: The Violence Profile. *Journal of Communication, 26*, 172–194.

Gerbner, G., Gross, L., Morgan, M., & Signorelli, N. (1986). Living with Television: The Dynamics of the Cultivation Process. In J. Bryant & D. Zillman (Eds.), *Perspectives on Media Effects* (pp. 17–40). Hillsdale, NJ: Erlbaum.

Gerbner, G., Morgan, M., Gross, L., Signorelli, N., & Shanahan, J. (2002). Growing Up with Television: Cultivation Processes. In J. Bryant & D. Zillman (Eds.), *Media Effects: Advances in Theory and Research* (2nd ed.). Hillsdale, NJ: Erlbaum.

Gerbner, G., & Signorielli, N. (1979). *Women and Minorities in Television Drama 1969–1978*. Philadelphia: Annenberg School of Communication, University of Pennsylvania.

Greenberg, B. S., Mastro, D., & Brand, J. E. (2002). Minorities and the Mass Media:

Television into the 21st century. In J. Bryant & D. Zillman (Eds.), *Media Effects: Advances in Theory and Research* (2nd ed., pp. 333–351). Hillsdale, NJ: Erlbaum.

Jhally, S. (1997). *George Gerbner on Media and Culture*. Northampton, MA: Media Education Foundation.

Jiwa, M. (2012). Doctors and the Media. *Australasian Medical Journal, 5*(11), 603–608. https://doi.org/10.4066/amj.2012.1562.

Ladson-Billings, G. (2009). "Who you callin' nappy-headed?": A Critical Race Theory Look at the Construction of Black Women. *Race Ethnicity and Education, 12*(1), 87–99. https://doi.org/10.1080/13613320802651012.

MacDonald, J. F. (1983). *Black and White TV: Afro-Americans in Television Since 1948*. Chicago: Nelson-Hall.

Mastro, D., & Greenberg, B. S. (2000). The Portrayal of Racial Minorities on Primetime Television. *Journal of Broadcasting and Electronic Media, 44*, 690–703.

Mclaughlin, J. (1975). The Doctor Shows. *Journal of Communication, 25*(3), 182–184.

Morreale, J. (Ed.). (2003). *Critiquing the Sitcom: A Reader* (1st ed). Syracuse: Syracuse University Press.

Punyanunt-Carter, N. M. (2008). The Perceived Realism of African American Portrayals on Television. *Howard Journal of Communications, 19*(3), 241–257. https://doi.org/10.1080/10646170802218263.

Quick, B. L. (2009). The Effects of Viewing *Grey's Anatomy* on Perceptions of Doctors and Patient Satisfaction. *Journal of Broadcasting and Electronic Media, 53*(1), 38–55. Retrieved from edshol.

Reynolds-Dobbs, W., Thomas, K. M., & Harrison, M. S. (2008). From Mammy to Superwoman: Images that Hinder Black Women's Career Development. *Journal of Career Development, 35*(2), 129–150. https://doi.org/10.1177/0894845308325645.

Rideout, V. (2008). *Television as a Health Educator: A Case Study of* Grey's Anatomy. Retrieved from Kaiser Family Foundation website: https://www.kff.org/other/television-as-a-health-educator-a-case/.

Rosette, A. S., & Livingston, R. W. (2012). Failure Is Not an Option for Black Women: Effects of Organizational Performance on Leaders with Single versus Dual-Subordinate Identities. *Journal of Experimental Social Psychology, 48*(5), 1162–1167. https://doi.org/10.1016/j.jesp.2012.05.002.

Sanborn, F. W. (2013). *A Cognitive Psychology of Mass Communication* (6th ed.). https://doi.org/10.4324/9780203110904.

Shrum, L. J. (2002). Media Consumption and Perceptions of Social Reality: Effects and Underlying Processes. In J. Bryant & D. Zillman (Eds.), *Media Effects: Advances in Theory and Research* (2nd ed., pp. 69–96). Mahwah, N.J: Erlbaum.

Sigelman, L., & Welch, S. (1993). The Contact Hypothesis Revisited: Black-White Interaction and Positive Racial Attitudes. *Social Forces, 71*, 781–795. Retrieved from edsbas.

Sims, D. (2014, September 16). Fifteen Years at County General: Definitively Ranking the Cast of *ER*. *The Atlantic*. Retrieved from https://www.theatlantic.com/entertainment/archive/2014/09/fifteen-years-at-county-general-definitively-ranking-all-of-ers-doctors-and-nurses/380164/.

Slater, M. (2002). Entertainment Education and the Persuasive Impact of Narratives. In M. C. Green, J. J. Strange, & T. C. Brock (Eds.), *Narrative Impact : Social and Cognitive Foundations* (pp. 157–181). Mahwah, N.J: Erlbaum Associates.

Springer, K. (2007). Divas, Evil Black Bitches, and Bitter Black Women: African American Women in Postfeminist and Post-Civil-Rights Popular Culture. In *Interrogating Postfeminism: Gender and the Politics of Popular Culture* (pp. 249–276). Durham, NC: Duke University Press.

Stinson, M. E., & Heischmidt, K. (2012). Patients' Perceptions of Physicians: A Pilot Study of the Influence of Prime-Time Fictional Medical Shows. *Health Marketing Quarterly, 29*(1), 66–81. https://doi.org/10.1080/07359683.2012.652579.

Tan, A., Fujioka, Y., & Lucht, N. (1997). Native American Stereotypes, TV Portrayals, and Personal Contact. *Journalism & Mass Communication Quarterly, 74*(2), 265–284. https://doi.org/10.1177/107769909707400203.

Wilson, C. C., Gutierrez, F., & Chao, L. M. (2003). *Racism, Sexism, and the Media: The Rise of Class Communication in Multicultural America*. Thousand Oaks, CA: Sage Publications.
World Health Organization. (2013). Definition and List of Health Professionals. In *Annex 1. Transforming and Scaling Up Health Professionals' Education and Training: World Health Organization Guidelines 2013*. Retrieved from https://www.ncbi.nlm.nih.gov/books/NBK298950/.

The Curious Case of the Black Male Doctor

Character Actualization and Moderate Blackness of ER's *Peter Benton*

LaToya T. Brackett

Introduction

There is a peculiar scene in the television series *ER* (1994–2009), a scene which classically demonstrates the complexities surrounding the characterization of Dr. Peter Benton (Eric LaSalle). These complexities prevailed throughout his character's tenure on this NBC series, and one could say that the more viewers learned about Benton, the more curious he became. In season 7, episode 5, "Flight of Fancy," this peculiar scene occurs, and it is peculiar because race is directly discussed, yet not discussed at all: "Your mother must be very proud," said an older Black woman, who was the patient of *ER*'s primary Black doctor, the young and distinguished Dr. Peter Benton. She had been lying down waiting to be seen for quite a while in the Emergency Room. Dr. Benton's proud and shy yet rarely seen smile embraced the older Black woman's affirmation. He put on his gloves to treat her. And before he could get the chance to place his helping hands on her, she spoke. She spoke to him, with a gentleness coinciding with firmness, "Before we get much further. I'd like to say that I would be more at ease with another doctor. You look like a fine young man, but I've always had white doctors. I've always felt more comfortable that way." "So you're saying that you only want to see a white doctor?" Dr. Benton clarified. "If it's all right with you." "It's fine. You'll just have to wait another three hours." Thus, she declined treatment from Peter Benton, M.D., African American son of a woman that so resembled the woman he attempted to treat. His smile slouched along with the rest of his body. His general demeanor that lacked any visible contentment reappeared as he took off his gloves and walked away.

Dr. Benton did not protest. He did not question the woman's use of whiteness as qualification. He did not express any feelings of rejection from a Black female elder. He simply moved on. Not once does Benton share this interaction with anyone else, not once does he process this experience. As he throws down his gloves, on the main ER desk, Dr. Carter (Noah Wyle) asks an administrative colleague, "What happened to him?" And she simply replies, "I don't know." And with white dismissal, that ends this amazingly deep scene, and never do the viewers see beyond Benton's veil. But this is scripted television, and one must ask, scripted by whom?

The character of Dr. Peter Benton on *ER* was introduced on a basic stereotypical level of a professionally driven Black man that holds one focus and thus one dimension. As the series evolved, so too did the attempt to further develop the character of Benton. This attempted development only truly began with a major catalyst initiated by Eriq La Salle to the production team on the series. La Salle's character's actualization on screen grew and shared with viewers various trials and tribulations in Benton's personal and professional life that elaborated on his hard exterior on the show. Despite Dr. Peter Benton's representation as over-eager, without emotions, individualistic, and for the lack of better words, scary and angry doctor, his various life experiences attempted to reveal to the television audience the intricacies that defined him. As Donald Bogle referenced, other characters on the series like Doug Ross (George Clooney), were actualized, so much so that he was seen as a womanizer and yet still as a caring pediatrician. Dr. Ross was never one dimensional but rather complex. But for Benton, despite "his intimate scenes with Boulet (Gloria Reuben), [he] remained remote, frustrating viewers all the more…. La Salle appeared unable to infuse a flat character with some personal warmth or idiosyncrasies. 'Benton is probably the most misunderstood [character],' … 'as he rarely allows his wall of defense to come down'" (Bogle, 2001, p. 444). It was Benton's turn to be complex and not simply a Black representation from the minds of white writers and creators. Without intricate details of Black experiences, writing a complex Black character often entails stereotypes and white understandings of Blackness, or simply placing a Black actor into a role written for a white doctor. This essay will discuss this curious case of Dr. Peter Benton through the lens of a concept known as moderate Blackness, coined by scholar Amy Wilkins in 2012, and the concept of character actualization. In assessing moments in the series that Benton fulfilled aspects of moderate Blackness, and storylines that were meant to make his character more actualized, it will be shown how, despite later attempts to better actualize Benton, the white lens of the writers and producers were unable to do so due to the assumption that most of their understanding of Black professional men is aligned with moderate Blackness. The suppression of emotions, which is required of moderate Blackness, disallows for true actualization of a Black male professional character who resides in a predominantly white work environment.

What Are Black Stories?

When analyzing the representation of African American characters on screen, there are many components to look at, but I posit that the most central questions are who created the character, who writes the character and who produces the series? Film and television remain white dominated, and thus film and television still maintain mostly white narratives and white audiences as central. Representation of African American lives on the big and small screen have increased over the decades, but when those who maintain control of the industry are not aware of such realities of Blackness, does a Black actor in a white narrative constitute a Black story? It is often Black writers and producers that make Black narratives visible. The lack of African American writers for the screen has enabled the continual perpetuation of African American stereotypes such as the Angry Black Man, which is aligned with aspects of Benton, but also one he attempts to rupture or at least avoid. I further ask if it is truly a representation of an African American experience if the character has no lines or is only known via one dimension? Additionally, if an African American narrative is written from whiteness, is it a Black story? The following section will give definition and foundation to the concepts being utilized in the analysis of *ER's* Peter Benton.

The Ava DuVernay Test: Is the Character Actualized?

In 1986 the Bechdel test was established in a comic strip by a cartoonist, Alison Bechdel. The Bechdel test relates to a feminist representation in film, of course evolving to more media mediums throughout the years. The very basic requirement of this test is that in a production there must be two women, they must hold a conversation, and it cannot place content focus on a man or men (Dargis, 2016). This test defined an actualized experience for women in films, and in 2016 a New York times columnist, Manohla Dargis, proposed the creation of an Ava DuVernay test, on a similar basis as the Bechdel test but in line with race, not gender (Child, 2016). The DuVernay test would also require that characters of color would have an actualized existence by having there be at least two characters of color who: 1. must have a conversation together and 2. the conversation must not centralize discussion around white people and the issues coinciding with the white race. Throughout the series, *ER* had various episodes which met the "DuVernay test," which is mostly successful due to the profession, as doctors, being central to most conversations on screen. The DuVernay test is a fine idea to the production of film and television that allows Black viewers to see their stories reflected back at them. But, is it not also potentially problematic to say that, in a series that is predominantly white, that a Black character is considered actualized even if they do not speak about race among their own people? This question leads up to the next concept to consider, one which is also curious, in how it is an accurate representation of Black realities, but it should not be used to write Black narratives that have a goal of character actualization.

Moderate Blackness: Black Males Fighting the Stereotype

Within the identity of African Americans there is this invisibility that is imposed upon them and also utilized by them to maintain a level of sanity within society. W.E.B. DuBois shed light on this role played by African Americans in his seminal text, *The Souls of Black Folk* in which he described a veil, and expressed a definition of African Americans as being a problem for white society, and further discussed the requirement of Blacks to wear a mask in order to survive and hopefully thrive within society. Masks that conceal "Black rage, anger, and fury" are used to please white preoccupations with Black people as a problem (Black Identity, 2005). An angry Black man is a problem.

Unproblematic, as defined by white dominant society, requires a lot of Black people to restrain their emotions. In her original research, Amy Wilkins gained insight into Black male college students at predominantly white institutions, on how they remain unproblematic and invisible to white harm. Utilizing grounded theory, she operationalized the concept of moderate Blackness.

> I call these strategies [to avoid white harm] "moderate Blackness." Moderate Blackness has three components: restrained, positive emotional standards; a temperate approach to Black politics; and the ability to get along with white people. It is thus moderate in two senses. First, it moderates the importance of Blackness to individual identities; for moderate Blacks, Blackness is one among many identity attributes. Second, it moderates racial discord, distancing itself from stereotypes of Blacks as angry and/or dangerous [Wilkins, 2012, p. 41].

In using this concept in relations to *ER*'s Benton, I align the Black male participants of Wilkins' study with Benton, due to both being considered educated, and both discussing their existence in predominantly white spaces such as Benton's work environment. Benton's character is definitively intimidating, and most likely angry, but he polices his demeanor, and thus he works toward moderate Blackness for his career success. Or rather the way his character is written is attempting this work.

> Middle-class Black men must avoid being stereotyped as "the angry Black man"—"a middle class, educated African American male, who despite his economic and occupational success, perceives racial discrimination everywhere and consequently is enraged"—by adhering to "racialized feeling rules" that both strenuously prohibit anger among African American men, and oblige them to deny race-based inequities. Successful participation in dominant institutions, then, requires Black men to exhibit extraordinary emotional restraint [p. 35].

Benton is not yet economically successful, but he aims for that goal, and he understands what he must do to enable it. He sees himself very individually, and throughout the series he is least likely to pull the race card, or allow someone else to pull it on him. He is a doctor first. And this I posit is a major issue with the actualization of the Benton character. How does one write the narrative of a Black doctor who places the needs of his white surroundings before his own? It is automatic when those who write the character are not Black, and perhaps are writing the character based on their own interactions with Black people, most likely Black folks who are resigned to relying on moderate Blackness for survival.

Maintaining the Veil: When White Writers Write Black Narratives

ER was based on the inner workings of the fictional County General Hospital's Emergency Room and Surgical Department. The original script for the series was written in 1974, and it was picked up twenty years later with a major push to NBC. The series was not like other television shows—it imparted a type of reality that incorporated a more honest interaction in the background of the main dialoging characters. The series also included a faster paced approach to the onscreen situations as in a real emergency room. Supporting characters were diverse and thus it better represented the potential demographics of medical professionals in Chicago. The inclusion of an African American main character, Benton, showed television progress, however Denzel Washington also headlined in *St. Elsewhere* (1982–1988) a decade earlier. *ER* was meant to be realistic across all fronts. But was it?

ER was first written by, and created by, a white man, Michael Crichton. It was the onboarding of another white man as producer, Steven Spielberg, that made NBC say yes to six episodes. Spielberg was not a continued asset on the series as it grew, but the two executive producers who produced all 331 episodes of the series were also white men; Crichton and John Wells. Crichton spoke greatly about his unexpected successful series, and in sharing some of the goals and desired outcomes of *ER* he revealed the nuanced realities of an inability for them to recognize that Benton's actualized story was missing. Crichton "pushed for a professional demeanor, which meant [that actors] not 'relate' to patients in expected ways. For example, it was hard to get the actors to look at the injury and not at the patients' faces, when they were talking to them. It goes against instinct. But professional behavior is a lot of what gives the show its realistic quality" (Spotlight on Michael Crichton's Television Career, 2020). Crichton, who had insight to the medical profession as a former medical student himself, focused on the profession of medicine, he centered the series on the doctors and that narrative first. The doctor narrative within U.S. socialization would by default be defined by those that make up the majority of doctors, white men. Crichton's own experience was as a white medical student as well. So how do you write for a narrative not your own? Christopher Chulack, a long-time producer on the series stated, "'Our idea from the start was to be an emotional action show.... The whole idea was to convey the pace of working in an actual ER. That, and studying the lives of the people who work in that emergency room and how this job impacted them'" (Spotlight on Michael Crichton's Television Career). Considering this goal, where was the emotion for Benton in the beginning? Where were the storylines that allowed the audience to understand, beyond a surface level, how Benton's work impacted his life, including his life as a Black man? It is not that Benton's character did not engage with his personal life on screen, but rather that so much was still missing, and often what was missing, I speculate is what Black viewers wondered about and white viewers did not.

Defining Dr. Peter Benton

Benton Is Missing: La Salle Requests Actualization

Eriq La Salle, in a white dominated career, broke with the desires for Black invisibility or moderate Blackness, and questioned the producers in their choices for Benton. La Salle even publicly shared the shortfalls of *ER's* production, with a juxtaposed recognition that things were indeed better. Eriq La Salle spoke on *The Today Show* about his character's newest developments and finally having an episode dedicated to Benton. La Salle shared that he did not understand why it took five seasons for the producers to focus on his character, "They've done it with every original member of the cast. They've actually done it multiple times.... I said, 'Okay, guys, I'm on the show too'" (Bogle, 2001, p. 445). La Salle's speaking up to producers and to the public is a prime example of how La Salle did not allow racism to affect him, and thus restrains what is most likely anger, and refuses to be instigated, even on a talk show.

In episode 16, of season 5, "Middle of Nowhere," the series focuses on Benton who takes on outside work in a rural area of Mississippi. Apparently, in this part of Mississippi, the idea of a "Black doctor" could not be accurate. Benton is hit with racism habitually throughout this episode and it is a prime example of how moderate Blackness is asserted into the writing of his character. In this episode he rises above the southern white racism consistently. He even allows for more friendly engagement with the white nurse he was there to support—a bit outside of his Chicago habits. Benton even breaks stereotypes about African American eating habits by revealing that he's a vegetarian. So even though the viewers get to know more about him in this dedicated episode, it seems to still be written with a purpose of being a manageable rendition of a Black man—moderately Black.

The other push that La Salle had for his character was to end the interracial relationship between Dr. Benton and Dr. Elizabeth Corday (Alex Kingston). La Salle stated: "So if the only time you show a balanced relationship is in an interracial relationship whether it's conscious or subconscious, it sends a message I'm not comfortable with … the only time that [Benton] becomes human and tender and vulnerable and open is when he falls in love with a white woman" (pp. 445-446). As African Americans viewed this series they saw Benton date several Black women, and even father a son with one of them, yet the relationships never worked. However, he later found romantic success in whiteness. This interracial relationship does puncture the most often non-interracial relationship narratives on television at the time, but it potentially created harm in how viewers interpreted it. It presents a narrative that for a professional Black man, a white professional woman is the only one who can satisfy him. After La Salle's request, the Corday-Benton affair concludes, and Benton finds love with a Black female *ER* doctor, Cleo Finch (Michael Michele). It is with Finch that Benton leaves the hospital, and the series, with a view of a better life ahead in season 8.

Glimpses of His Anger, Shadowed in Humanity

It is interesting that most of the deep engagement with colleagues for Benton is not with a peer, nor a person of color but with Dr. John Carter, his former intern. This is one of the most unique relationships on television. Based on the DuVernay test, their relationship and interactions are not actualizations as a Black man, but they definitely reveal his professional expectations storyline the most.

It is with Carter that Benton releases aspects of his anger, but still his anger does not revolve around race, but work. After Carter's year as a surgical resident under the leadership of Benton, Carter decided to move his specialty to emergency medicine. Benton is very disappointed in this, and very much dismisses Carter. The two argue about his decision. Carter feels that he had worked hard for three years and had earned Benton's respect. Benton believes that because of this decision, his hard work was wasted. Carter feels it is not about the work but because he chose emergency medicine and Benton chose surgical residency.

> **CARTER:** This isn't about your time, this is about your egotism.
> **BENTON:** Yeah, yeah right, yeah Carter I'm egotistical. You know what, I got a lot of people that worked hard to make sure I am where I am. And for them I got to be self-centered, I don't take time for anything, but for you man, man, I did for you, Carter. I did man.

This interaction reveals more about Benton's approach to his career, and why it matters so much, than any other interactions on the series. Yet again it falls short to extend discussion about how, who Benton is as a Black man, potentially requires his extreme work focus and required success. Peter Benton is self-centered because he cannot fail, otherwise he'd be letting those who led the way for him down. He is prideful, which often can be seen from white onlookers as anger, because they cannot see past the veil that shields them from the realities of being Black in America. So, when Benton first introduced Carter to the chief of surgery in the pilot episode, and the chief said: "Dr. Benton is one of the best residents we have. Learn everything you can from him. Except his attitude," so much context is missing, and in reality it is never fully uncovered in Benton's tenure on the series.

Race Does Matter, but It Doesn't Have To

Peter Benton was a Black character who rarely spoke about race, Bogle references this when he highlights how African American viewers were waiting to know what this professional Black man thought about race, and what he thought about being the only Black male doctor.

> Many Black men experienced gendered racism in the form of countering white colleagues' perceptions of them as threatening, menacing, or overly aggressive, or as many respondents described, the image of the "angry Black man." As respondents described

it, the angry Black man image is a middle-class, educated African American male who, despite his economic and occupational successes, perceives racial discrimination everywhere and consequently is always enraged.... Many respondents perceived that white colleagues and superiors expected them to fit this image. As such, they took pains to avoid engaging in any behavior that might reflect it [Wingfield, 2007, p. 205].

In season three, Dr. Dennis Gant (Omar Epps) joins the cast as a surgery intern. Gant was extremely emotional, and outwardly so. He definitely fit what Wingfield's respondents defined as an angry Black man. In a disagreement fostered by Gant, Benton asks if Gant had checked Black as his race on his medical school application, and when he affirmed he had, "Benton informs him that everyone will assume Gant is there because of a quota system, not because of merit. Therefore Gant must work harder and be better to prove them wrong" (Bogle, p. 445). Benton is making reference to Affirmative Action, and the negative stereotyping of a person of color being less capable. Benton consistently focused on being the best. Benton's one-on-one advice to another Black male doctor to suppress his emotions, aligns directly with the strategies of moderate Blackness.

To be sure, moderate Black men do not deny that racism exists, but instead claim that racism does not affect their daily lives or life chances. They enact a range of emotion strategies to create and sustain this view: defining racism narrowly; imagining that racism happens to other people, but not to them; framing race-based interactions as unimportant; and interpreting perpetrators as innocent or ignorant. Together, these strategies allow them to displace racism from their everyday lives, and to see the campus as a welcoming place [Wilkins, p. 45].

Benton knows that there is racism, but he refuses to let it affect his professional success. For Benton throughout most of his time on the series he is certain that his acceptance into medical school, and the career that follows, was on his own merit alone.

In the seventh season, in episode 12, "Surrender," Benton is tricked into being the director of diversity for the medical school by a truly angry and unliked man Dr. Robert Romano (Paul McCrane)—as a white man, he can be angry, mean, and even unethical and still be a successful character on TV. Benton had reported Romano for unethical medical practice, and in response Romano deleted the attending position in surgery that Benton was slated to fill. Additionally, Romano black-balled Benton from getting other positions, until Benton had no other choice but to be a per diem physician at County General with no benefits or guarantees. Always looking for more financial enhancement, due to Romano's personal angst against Benton, Benton has no other choice but to embrace the director of diversity position when Romano announces the title of the position to Benton and a room of reporters at the same time. Benton did later in the episode reject the job, because he stated it was only because he was Black. Romano admitted that Benton was right about Romano's reasons, but also the reality that he had no one else and thus the position was created to make a difference on the issue of diverse doctors.

It's interesting how from the beginning of *ER* Benton was always a rock star, all his skills related to him being brilliant, nothing was mentioned about his ability to do his job for anything other than if he truly was medically qualified, except by that one elderly Black female patient. And the interesting part comes, in episode 14 of season 7, "A Walk in the Woods," when as director of diversity, Benton finds his medical school application under the category of Affirmative Action. Despite the continued projection to the viewers of how competent Benton was, for some reason the white producers desired to give a background story on Benton that makes them wonder about his capabilities. He had a reputation at the hospital, particularly among those he'd supervised, as stated in episode 1, of season 3, "Dr. Carter, I Presume": "Dr. Benton is an intern's worst nightmare. He's smarter than you, he never eats, he never sleeps, and he reads every medical journal no matter how obscure ... and you will wake up every morning praying for his approval. You won't get it." Obviously, it shouldn't matter at this later point in his career, but even as Benton told Gant, people will wonder. Benton did not discuss this new information with anyone, so the characters on the series didn't suddenly have a reason to question Benton's abilities, yet now the viewers did.

Peter Benton, MD: An Unfinished Black Story

In Benton's final appearance as a regular, episode 10 of season 8, "I'll Be Home for Christmas," Carter tracks Benton down on his morning run to inform him of how much Benton means to Carter. Benton planned to leave with no real goodbyes, not even to his closest colleague, and dare we say friend. Carter hands Benton a gift, containing a L-token Benton had given Carter years ago. The L-token is a reference to a major moment in Carter's career facilitated by Benton. As Carter gives Benton the token, he says: "... you can use it to come back." Benton laughs his smirky, dismissive laugh, "Carter, they don't use tokens anymore." "Then call and I'll come pick you up." As Benton excuses himself by stating he's getting cold, Carter tells him, "I'm a good doctor because of you." Benton responds: "No you're not ... but keep trying." And after eight seasons, Benton simply jogs off, no hug, no emotion, no attachment.

Dr. Peter Benton, played by Eriq La Salle, from 1994 to 2001, was a curious character, because no matter the various attempts throughout the series to unveil the undergirding that defined his realities, so much about why he was the way he was, was never actualized. As a Black character on a predominantly white series, the majority of the audience watching were also white, and stereotypes of Benton being an angry Black man, and being unemotional, uncaring and self-centered needed to have an explanatory narrative shared—it never truly was told. His Black story was missing. Despite attempts to further develop Benton's character in the series, so much was still underdeveloped, or oversimplified, due to the lens from which it was written—a white one. Perhaps, despite La Salle's attempt to have his character puncture stereotypes of African Americans, it was too late, because the original premise of his character was never truly developed as a Black story but as a doctor story with a Black actor playing the part. Whiteness told Benton's story from how white individuals in predominantly white educated spaces, witness Black men engaging—with moderate Blackness. Thus, in the end, Peter Benton is a curious case, because a professional Black man creates curiosity for white spaces and people he must exist around, and so any stories told about a Black man never investigate why he seems so curious to them. White producers and writers can continue to attempt this Black character actualization, but the reality is, they will never see past the veil.

References

Black Identity. (2005). In G. D. Jaynes, *Encyclopedia of African American Society Volume 2* (p. 354). Thousand Oaks:, CA Sage Publication.

Bogle, D. (2001). *Primetime Blues: African Americans on Network Television.* New York: Farrar, Straus and Giroux.

Child, B. (2016, February 1). Ava DuVernay Backs "DuVernay Test" to Monitor Racial Diversity in Hollywood. Retrieved from The Guardian : https://www.theguardian.com/film/2016/feb/01/ava-duvernay-test-racial-diversity-hollywood-selma-director-oscars.

Dargis, M. (2016, January 29). Sundance Fights Tide with Films Like "The Birth of a Nation." Retrieved from The New York Times: https://www.nytimes.com/2016/01/30/movies/sundance-fights-tide-with-films-like-the-birth-of-a-nation.html.

Spotlight on Michael Crichton's Television Career. (2020, May 23). Retrieved from The Official Site of Michael Crichton: http://www.michaelcrichton.com/television/.

Wilkins, A. (2012). "Not Out to Start a Revolution": Race, Gender, and Emotional Restraint Among Black University Men. *Journal of Contemporary Ethnography*, 34–65.

Wingfield, A. H. (2007). The Modern Mammy and the Angry Black Man: African American Proffesionals' Experiences with Gendered Racism in the Workplace. *Race, Gender, & Class*, 196–212.

PART IV

Educators
and the Educated

Anti-Blackness and Colorblindness in Post-Cosby Sitcoms

Likeable Black Teachers, Exceptional Black Students but/and Everybody Hates Chris

Amir Asim Gilmore

The anti–Black representations of Black teachers are crucial to understand. Not only are Black teachers underrepresented in the professional job market, but they are misrepresented within television shows (Figilo, 2018). Television shows are a significant social and cultural influencer, because not only do they shape the educational and professional outlook of Black children, but they also have the potential to shape racist public perceptions, attitudes, and stereotypes that can be potentially detrimental to Black children (Bell & Janis, 2011). When Black children watch television shows, little emphasis is placed on Black education or the importance of a Black teacher. Therefore, when television shows underrepresent or misrepresent the value of Black education and the professionalism of Black teachers, the effects are felt, especially with children. If Black children do not see a professional that looks like them within the classroom, what value would they place in becoming a teacher? This divestment towards education is reinforced in Black education-based television shows by Black media-teachers. Media-teachers defined by Swetnam (1992) are, "teachers showcased in fictional television programs and films" (p. 30). The Black media-teachers on these shows were portrayed as incompetent, comedic, hypersexual, indifferent, and unprofessional. The conveyed message is that Black teachers and Black children are not valued for their intellectual contributions (Bell & Janis, 2011).

136

Black education's devaluation is not a new phenomenon, but a persistent, racist, and calculated issue that was entrenched centuries ago (Hartman, 2008).

In Saidiya Hartman's (2008) *Lose Your Mother: A Journey Along the Atlantic Slave Route*, Hartman described how Black people live in the "afterlife of slavery" (p. 6). The afterlife of slavery is a critical and political orientation that explores the relationship between the Black past and the Black present and insists that those historical links "echo" across institutions, ideologies, and policies (Womack, 2017). It is an examination of how slavery, and its afterlife lingers, thrives, and haunts Black people, causing them to suffer. To study these historical links, utilizing Black Critical Race (BlackCrit) theory is necessary to interrogate slavery's enduring presence in the twenty-first century; its persistent denial of Black civil and social rights, and to trace the hauntings of slavery in Black education and contemporary Black education-based television shows (Womack, 2017). This chapter will connect how the "racial calculus" of anti–Blackness erased the importance of Black teachers during the Civil Rights Movement and how anti–Blackness (mis)represents Black teachers as unprofessional in Black education-based sitcoms such as, *The Steve Harvey Show, Hanging with Mr. Cooper, Smart Guy,* and *Everybody Hates Chris.*

The Importance of Black Critical Race Theory in Education

BlackCrit is a theoretical race-based framework that provides an understanding of being a Black person in an anti–Black society (More, 2012). BlackCrit analyzes how the Black/Non-Black binary affects Blackness and the lived experiences of Black people (Roberts, 1999; Dumas & Ross, 2016). Moreover, BlackCrit interrogates *anti–Blackness,* an ever-present condition of Black social suffering (Dumas, 2018). Blackness and Black people, through this framework, are not only casted as "other," but other than human (Dumas, 2016). Democratic societies employ anti–Blackness by "othering" Black people from their subjectivity and citizenship (Sexton, 2016, as cited in Ray et. al, 2017). This is evident within the contexts of education, schooling, and television shows.

Black children suffer within education because schools, "revolve around middle-class white norms and expectations" (Majors & Billson, 1994, p. 14). The suffering of Black children is invisible and largely insignificant because the notions of meritocracy and "racial progress" within schooling does not value the humanity of Black life. BlackCrit *invites* and *calls* for people to understand why Black children are devalued and envisions liberatory spaces for Black children beyond the notion of racial justice (Dumas, 2018). The first step to creating those spaces is to interrogate the Black educational experiences of teachers and students, as well as examine how those experiences are represented on television.

Black Like Me: The Importance of Black Educators

Educators are vital to a child's socio-cognitive development, as they help students embody ethical and equitable practices; understand factual information, develop critical thinking skills, improve verbal and written communication, and foster better time management skills (Sleigh & Ritzer, 2004). These skills help students maximize their potential, both personally, socially, and professionally, as they are critical for future academic and nonacademic success (Sleigh & Ritzer, 2004). Moreover, educators can provide students access to opportunities such as scholarships, internships, and additional educational experiences (i.e., college) through recommendations and guidance. In essence, educators have a tremendous amount of power to alter and influence a child's life. That power and influence is magnified within the context of race.

Prior to 1954, Black educators played powerful professional roles as models and advocates for Black children. The abundance of skilled Black teachers resulted in Black children receiving robust education, and wisdom from their Black elders about "the ways of the world" (Lutz, 2017). Black educators developed relationships with Black students by sharing how they overcame life challenges and obstacles (Griffin & Tackie, 2016). Moreover, Black educators were more likely than white teachers to recognize their students' competence (Staples, 2017). Staples (2017) noted "that children who encounter African-American teachers are more likely to be recognized as bright enough for gifted and talented programs, more likely to be viewed as capable of success and more likely to graduate from high school and aim for college. That dynamic changed after 1954, as Black teachers began to "disappear."

The Afterlife of Segregation: The Unrecognized Failures of Brown v. Board of Education

Dumas (2018) stated that, "justice in education in no way promises an end to Black suffering" as racial justice seeks "not to dismantle or destroy the system, but to seek redress" (p. 30–31). This was evident in the landmark

Supreme Court decision of *Brown v. Board of Education of Topeka* (1954). The decision had a devastating effect on Black education. In an effort to upend Jim Crow segregation to the "graveyard," its "afterlife" mutated into something less tangible and far more durable (Cobb, 2014). Though *Brown v. Board* mandated desegregation, it created "second-class integration," for Black children and led to a calculated divestment and erasure of Black teachers (Oakley, Stowell, & Logan, 2009; Anderson, 2018). After *Brown v. Board,* Black teachers were fired, and Black teacher retention was omitted in federal legislation, such as the Civil Rights Act of 1964 and the subsequent federal desegregation guidelines of 1966 (Lutz, 2017; Oakley, Stowell, Logan, 2009). Lutz (2017) stated that Black students were impacted because they, "lost role models who not only knew them on a personal level, but had a unique understanding of their communities, cultural identities, and individual situations." Without Black teachers representing and advocating for the equal rights of Black students, mass media controlled the narrative of "racial progress" and projected how to perceive and interact with Black children.

The Afterlife of Minstrels: Black Sitcoms

Mass media has been criticized for their representations of Black people on television, as Black images can cause viewers to conceive, alter, or even reinforce their beliefs and opinions about Black people (Punyanunt-Carter, 2008). This criticism is evident with Black situational comedies (sitcoms). Means-Coleman (2003) defined Black sitcoms as those that star Black Americans, and works to "illuminate Black cultural, artistic, political and economic experiences" (as cited in Vickers, 2018). While supposedly having more Black media representation could be seen as a positive, Black sitcoms have been problematic because they are the "afterlife" of vaudevillian minstrel shows dating back to the 1830s. Minstrel shows were a racist form of entertainment, where white (and sometimes Black) performers portrayed themselves as a "stereotypical" plantation slave. Performers would achieve this by painting their face Black, which is known as "Blackface" (Taylor & Austen, 2012). In Blackface, performers depicted Black people as being thoughtless and comical, living a carefree life, liberated from oppression, responsibilities, and burdens (Taylor & Austen, 2012). These persistent stereotypes that were depicted in minstrel shows have also been present in Black sitcoms. Moreover, Black sitcoms have been problematic because the legitimacy and seriousness of Black suffering were commodified to be humorous for white audiences (Vickers, 2018). Black sitcoms have conveyed that Black social suffering was ordinary, comical, and became a tool to "get over" the past (Womack, 2017). *The Cosby Show* perfected this commodification.

The Cosby Show *and* The Cosby Effect

The Cosby Show (1984–1992) was the first Black sitcom that depicted an affluent Black family (Crooks, 2014). Dr. Heathcliff Huxtable (Bill Cosby), an obstetrician married to his wife, Clair (Phylicia Rashad), an attorney, lived with their five children in a Brownstone in New York City (Inniss & Feagin, 1995). *The Cosby Show* set a standard for Black sitcoms because it departed from the formula of minstrel-era stereotypes and took a "color-blindness" approach (Crooks, 2014). Crooks (2014) noted that Bill Cosby, "wanted to depict a middle-class family who happened to be Black, so that the television show could avoid racialization and depict middle-class values through the lenses of colorblindness" (p.5). Cosby's "humorous" colorblindness approach made the Huxtables *likeable* for white audiences. As America's leading Black family, the Huxtables were non-threatening, educated, courteous, graceful, and apolitical (Agada, 2015). Though Cosby's prescribed approach to the Black family image seemed like a positive, its "formula" echoed anti–Black sentiments.

The "Cosby formula," was a concoction of *Black Exceptionalism* rooted in respectability politics. Respectability politics is a self-presentation strategy of appealing to dominant white society in order to receive better treatment. Connecting respectability politics to Black exceptionalism, Agada (2015) stated that Black exceptionalism is, "the mythical notion that Black people who are educated, smart, articulate, and poised are atypical or rarities among the general Black population." Black people that "defied" dominant racist stereotypes are deemed "exceptional." This notion polices Black people through a hierarchy of Black life, as it distinguishes *good* Black people from *bad* Black people (Armour, 2000). Only those that defy the stereotypes are worthy of praise. The Huxtables were "worthy of praise" because they were uncharacteristic. Lewis and Jhally's (1992) *Enlightened Racism*, highlighted these notions as their white focus groups believed that the "Huxtables were not like most Black Americans," that institutional discrimination no longer exists because the Huxtables "defied the odds," and that Black failure was based on Black people not working hard enough to achieve the "American Dream" (p. 95; Crooks, 2014; Inniss & Feagin, 1995). The show created the "Cosby effect," a formula that Black sitcoms had to follow in order to be successful. This formula was evident in *The Steve Harvey Show, Hanging with Mr. Cooper, Smart Guy*, and *Everybody Hates Chris*.

Are They Teachers: Exploring The Steve Harvey Show *and* Hangin' with Mr. Cooper

Swetnam's (1992) research on the distortion of media-teachers was extended by Williams' (2017) research on the representation of Black media-teachers. Black media representation is often a challenge because of the narrow portrayals of Black lived experiences. Black male media-teachers on Black sitcoms such as in *The Steve Harvey Show* and *Hanging with Mr. Cooper* did little to uplift perceptions of Black male teachers. The shows conveyed contradictory messages about the professional life of teachers and evoked anti–Black sentiments.

Steve Hightower (Steve Harvey) from *The Steve Harvey Show* and Mark Cooper (Mark Curry) from *Hanging with Mr. Cooper* both embody problematic representations of Black male media-teachers. Hightower and Cooper fall into Neal's (2013) "race men" stereotype, a term that described an elite class of Black men of stature and integrity. Race men were perceived as "well-mannered" and "good intentioned" (Neal, 2013; Williams, 2017). The race men stereotype is linked to Black exceptionalism and the respect-ability politics that *The Cosby Show* projected. Hightower and Cooper were appealing to white audiences because they were non-threatening Black men, who were graceful, eloquent, humorous, and apolitical. For Black media-teachers to be depicted as apolitical, erases the legacy and impact of real-life Black educators. Brazilian educator and philosopher Paulo Freire (1980) described that teaching is a political act, as teachers have the power to build relationships with students, be their advocates, provide them with opportunities, and help them navigate systemic barriers. Education is not a neutral site and not seeing Hightower and Cooper as political "agents of change," was a missed opportunity on both television shows' part.

Aside from their neutrality, Hightower and Cooper perpetuated media-teacher stereotypes, such as, that anyone can teach and that teach-ers are indifferent, even comical (Swetnam, 1992). Moreover, these shows stereotyped Black male media-teachers as hypersexual, incompetent, and unprofessional (Williams, 2017). Teaching was not the first profession for Hightower or Cooper, as they just "fell" into teaching. Hightower was a "funk legend" who took on teaching music, art, and drama to make ends meet. Cooper was a former NBA player who became a high school gym teacher after a tragic turn of events (Williams, 2017). Despite the shows being "teacher-centered," there is more emphasis placed on the romantic lives of the teachers, than on teaching. Hightower and Cooper are depicted as hypersexual Black male media-teachers. Williams (2017) stated that Hightower was, "depicted as a conniving womanizer" (p. 58) because he is shown pursing romantic relationships with multiple women, until he begins a monogamous relationship with principal Regina Grier (Wendy Raquel Robinson). Cooper, like Hightower, is depicted pursuing romantic relationships throughout the show until Cooper becomes engaged and married to his roommate, Vanessa (Holly Robinson Peete). This created a disingenuous perception about teaching, as it conveyed that teaching is not a priority for Black male teachers and that teaching is an easy alternative career choice. Moreover, it conveyed that Black students are not worthy of educators that are dedicated to the teaching profession and that anyone without teaching pedagogy or curriculum instruction can teach Black students. With Black male teachers in short supply, these narrow representations of Black male media-teachers are not beneficial.

Who Helps the Smart Guy?

Smart Guy (1997–1999) is a Black sitcom that revolved around the life of T.J. Henderson (Tahj Mowry), a Black 10-year-old intellectual genius (IMDB, 1997). *Smart Guy* perpetuates the myth of Black exceptionalism, as T.J. is not like "other Black children" because he is "smart and gifted"— labels usually attributed to white children. The show conveys that intelligence is inextricably linked to whiteness. Moreover, T.J. is the 10-year-old equivalent of Neal's (2013) "race men" because he is well-mannered, well-groomed, and articulate. What T.J. projects is "problematic," because academic success for Black male youth is a complicated matter. Within the United States, Black male youth have been scapegoated through the legacies of institutionalized racism and educational discrimination.

Deficit-oriented social science research on Black male youth has dominated academic literature and has shaped white teachers' beliefs about them as not being smart enough. Black male youth are socialized to believe that they are unintelligent, and that school is not for *them*. *Smart Guy* established a hierarchy of Black worth by conveying that not *all* Black children are capable of being intelligent, but only a select *few*, and those few must embody whiteness. Being labeled the "smart" one in the Henderson family creates the perception that T.J.'s brother Marcus (Jason Weaver), his sister Tasha (Essence Atkins), and family friend "Mo" (Omar Gooding), are not smart. At times, Tasha, Marcus, and Mo are annoyed with T.J.'s intelligence and episode 1 of season 1, "Pilot" (1997) is a great example showcasing this. In the episode, Marcus is aggravated and talking to his dad, Floyd Henderson (John Marshall Jones) about how T.J.'s presence is diminishing his "place" at the high school:

> **FLOYD HENDERSON:** …but eventually T.J.'s going to find a place of his own and everything will get back to being normal.

MARCUS: It'll never be normal. Do you realize that he's not normal? Nobody thinks he's normal. He's just one smart little pain in the butt, and he's ruining my life [Kallis, 1997].

Dumas (2018) stated that, "Black suffering also takes the form of aesthetic assault, in which the Black body is constructed as wrong, inappropriate, not enough" (p. 39). Not only does the pilot episode capture that T.J.'s intelligence as a Black child is an abnormality, but that Marcus' worth is "not enough," because he lacks what T.J. has. Both boys are oppressed and devalued through Black exceptionalism.

As a show centered on schooling, the question becomes, "who helps the 'smart' guy on his academic journey?" The Black educators within *Smart Guy* play a minor role within T.J.'s life. Ms. Williams (Anne-Marie Johnson), T.J.'s Black guidance counselor only appears in the pilot episode and is written out of the show. Her absence connects to the lack of real-life guidance counselors that work with first-generation and underrepresented students (Murphy, 2016). T.J.'s Black principal, Principal Dowling (Marsha Warfield) is featured in two episodes and only appeared when either T.J., Marcus, or Mo need to be disciplined. The implications of this are far-reaching because Black educators have expressed that they are not valued for their pedagogy but are utilized for their assumed skill of managing and discipling Black children (Griffin & Tackie, 2017). Delegitimized as experts and professionals, Black educators are relegated as classroom managers. T.J.'s father, Floyd, though not a professional educator, provides T.J. life skills and moral advice throughout the show. In episode 15 of season 2, "Bad Boyz" (1998), Floyd demands that T.J. not associate himself with "certain" Black children because they are "urban" and dress like "thugs." Floyd's anti–Black sentiments are rooted in Black exceptionalism. Floyd deemed those children as "unworthy" to interact with T.J. because he saw them as "bad." What Floyd conveyed to the audience was that *certain* Black children are criminals. Dumas (2018) stated that, "anti–Blackness positions dark bodies as already bad; to be Black is to be always bad, and to be in urgent need of disciplining" (p. 38). This episode reinforces the notion that Black youth can easily be (re)labeled "troublemakers" if their "behavior" and their "appearance" affirm racist notions of Black deviance.

Who's Laughing: Chris' Racial Humor in Lieu of Black Suffering

Everybody Hates Chris (2005–2009) is a Black sitcom based on the adolescent life of comedian Chris Rock, growing up in Brooklyn, New York (IMDB, 2005). Referencing his life, Rock uses narration as humor to detail his racist experiences within predominantly white schools. Chris' (Tyler James Williams) racist conversations and interactions with his white female teacher, Ms. Morello (Jacqueline Mazarella), convey how Black children are devalued and suffer within school. In an attempt to "relate to" Chris, Ms. Morello has proudly pumped a Black power fist, given cans of food to his "ghetto" family at Christmas, and called him a "Sweet Sweetback" (Snook, 2006). Morello's colorblind racism is embedded into her white paternalism for Black students. In essence, Ms. Morello is a "Miss Ann." A Miss Ann is a white woman who is inquisitive towards Black people (especially men), but "always has [a] pernicious way of expressing her fear and resentment of Black people" (Alexander, 2016). Chris' interactions with Ms. Morello paints a vivid picture of how certain white teachers see, speak to, value, and (mis)understand their Black students.

Rock's use of racial humor to rectify Black suffering is well-connected to how Black sitcoms must operate to be successful. Rock's show provides a glimpse of the varying degrees of trauma that Black children endure in school. Dumas (2014) noted that a "school is a site of Black suffering" (p. 2) and *Everybody Hates Chris* affirms that. In similarity to *Smart Guy* there was a lack of Black educators in Chris' life. Chris had no one to help him navigate his adolescence or the racist experiences that he endured. What happened to Chris and what is happening to so many other Black children in schools is Black social suffering (Dumas, 2014). Black students are told that schooling is not suffering, as it is an opportunity to better your life, but then are forced to endure the daily onslaught of anti–Blackness. If they do not succeed, Black students are told they did not "take advantage of school," that they are "lazy," or that they lack the ability to succeed (Dumas, 2014, as cited in Pabon, 2016). Under the guise of meritocracy and racial progress, there is a fondness to dismiss Black suffering, because it is presumed to only occur in the past (Dumas, 2018). Without examining the current experiences of Black students, Black suffering becomes mundane—it becomes assumed—it becomes invisible. Black suffering is so ever-present that a Black person watching Rock's "humorous" schooling experience, could say to oneself: "This was me."

Conclusion and Implications for the Future of Black Education

In this "afterlife of slavery," the ever-present nature of anti–Blackness permeates within Black education and Black education-based television shows. The devaluing and stereotyping of Black people are not just a phenomenon of the past, but a mark of the present (Vickers, 2018). Under the banner of "racial progress," the value of Black teachers was erased and the disingenuous representations of Black people within Black sitcoms such as *The Cosby Show, The Steve Harvey Show, Hanging with Mr. Cooper, Smart Guy,* and *Everybody Hates Chris,* negatively shaped the public perception of Black children and Black teachers. While television shows might be entertaining to some, Black families do not have enough television shows that represent their lived experiences to simply say, that it is just "television" (Williams, 2017). The negative stereotypes within these Black television shows were not only damaging, but ineffective by any professional standards. It is imperative that people continue to interrogate the nuances of Black representation to create liberatory spaces for Black children. Black representation must always matter, because if Black children cannot envision it, how can they be it?

REFERENCES

Agada, E. (2015). Sidney Poitier, Mike Brown, and the Myth of Black Exceptionalism. Retrieved from http://celluloidinBlackandwhite.blogspot.com/2015/01/sidney-poitier-mike-brown-and-myth-of.html.

Alexander, A. (2017). Miss Ann's Revenge. Retrieved from https://www.theroot.com/miss-ann-s-revenge-1790857709.

Anderson, M. (2016). Sixty Years After Brown V. Board, Black Teachers Are Disappearing-Again. Retrieved from https://www.ebony.com/news-views/sixty-years-after-brown-v-board-Black-teachers-are-disappearing-again-304.

Anderson, M. D. (2018). The Secret Network of Black Teachers Behind the Fight for Desegregation. Retrieved from https://www.theatlantic.com/education/archive/2018/08/Black-educators-hidden-provocateurs/567065/.

Armour, J. D. (2000). *Negrophobia and Reasonable Racism: The Hidden Costs of Being Black in America.* New York: New York University Press.

Bell, J. D., & Janis, E. D. (2011). Media Representations and Impact on the Lives of Black Men and Boys(Rep.). Retrieved https://opportunityagenda.org/explore/resources-publications/media-representations-impact-Black-men/media-portrayals.

Carsey, M. (Executive Producer), & Werner, T. (Executive Producer). (1984). *The Cosby Show* [Television series]. New York: Viacom Enterprises.

Cobb, J. (2017). The Failure of Desegregation. Retrieved from https://www.newyorker.com/news/news-desk/the-failure-of-desegregation.

Coleman, R. R. (2003). Bringing Diversity and Activism to Media Education Through African American-Centered Pedagogical Cases. *Television & New Media,4*(4), 411–438. doi:10.1177/1527476403255805.

Crooks, R. (2014). Enlightened Racism and *The Cosby Show. The Owl | The Florida State University Undergraduate Research Journal,4*(1), 4–13.

Dumas, M. J. (2014). "Losing an Arm": Schooling as a Site of Black Suffering. *Race Ethnicity and Education,17*(1), 1–29. doi:10.1080/13613324.2013.850412.

Dumas, M. J. (2016). Against the Dark: Anti-Blackness in Education Policy and Discourse. Theory into Practice, 11–19. DOI: 10.1080/00405841.2016.1116852.

Dumas, M. J. (2018). Beginning and Ending with Black Suffering: A Meditation On and Against Racial Justice in Education. In E. Tuck & K. Yang (Ed.), *Towards What Justice? Describing Diverse Dreams of Justice in Education*(pp. 29–46). Taylor & Francis.

Dumas, M. J., & Ross, K. M. (2016). Be Real Black for Me. *Urban Education,51*(4), 415–442. doi:10.1177/0042085916628611

Figlio, D. (2018). The Importance of a Diverse Teaching Force. Retrieved from https://www.brookings.edu/research/the-importance-of-a-diverse-teaching-force/.

Franklin, J. (Executive Producer). (1997). *Hangin' with Mr. Cooper* [Television series]. Burbank, CA: Warner Bros. Domestic Television Distribution.

Grey, B. (Executive Producer), & Brillstein, B. (Executive Producer), & Harvey, W. (Executive Producer, & Lathan, S. (Executive Producer). (1996). *The Steve Harvey Show* [Television series]. Culver City, CA: Sony Pictures Television.

Griffin, A., & Tackie, H. (2017). Through Our Eyes. *Phi Delta Kappan,98*(5), 36–40. doi:10.1177/0031721717690363.

Hartman, S. V. (2008). *Lose Your Mother: A Journey Along the Atlantic Slave Route*. New York: Farrar, Straus & Giroux.

IMDB. (1997). *Smart Guy*. Retrieved from https://www.imdb.com/title/tt0118466/.

IMDB. (2005). *Everybody Hates Chris*. Retrieved from https://www.imdb.com/title/tt0460637/?ref_=nv_sr_5?ref_.

Inniss, L. B., & Feagin, J. R. (1995). The Cosby Show: The View from the Black Middle-Class. *Journal of Black Studies,25*(6), 692–711. doi:10.1177/002193479502500604.

Jhally, S., & Lewis, J. (1992). *Enlightened Racism: The Cosby Show, Audiences, and the Myth of the American Dream*. Boulder: Westview.

Kallis, D. (Executive Producer). (1997). *Smart Guy* [Television series]. Burbank, CA: Buena Vista Television.

Lutz, M. (2017). The Hidden Cost of Brown v. Board: African American Educators Resistance to Desegregating Schools. *Online Journal of Rural Research & Policy,12*(4). doi:10.4148/1936–0487.1085.

Majors, R., & Billson, J. M. (1993). *Cool Pose: The Dilemmas of Black Manhood in America*. Simon & Schuster.

More, M. (2012). Black Consciousness Movement's Ontology: The Politics of Being. *Philosophia Africana,14*(1), 23–40.

Murphy, J. S. (2016). The Neglected Link in the High-School-to-College Pipeline. Retrieved from https://www.theatlantic.com/education/archive/2016/09/the-neglected-link-in-the-high-school-to-college-pipeline/500213/.

Neal, M. A. (2013). *Looking for Leroy: Illegible Black Masculinities*. New York: New York University Press.

Oakley, D., Stowell, J., & Logan, J. R. (2009). The Impact of Desegregation on Black Teachers in the Metropolis, 1970–2000. *Ethnic and Racial Studies, 39*(9), 1576–1598. http://doi.org/10.1080/01419870902780997.

Pabon, A. J. (2016). In Hindsight and Now Again: Black Male Teachers' Recollections on the Suffering of Black Male Youth in US Public Schools. *Race Ethnicity and Education,20*(6), 766–780. doi:10.1080/13613324.2016.1195359.

Punyanunt-Carter, N. M. (2008). The Perceived Realism of African American Portrayals on Television. *Howard Journal of Communications,19*(3), 241–257. doi:10.1080/10646170802218263.

Ray, V. E., Randolph, A., Underhill, M., & Luke, D. (2017). Critical Race Theory, Afro-Pessimism, and Racial Progress Narratives. *Sociology of Race and Ethnicity,1*–12. doi:10.1177/2332649217692557.

Roberts, D. E. (1999). BlackCrit Theory and the Problem of Essentialism. *University of Miami Law Review,53*(4), 855–862.

Rock, C. (Executive Producer), & LeRoi, A. (Executive Producer). (2005). *Everybody Hates Chris* [Television series]. Santa Monica, CA: CBS Television Distribution.

Sexton, J. (2016). Afro-Pessimism: The Unclear Word. *Rhizomes: Cultural Studies in Emerging Knowledge,*(29). doi:10.20415/rhiz/029.e02.

Sleigh, J., & Ritzer, D. R. (2004). Beyond the Classroom: Developing Students' Professional Social Skills. Retrieved from https://www.psychologicalscience.org/observer/beyond-the-classroomdeveloping-students-professional-social-skills.

Snook, R. (2006). *Everybody Hates Chris'* Ms. Morello Teaches Us a Lesson | TV Guide. Retrieved from https://www.tvguide.com/news/everybody-hates-chris-38467/.

Staples, B. (2017). Where Did All the Black Teachers Go? Retrieved from https://www.nytimes.com/2017/04/20/opinion/where-did-all-the-Black-teachers-go.html.

Swetnam, L. (1992). Media Distortion of the Teacher Image. *The Clearing House, 66*(1), 30–32. Retrieved from http://www.jstor.org/stable/30188962.

Taylor, Y., & Austen, J. (2012). Darkest America: Black Minstrelsy from Slavery to Hip-Hop. Retrieved September 10, 2016, from http://www.popmatters.com/feature/162955-darkest-america-Black-minstrelsy-from-slavery-to-hip-hop/.

Vickers, J. (2018). *Black or Black-ish: Decoding Black-ish and Its Place in the Conversation of Diversity* (Master's thesis, Syracuse University, 2018). Surface.

Williams, M. L. (2017). "Ain't I a Teacher?": A Television Analysis of Black Male Media-Teachers on *The Steve Harvey Show*. Retrieved from https://muse.jhu.edu/article/660540/pdf.

Womack, A. (2017). Visuality, Surveillance, and the Afterlife of Slavery. *American Literary History*, 191–204. doi:10.1093/alh/ajw061.

"Dear White People: It truly is A Different World"

Representations of Black Male Faculty in Television Series

DOMINICK N. QUINNEY

Historically, the relationship between Blacks and higher education has been one complete with lack of access, denial, rejection, or adversity. By extension the experiences of Blacks in the academy as faculty professionals have been sparse in representation. According to the U.S. Department of Education, Black Americans constitute 6 percent of the professoriate, which adds to the complexities of the experience of life in the academy. These complexities, complete with, "institutional racism, microaggressions, and marginalization ... lower academic status, comparably lower salaries, stunted advancement, and heavier workloads" compile some of the challenges Black professionals in the academy encounter in their matriculation towards tenure or other avenues of advancement (Louis & Freeman, 2018, p. 21). The linkages between racial hegemony and access to higher education have been major barriers to the education of Blacks. As Ladson-Billings (1995) highlights, "in schooling, the absolute right to exclude was demonstrated by denying Blacks access to schooling altogether. Later it was demonstrated by the creation and maintenance of separate schools" (p. 60). The struggle for equitable opportunity for Black professional faculty in the academy serves as a testament to the importance of representation.

As previously stated, representation matters, particularly within the scope of Black professionals in popular culture. The experiences of Blacks in higher education as it relates to imagery in popular culture has been one that has been fairly new in the scope of entertainment and varying forms of media. Most of the attention brought to this scope has been through the experiences of students attending various institutions, and rarely a focus on the experience on the faculty and administration that interact with students. Faculty, and particularly those of color provide a unique perspective that often goes unnoticed yet it is a needed experience to provide a holistic meaning to "the college experience."

Through the exploration of television shows including *A Different World* (1987–1993), a show situated on the campus of a Historically Black College/University (HBCU), the Black faculty of the fictional private liberal arts institution Winchester University on *Dear White People* (2017–present), and the adjunct faculty at Cal-U on *Grown-ish* (2017–present), this essay will delve into the campus experiences and relationships Black male faculty and staff take on in the development of student success in each of their respective television shows and subsequently their experiences they have in their respective fictive roles. It is important to note that while *A Different World* falls out of the timeline of shows highlighted throughout the book, the show's characters continue to have a profound impact on the representation of Black faculty and staff in higher education since its debut on NBC in 1987. It should also be noted that this essay focuses its analyses on Black men professionals in higher education. The reality is that they are seen more in such roles on television over time, and definitely possess more developed characters than their counterparts. A brief analysis is also shared at the end of this essay discussing this difference in gender representation.

"Dr. War"

One of the most notable examples of Black faculty having a profound impact on students in a television series would be that of Colonel Bradford Taylor (Glenn Turman) on the hit television series, *A Different World* (1987–1993). The show had such a profound impact beyond the screen with respect to the scope of higher education, boosting enrollment at HBCUs[1] by 24.3 percent (Watson, 2016). A Vietnam War veteran, Col. Taylor served as head of Hillman College's (a fictional historical Black Liberal Arts College) Mathematics Department and as Commander of the campus' Reserve Officers' Training Corps (ROTC). Col. Taylor's presence was felt across campus—be it as a professor in the classroom, to having lunch at the campus eatery "The Pit" or imparting life wisdom to colleagues and students alike. He earned the nickname "Dr. War" not only because of his connection to the military, but also because of his reputation for having high standards for students. Col. Taylor embodied the culture of many HBCU institutions in that he encouraged and motivated students throughout their undergraduate and graduate school experience as well as beyond the confines of a classroom. Gallien (2005) posits, "African American students continuously maintain that they respond best to professors who care about them. This feeling of care and concern is a serious issue in the retention and eventual graduation rate of African American students across the country" (p. 9–10). Colonel Taylor throughout his run on the series embodied care and concern with each of his students, which was shown through mentorship, teaching, and offering life lessons that often went beyond the basic duty of a college professor.

As previously mentioned, Col. Taylor's relationship with students went beyond the scope of the classroom and often gave insight that related to their real-life experiences in ways that allowed Col. Taylor to see the humanity in his students. In episode 12, season 4, "War and Peace,"[2] Taylor connects with main character Dwayne Wayne's (Kadeem Hardison) childhood friend Zelmer Collier (Blair Underwood), an alumnus of Hillman who is in the Army Reserves and is going into active duty in the Persian Gulf. Throughout the episode Collier gives the appearance that he is okay with the possibility of going into combat, and that serving would be a show of honor, patriotism, and a way to pay back federal student loans. Collier's pride and happiness turned into fear and uncertainty when he meets with Colonel Taylor to discuss his unknown future in military combat. The episode culminates with Col. Taylor meeting with Zelmer, and sharing a story with him about a friend who overcame adversities in the face of a fearful situation. Zelmer, unsure of what the significance of the story fires back, "That story didn't help me too much, Colonel." Col. Taylor responds that the story wasn't for Zelmer, but rather a segue to his follow up statement to the young soldier: "Find your own source of inspiration." Hurtado, Cabrera, Lin, Arellano, & Espinoza (2009, p. 201) posit that "validating experiences and recognition," allows for the cultivation of students' success. Col. Taylor was able to connect and empathize with Zelmer in a manner that validated his experiences, above and beyond what most faculty members put into their work. By having a shared lived experience both with race and other intersections of identity, Black faculty are better able to connect with Black students to foster a stronger relationship that enhances the overall academic experience. Col. Taylor represented this important connection in a well watched television series.

A visible and influential faculty member on the fictive Hillman campus, one of the most memorable relationships Col. Taylor had was with student and mentee Dwayne C. Wayne. Dwayne entered the campus an eager freshman that tried to avoid at all costs encountering Col. Taylor, hearing rumors of the strong work ethic he had around campus, and the responsibility that it carried as a student. Upon their first encounter in earlier seasons of the show, it became clear their relationship would be of merit, and it would shape many of the successes Dwayne would experience on campus. Their relationship was so strong that Wayne declared mathematics as his major, and upon completion of his bachelor's degree worked in the math department as a graduate instructor, following in the footsteps of his mentor and forging relationships with incoming students in the same manner that was done for him. Astin (1993) states that through interaction with faculty, students have a higher probability of remaining enrolled at their respective institution. As such, Col. Taylor's relationship with Dwayne showed one of the ways in which strong mentoring relationships between faculty and students is essential toward understanding persistence in a collegiate program. Watching a show such as *A Different World* would showcase the importance of mentoring as a strong component of the undergraduate student experience, and the embodiment of the adage, "lift as you climb."

Dean Fairbanks

A more recent depiction of Black faculty in higher education would be that of Dean Walter Fairbanks (Obba Babatunde) of the show, *Dear White People* (2017–present). A spinoff of the successful motion picture film directed by Justin Simien, the Netflix series focuses on the lived experiences of Black students at Winchester College, a fictitious predominantly White Institution (PWI). This show takes a different approach than that of *A Different World* in that it explores some of the realities Black students encounter that are marginalized on often very-white campuses, particularly at liberal arts institutions. Dean Fairbanks' role offers several representations on their campus—a Black, high-ranking administrator, mentor, and an example of one who "made it" through the matriculation of a PWI. In many respects he serves as a guide to many of the students as one who not only functions, but is able to thrive in what can be a hostile and tense environment.

In many respects, Dean Fairbanks was immersed in what Padilla (1994) calls cultural taxation, wherein faculty of color are ladened with additional responsibilities because of their racial and/or ethnic identities. This often comes in the form of serving as an (un)official mentor and advocate for students of color, sharing perspectives with colleagues, or serving in a capacity related to diversity, multiculturalism, or inclusion. Often these responsibilities come at the expense of work not being recognized by the academy as "quantifiable work," adding to the pressures of the workload.

Dean Fairbanks' role and representation in the series shows more prominently in the series with his relationship with his biological son Troy

(Brandon P. Bell), and another fellow student Reggie Green (Marque Richardson). In the first season, Reggie attended a campus party where campus security draws a gun on him, stating he needed to show identification, thinking he is not a student at Winchester. As a follow up to this episode, Reggie is required to attend a number of therapy sessions to deal with the traumatic event. Dean Fairbanks attempts to reach beyond his campus duties and reach out and connect to Reggie on a more personal level, specifically relating to Reggie being a Black man on a predominantly white campus. In an impromptu meeting, he says to Reggie:

> Son, my job basically is to approve student events, glad-hand donors, and try to stay awake during board meetings. I'm talking to you from my heart. We don't always have someone who understands where we're coming from. I want you to be in the right head space so you can succeed.

Reggie appreciates the offer of mentorship and guidance, and reluctantly takes up the Dean on the suggestion. In this exchange we can see Dean Fairbanks extending beyond the job duties as Dean of Students into one of mentor for Reggie. Fairbanks' usage of the word "son" to a person that is not biologically his child adds a component of chosen familial guardianship that is meant to serve as an added care that Black students often fail to receive at Predominantly White Institutions (Guiffrida, 2005). Over time their relationship begins to develop, and Dean Fairbanks shares his experiences being one of only a few Black students on the campus of Winchester when he attended as an undergraduate. Fairbanks' goal was to show Reggie that not only was he not alone, but that these experiences with being a Black man at a Predominantly White Institution is not a new phenomenon. Sinanan (2012) notes African American males' perceptions of their college campus, as well as how they themselves are perceived can have quite an impact on the students' learning experience. Furthermore, Black men, because of their low populations on the campuses of PWIs may be more susceptible to the impacts of discrimination and racism, in that they are, "more hyper-visible and less socially connected" (Sinanan, 2016, p. 160). This was indeed the case for Reggie and in some respects Dean Fairbanks. Dean Fairbanks in trying to share his experiences on the same campus worked to not only mentor Reggie, but also to prepare him for the hyper-visibility and abrasiveness of discrimination that Black men experience on college campuses in an attempt to make a connection of shared experience with him. The relationship between Reggie and Dean Fairbanks in the Netflix series represents what the relationships on the campuses of Predominantly White Institutions look like between Black faculty and students of color: one of mutual reciprocity. Because PWIs can be isolating and challenging for both Black faculty and students alike, the symbiotic relationship allows for mutual support, respect, and a shared experience in what can be a sequestering place. Reddick (2005) found that Black professors tend to have a special connection with their Black students because of their shared experiences and often gain a sense of satisfaction from mentoring them. While Fairbanks wanted all students to succeed at Winchester, he was particular in wanting students of color to be successful.

Interestingly, Dean Fairbanks serves in a rare space in that not only is he a part of the administration of the institution, but he is also an alumnus, which by extension makes his son Troy, a legacy. Fairbanks is among a small number of Blacks who attended Winchester, a school noted for its connection to slavery and the upholding of white supremacy. As Wilder (2014) notes, "the academy never stood apart from American slavery—in fact, it stood beside church and state as the third pillar of a civilization built on bondage" (p.11). Despite changing demographics and social landscape, institutions of higher education maintain a past rooted in an ugly truth that included the bondage and violence of Black people. His relationship with his son is different in that his interactions with Troy are mostly that of protecting the family name, legacy and reputation at the institution. Dean Fairbanks is so invested in his son's success at Winchester that he sends him to a secret, exclusive meeting of Black Winchester alum to have them offer their experiences and advice to the young student. Dean Fairbanks' privilege in this case shows the impact of Black legacies on college campuses. The demographics of legacies, a space historically noted for White college alum and their children, has begun to change with the changing tides of campus populations as they begin to diversify (Howell & Turner, 2004). The Dean's unique (and also rare) position of both a campus legacy and administrator represent a small number of Blacks' experiences in the academy. These multiple consciousness' give way to a unique experience that often goes unnoticed in the realm of the Black experience.

Professor Telphy

Professor Charlie Telphy (Deon Cole) is an adjunct professor at Cal U on the hit television series *Grown-ish*. On the series he teaches a nighttime course on "Digital Marketing Strategies" with an emphasis on drones. Telphy's character represents a larger growing population of instructors on college campuses in reality—that of adjunct faculty. While all educators contribute important aspects of college life and learning, the growing trend of institutions hiring adjuncts instead of full-time and tenure track faculty represents largely the experiences of instructors, primarily of color. According to the National Center for Education Statistics (2017), Black men represent roughly three percent of the professoriate, the larger being in non-tenure track positions, part-time, or non-guaranteed reemployment. More often, institutions hire faculty of color in adjunct positions often resulting in a heavier teaching load, more service work, and lesser abilities to climb the faculty rankings. On the surface, institutions give the appearance that they value diversity and inclusion; all while the burden of work is unfairly placed upon faculty of color. In the same vein, while the unfair burden exists, financial compensation and the challenge of quantifying service work for Black faculty continue to be issues that remain unaddressed. Additionally, faculty of color face challenges including students and faculty alike questioning their credibility and authority in classrooms, or the validity of their research agendas particularly ones with a focus on race and ethnicity (Tuitt, Hanna, Martinez, Salazar, & Griffin, 2008). These experiences make college campuses isolating and difficult to navigate.

Professor Telphy's role in *Grown-ish*, albeit limited in screen time, largely represents how institutions of higher learning approach the capacity of Black faculty—limited (Allen, Epps, Guillony, Suh, & Bonous-Hammanth, 2000; Frazier, 2011; Padilla, 1994; Shavers, Butler, & Moore, 2014; Eagan & Garvey, 2015). To add to his representation, Professor Telphy's representation adds other dimensions of complexity to the role. Telphy notes his credentials or lack thereof may be an issue in the show's first episode, which adds to the stereotyped depictions of Blacks in education. Telphy is present in the academic space, however his contributions to intellectual thought are very limited in scope, which pulls back the level of professionalism of being a college professor. Additionally, this creates a less impactful representation of Black faculty on screen.

Further Representation of Black Faculty on TV

While these images in media offer a glimpse into the experiences of Black faculty at a variation of college campuses, there are other representations that offered nuanced experiences of the professoriate experience. *The Parkers* (1999–2004) highlighted Stanley Oglevee (actor Dorien Wilson) as a professor of African American Studies at Santa Monica Community College. Oglevee closely matched the experiences to that of Col. Taylor in that he was present in the lives of his students—eating in the commons area, being in the same fraternity as his mentees, or teaching a class that is one of the more popular courses on campus. The character, however, was rarely shown in the capacity of professor but rather in the many other capacities that Black faculty are often expected to carry out as responsibilities at institutions of higher education, that include the pressures of cultural taxation, as previously mentioned.

It is important to note that the experiences and representations of Black women in faculty positions have rarely if at all been depicted in media, which by extension can affect the experiences of students on a college campus. The *Digest of Education Statistics* (2012) reported that Black women constitute four of the total seven percent of Black faculty on college campuses. At the same time, it is noteworthy to mention that Black women earn graduate degrees at a higher rate than Black men, 8.5 percent compared to 6.3 percent for that of Black men (Naylor, Wyatt-Nichol, & Brown, 2015). As Howard-Vital (1989) notes, "there is a need for a continuous generation of paradigms to determine how they illuminate, obscure, or predict experiences of African American women in different higher education milieus. Without this intellectual activity, African-American women will become invisible, isolated, and powerless" (p. 189). Shows like BET's *The Quad* (2017–2018) attempt to disrupt the lack of representation in this narrative, however the work for more disruption of this narrative is ever ongoing.[3]

Representation matters—on actual college campuses, as well as within media outlets. The roles of Dr. Colonel Taylor, Dean Fairbanks, Professor Telphy and other Black college faculty further extend the importance of understanding Black experiences in academic spaces. These depictions, though few and sparse, should serve as motivation toward more, vast, and complex identities within media and real life. Additionally, the narratives and experiences of Black faculty have the ability to promote more diverse and inclusive environments, mentor and advise Black students, as well as provide insight and intellect that often goes unnoticed in what have been traditionally white spaces.

NOTES

1. Contrary to the title of a Historically Black College or University, the institutions have never been exclusionary to any particular race or ethnicity; they were created to serve a population that was excluded by dominant institutions.

2. One week after the episode aired, the U.S. launched an aerial assault on Iraq on January 17th, 1991. This event reiterates for the viewers the seriousness of Collier's fear, within a scripted series' connection to current political issues.

3. There are also other shows and characters that highlight Black women in the professoriate, including but not limited to: Dean Dorothy Davenport (*A Different World*), whose character was developed later in the television series, Dr. Vivian Banks, whose career is mostly mentioned not showcased (*The Fresh Prince of Bel-Air*), and Annalise Keating, Esq. whose professor role gets blurred into a more focused storyline as an attorney solving cases (*How to Get Away with Murder*) who will be highlighted in another essay of this book.

REFERENCES

Allen, W. R., Epps, E. G., Guillory, E. A., Suh, S. A., & Bonous-Hammarth, M. (2000). The Black Academic: Faculty Status Among African Americans in US Higher Education. *Journal of Negro Education*, 112–127.

Eagan Jr, M. K., & Garvey, J. C. (2015). Stressing Out: Connecting Race, Gender, and Stress with Faculty Productivity. *The Journal of Higher Education*, 86(6), 923–954.

Guiffrida, D. (2005). To Break Away or Strengthen Ties to Home: A Complex Issue for African American College Students Attending a Predominantly White Institution. *Equity & Excellence in Education*, 38(1), 49–60.

Howard-Vital, M. R. (1989). African-American Women in Higher Education: Struggling to Gain Identity. *Journal of Black Studies*, 20(2), 180–191.

Howell, C., & Turner, S. E. (2004). Legacies in Black and White: The Racial Composition of the Legacy Pool. *Research in Higher Education*, 45(4), 325–351.

Hurtado, S. Cabrera, N.L., Lin, M.H., Arellano, L., & Espinosa, L.L. (2009). Diversifying Science: Underrepresented Student Experiences in Structured Research Programs. *Research in Higher Education*. 50, 189–214.

Ladson-Billings, G., & Tate. W. (1995). *Toward a Critical Race Theory of Education*. Teachers College Record, 97(1), 47–68.

Louis, D. A., & Freeman Jr, S. (2018). Mentoring and the Passion for Propagation: Narratives of Two Black Male Faculty Members Who Emerged From Higher Education and Student Affairs Leadership. *Journal of African American Males in Education*, 9(1).

National Center for Education Statistics, Institute of Education Sciences (2012). Digest of education statistics 2011. Washington, D.C.: U.S. Department of Education.

Naylor, L. A., Wyatt-Nichol, H., & Brown, S. L. (2015). Inequality: Underrepresentation of African American Males in US Higher Education. *Journal of Public Affairs Education*, 21(4), 523–538.

Padilla, A.M. (1994). Ethnic Minority Scholars, Research, and Mentoring: Current and Future Issues. *Educational Researcher* 23(4), 24–47.

Reddick, R.J. (2005). "Ultimately, It's About Love": African-American Faculty and Their Mentoring Relationships with African-American Students. Retrieved from http://gseacademic.harvard.edu/~reddicri/Documents/Reddick_Ultimately_Its_About_Love.pdf.

Shavers, M. C., Butler, J. Y., & Moore III, J. L. (2014). Cultural Taxation and the Over Commitment of Service at Predominantly White Institutions. *Black Faculty in the Academy: Narratives for Negotiating Identity and Achieving Career Success*, 41–51. New York: Routledge.

Sinanan, A. (2012). Still Here: African American Male Perceptions of Social and Academic Engagement at a 4-year, Predominantly White Institution of Higher Learning in Southern New Jersey. *Sage Open*, 2, 1–7.

Sinanan, A. (2016). The Value and Necessity of Mentoring African American College Students at PWI's. *Journal of Pan African Studies*, 9(8), 155–166.

Tinto, V. (1993). *Leaving College: Rethinking the Causes and Cures for Student Attrition*. Chicago: University of Chicago.

Tuitt, F., Hanna, M., Martinez, L. M., Salazar, M., & Griffin, R. (2009). Teaching in the Line of Fire: Faculty of Color in the Academy. *Thought & Action*, 25, 65–74.

U.S. Department of Education, National Center for Education Statistics. (2017). *The Condition of Education 2017* (NCES 2017–144), Characteristics of Postsecondary Faculty. (https://nces.ed.gov/fastfacts/display.asp?id=61).

Watson, J. E. (2016, August 18). "A Different World" Still Pulls Fans into HBCU Experience. Retrieved September 12, 2018, from https://diverseeducation.com/article/86111/.

Wilder, C. S. (2014). *Ebony and Ivy: Race, Slavery, and the Troubled History of America's Universities*. Bloomsbury Publishing USA.

PART V

Policing and Politics

Not So Black and White

Race, Police and Double Standards in The Shield

Saravanan Mani

When considering the modern TV landscape for distinctive portrayals of African American police officers, *The Shield* (FX, 2002–2008) may not be on the top of many lists. Created by *Nash Bridges* and *Angel* alum Shawn Ryan, *The Shield* explores the violent side of law-enforcement where corrupt cops use unethical policing methods in the face of overwhelming law and order problems of Los Angeles, California. In this show, people of color are often reduced to the criminal element that needs to be neutralized by the show's all-white Strike Team. Spearheaded by their corrupt leader, Vic Mackey (Michael Chiklis), the team pursues "natural justice" through brutal methods that exceed the limits of police procedure and are justified by their effective results. The thrilling narrative and the fast-paced action align the viewers to enjoy the illegal actions of the Strike Team. Critical commentators have observed that *The Shield* tends to privilege the power of natural justice to the paternalistic white male antihero, Vic Mackey. Despite seeming to align the viewers with the vigilante authoritarianism of Mackey, the show uses two Black police officers, Detective Claudette Wyms (CCH Pounder) and Lieutenant Jon Kavanaugh (Forrest Whittaker), to challenge the legitimacy of Mackey's methods. The conflict of policing style also exposes the double standards imposed along racial lines for characters who behave in similar ways. Therefore, despite its problematic relationship with race—and at times directly because of it—*The Shield* serves as an interesting case study for the portrayal of African American professionalisms.

In the wider context of TV drama, African Americans seem well-represented in police dramas compared to other genres. Adilifu Nama (2003) notes that nearly two-thirds of all prime-time law enforcement dramas feature at least one African American series regular, whereas half of all TV dramas do not feature any (p. 29). However, Nama is skeptical of token representations which serve only to "enhance the 'look' of the internal reality of the show" (p. 34). He takes exception to police dramas which used African American characters to "[elicit] recognition from the viewing audience that the television police set was 'realistic' in its resemblance to a real urban police station" (p. 34). Mike Chopra-Gant (2012) observes a similar decline of African American characters in TV by the end of the 1990s (p. 130). Even in the crime drama genre where "there is a reasonably good presence of non-white characters in key roles" Chopra-Gant notes that those roles are crafted to "not problematize race or ethnicity" as they aim to "transcend race," ironically "[rendering] race and ethnicity almost invisible despite increasing the number of roles for nonwhite characters" (p. 131). It then follows that African American police officers in popular culture are reduced to playing a small repertoire of portrayals that ranges from the wise-cracking detective (Odafin Tutuola from *Law & Order*), the tough angry cop (Luther from *Luther*) to the no-nonsense authority figure (Maria LaGuerta from *Dexter,* Al Giardello from *Homicide: Life on the Street*).

These routine portrayals are a critical problem, as Stuart Hall (1989) rightly points out the key role played by representation in the relation between identity and cultural production. He argues that

> identity is not as transparent or unproblematic as we think. Perhaps, instead of thinking of identity as an already accomplished historical fact, which the new cinematic discourses then represent, we should think, instead, of identity as a "production" which is never complete, always in process, and always constituted within, not outside, representation [p. 68].

To extend Hall's argument, representations on TV are as important, if not more important than cinematic images, for TV is a part of everyday domestic life. Considering its reach and the role it plays in constructing the popular imagination, Hall (1992) observes that "popular culture always has its base in experiences, the pleasures, the memories, the traditions of the people. It has connections with local hopes and aspirations, local tragedies and local scenarios that are the everyday practices and everyday experiences of ordinary folks" (p. 108). Hall contends that it is important to be represented in popular culture, despite its contradictory nature. Hall stresses the importance of retaining Black expressivity and experience in popular culture. Ironically, TV offers caricatures of Black experiences resulting in a further deepening of the racial divide. A close examination of the role played by such texts can be used to recuperate racial understanding as well.

Initially, *The Shield's* prominent African American characters, including the Internal Affairs Lieutenant Jon Kavanaugh and Detective Claudette Wyms, also seem to be recycled versions of popular Black stereotypes who reaffirm the power given to the white characters. Michael Wayne (2014) notes that the academic reception of *The Shield* has either affirmed the show as a realistic portrayal of a multicultural city or denounced it as a regressive text that relies upon problematic racial hierarchies (p. 183–184). Wayne further expands on the problematic racial structures in the show by stating that "Farmington's minority populace remains largely invisible when not serving a narrative function related to the district's primarily White police force" (p. 185). By positioning Kavanaugh and Wyms against the Strike Team, the show questions the viewers' alignment with unlawful police methods. The professional ethics of these two characters allow them to overcome simplistic and stereotypical portrayals that have long since plagued African American police officers in popular culture.

"*Whatever it takes*": Policing in The Shield

The Shield's central protagonist, Vic Mackey, is a macho white cop who uses violent and illegal shortcuts ranging from planting evidence to unauthorized searches to maintain the peace of the fictional Farmington district. Based on the notorious real-life Rampart scandal that exposed the deep-rooted corruption in the LAPD, *The Shield* examines the distance between effective policing and ethical police practice. Mackey is an attractive, if ambivalent protagonist, because he delivers quick results in contrast to the glacial pace of the legal system. From the beginning of the show, he is portrayed as someone who is willing to do things that others would not, in his quest to protect the innocent. Nicholas Ray (2012) argues that Mackey's exceptional methods, even when they make the viewers uncomfortable, inadvertently sanction his methods by rewarding him with positive outcomes. He contends that while Mackey's tactics may be "discomforting [to] the audience" *The Shield's* narrative is structured in a way where Mackey's suspension of the law "in the name of law" results in the restoration of the peace (p. 181). Ray channels Theodore Adorno's (1954) reading of Television which distinguishes the "pseudorealistic" attitudes at the surface from "a number of repressed gratifications" (p. 222). In Ray's reading, the audience becomes complicit to Mackey's extrajudicial ways and reframe questions of ethics into narrative puzzles that need to be and are solved by the end of every episode and every season.

Over the course of seven seasons, the viewers are compelled to confront Mackey's constant failure to uphold the limits of his own legal authority. His actions are often part of a manipulative scheme and his intentions reveal themselves to be self-serving. As the viewers are invested in the narrative outcomes for Mackey, individual rights become secondary to his roughshod style of policing, and characters who stand up for ethical policing are made to seem villainous for simply going against Mackey. Interestingly, this antagonistic position is occupied by characters of color more than once. Despite not directly addressing the complicated racial relationships in the LAPD, these conflicts of policing style expose the double standards of police ethics enacted along racial lines.

In fact, there are many moments where *The Shield* reveals a nuanced approach to race, which challenges conventional power structures. The effects and significance of the complex portrayal of race, however, is up for debate. Mike Chopra-Gant notes that

> although minority characters are invested with legal and moral authority, this sense of "natural" justice is unambiguously the possession of the middle-aged white man: Vic Mackey … by constantly privileging Mackey's maverick solutions to the problem of law enforcement, it elevates those solutions to a position of privilege over the values of law and morality represented by [David] Aceveda [the captain], Wyms and the other ethnically and sexually marked characters who stand in opposition to Mackey [p. 132].

Chopra-Gant's observations ring true when considering characters like Jon Kavanaugh, an African American Internal Affairs officer who investigates Mackey and drives him to the edge of defeat, before Mackey devises yet another solution to escape the threat. He has his authority questioned, as Chopra-Gant points out, while Mackey moves from one position of strength to another. Indeed, Kavanaugh is an isolated figure within the department, and he is treated with a certain reservation for being a well-spoken and high-ranking Black police officer, although those reasons are never openly discussed. Kavanaugh's motivations are revealed to be the desire to succeed where others have failed in nabbing Mackey and his team, ironically leading him to embrace the same "at whatever cost" tactics that he despises in Mackey. While Kavanaugh is a marginal figure, by mirroring Mackey, he compels the viewers to recognize the cognitive dissonance of backing the series protagonist.

Kavanaugh is initially presented as a character with unimpeachable ethics. In episode 8 of season 5, "Kavanaugh" (2006), Kavanaugh's mentally ill wife Sadie (Gina Torres) begs him not to book her for filing a false police report, to which an emotionally distraught Kavanaugh replies "I can't, there are rules…. What I do is stop cops from breaking the rules. I can't stop them if I can't stop myself." However, Kavanaugh's personal code deteriorates over the course of the story as he becomes obsessed with Mackey's downfall. Kavanaugh manufactures a false witness, plants evidence, and tries to derail cops who are suspicious about the all-too convenient nature in which he seems to close in on Mackey. Contrary to Chopra-Gant's assessment, Kavanaugh's ambiguous actions do not undermine his moral authority, because unlike Mackey, he surrenders his investigative authority when he recognizes that he has betrayed his principles. When he sees his witness falling apart under interrogation, Kavanaugh intervenes and stops the questioning by admitting his guilt by saying that "[he] framed a guilty man" (episode 2, season 6, "Baptism by Fire"). Kavanaugh's admittance is not so much a concession of defeat to Mackey, but rather a recognition that he has failed his own moral standards. Thus, Kavanaugh partially recovers his moral authority in the face of narrative failure, whereas Mackey is ultimately condemned despite repeatedly evading the law.

The function that Kavanaugh performs in the show is to challenge Mackey's methods and call for reform of police oversight. Show-creator and lead writer Shawn Ryan's wry observation about the Kavanaugh-Mackey storyline also seems to imply that Kavanaugh's authority is challenged by Mackey. He says:

> If I said to you: I'm going to have a story about a corrupt cop who murdered another cop and stole a bunch of money. And that there's a pretty virtuous Internal Affairs detective who starts digging into the case and becomes hell-bent on bringing this man to justice. Who would be the hero of the piece? But our audience viewed Vic as the hero…. They found every negative thing to say about Whitaker's character they could think of…. They knew who to root for [qtd. in *Difficult Men* by Brett Martin, 2013: 226].

Ryan, like Chopra-Gant, conflates the viewers' desire to root for someone and the viewers' moral evaluation of their actions. The viewers' desire for narrative pay-off seems to suppress their knowledge of the character's virtues. Both Chopra-Gant and Ryan do not account for the relationships that viewers have cultivated with the characters over time. I argue that people root for Mackey not because of their desire to see a middle-aged white male to be reaffirmed as the dominant figure, but rather because they are invested in the outcomes of Mackey's actions over time. Nor is the viewer alignment an endorsement of the power relationship where he continues to exceed the law for selfish outcomes. The viewer's alignment with Mackey does not prohibit them from evaluating his actions. In fact, it only deepens their examination as they position Mackey's present action in the context of his previous misdeeds. The serial engagement calls the viewer to evaluate their enjoyment of Mackey's actions.

Another crucial aspect of Kavanaugh's character that Ryan glosses over is that he is designed to make the viewers hate him. Quentin Huff (2007) notes that "Kavanaugh must be the 'bad' guy because success for him means disappointment for the viewers." Despite his righteous cause, he ruthlessly harasses Mackey's friends and family for not cooperating with the investigation. While well within his jurisdiction, his attempted coercion of Mackey's wife and Strike Team partners mirrors Mackey in ignoring their individual rights. The viewers' alignment against Kavanaugh makes his final moment of recognition more poignant. His concession that he is willing to lose his case rather than stooping to Mackey's level draws the viewers' reluctant admiration, as they have witnessed both his absolute moral certainty and compromised moments. Significantly, the show does not obscure Kavanaugh's contradictory role as a Black police-officer. A drug-dealer in the show casually identifies Kavanaugh as "the right color … [but he] feels that you're working on the wrong side, brother." He will never stop being treated differently for doing the same things as the white protagonist. His transformation from strict moral authority to vindictive police officer who could not "stop himself" allows the viewers to question their own alignment with Mackey. Instead of copying Mackey's criminal exceptionalism, Kavanaugh acknowledges his terrible actions; highlighting that Vic Mackey's actions go unchecked. The contrasting images of morally compromised police officers reveal the double standards of ethics enforced for African American police officers.

Uncompromisingly Moral Policing

Where Jon Kavanaugh failed in his bid to end Mackey's illegal ways, Claudette Wyms, who grows from a detective to the precinct's captain during the series, rises above the shady practices in day-to-day policing. At the early stages of the show, Wyms appears to be a supporting figure who offers sagely and non-committal advice to characters. However, as the series progresses, Wyms evolves to the role of a central protagonist whose integrity and professionalism becomes an alternative to Mackey's methods. She is presented as the ultimate moral authority in a narrative world full of terrible police officers. Jason P. Vest notes that "Wyms is not only *The Shield*'s most intriguing principal female character, but also the person whose experience exemplifies the show's approach to female agency" (p. 147). Wyms battles the double bias against her for being both a woman and an African American. She does not allow the police district's day-to-day politics to corrupt her principles of policing. When she does not abet the shortcuts proposed by her superiors, she is punished by being looked over for a rightfully earned promotion. However, Wyms' capacity as a moral leader and an enforcer of ethics ensures that her value is recognized. In season 3, despite punishing her by denying a promotion, Captain Aceveda puts Wyms in charge of the Strike Team and the decoy squad, as he values her ability to lead. Eventually, Wyms rises through the ranks on her own merit to become the Captain and enforces rigorous scrutiny to prevent further wrongdoing by Mackey and his team. Wyms is the character who is vested with the moral authority in the closing moments of the series, because she never loses sight of the fact that only ethical policing can bring down a corrupt cop.

In the show's pilot, Wyms seems to support Mackey's methods. When the precincts' captain compares Mackey to Al Capone, she retorts,

> Al Capone made money by giving people what they wanted. What people want these days is to make it to their cars without getting mugged. Come home from work, see their stereo still there. Hear about some murder in the barrio, find out the next day the police caught the guy. If having all those things means some cop roughs up some nigger or some spic in the ghetto, well, as far as most people are concerned, it's "don't ask, don't tell" [episode 1, season 1, "Pilot"].

Vest reads Wyms' harsh words as "[she] does not approve of Mackey's brutality, but in this situation, she cannot suggest a more expedient alternative" (p. 148). Vest's analysis paints Wyms as a pragmatic veteran who has lived through the everyday constrains on policing to the point that she is willing to compromise her ethics. However, her words are loaded with bitter cynicism directed towards the callous tyranny of the police towards people of color and the conspiratorial silence of the upper-middle class who are willing to turn a blind eye to police brutality as long as it does not affect them. Wyms' words are not an endorsement of Mackey's methods but rather an exasperated outburst at the conditions that have allowed for people like Mackey to become key players in the police department. Wyms spits out the racial slurs as an expression of her suppressed anger against a department which tolerates and rewards of Mackey's methods, which often target people of color as its victims. Wyms is practical enough to understand that under extraordinary circumstances, extra-legal methods are an inevitable part of the job. However, she does not endorse it as a legitimate method of fighting crime.

The most crucial test of Wyms' professionalism comes when she is forced to choose between her ethics and her career. In episode 15 of season 3, "On Tilt" (2004), during a murder investigation, Wyms and her partner Dutch Wagenbach (Jay Karnes) find out that the victim Lisa Kensit was a public defender who abused the drug Oxycontin for the past three years. Despite explicit warnings from her superiors to suppress this information, lest defendants who were represented by Kensit may have their judgments overturned or cases retried due to the deceased being an unfit legal counsel, Wyms decides to press on with her case because she is willing to let "as many [guilty people] as it takes to fix a wrong [conviction]." Wyms succeeds in ensuring that an innocent suspect is exonerated, but her ethics costs her a professional setback. In contrast, her white male partner, Wagenbach, is offered the captaincy at the end of season 4 despite being an equal participant in their decision to pursue the Kensit case, subtly revealing that his punishment is more easily forgiven.

Claudette Wyms proves herself to be a figure of unimpeachable moral authority time and again. In the Kavanaugh investigation, she confronts her partner Wagenbach and asks if he is reluctant to pursue the inconsistencies in the case against Mackey because he believes that Mackey deserves to be framed. She insists that "the truth may not lead us down the path we want, but it's the only way to fix this place" (season 6, episode 2, "Baptism by Fire") and refuses to gloss over minor but critical details. And yet, Wyms is not reduced to a virtuous-minority stereotype, as she is a fully rounded character who acts selfishly by preventing her daughter from being called as a witness in a case or lashes out at her partner when she suffers from intense bouts of pain from her critical illness. However, she does not use her circumstances to justify illegal methods. She remains incorruptible and despite being undermined by Mackey at times, she proves herself to be the ultimate moral figure in the show through her diligence and skillful detective work.

In retrospect, Claudette Wyms is the foil to Mackey's moral decline. Like Kavanaugh, she is also judged by her race, but she uses her professionalism to overcome stereotypes. We evaluate her accomplishments not in the many little narrative failures where Mackey might have shown her up, but in the one final interrogation where she holds him responsible for his actions. She overcomes the obstacles of vindictive superiors and a biased police administration to become the captain of the precinct. Her plans have been foiled by Mackey's exceptionalism over the course of the series, but that does not take away from her moral authority; it only strengthens her resolve amidst the wave of unchecked corruption. She is offered as a counterpoint to former Captain David Aceveda (Benito Martinez), who also surrenders his moral authority by allowing his political ambitions dictate his behavior. In the final moments of the show, Captain Claudette Wyms calls Vic Mackey to confront his moral failure and displays the devastation he has caused on his family and his team, making it clear that while he has found a loophole to escape legal repercussion, he will forever be condemned in the eyes of the natural justice that he prided in serving. Despite *The Shield's* predictably unsatisfying casting conceit, the writers allow Wyms a moral clarity and dignity that Mackey cannot match. While the "nobility" or wisdom of people of color is another troubling trope, the show's handling of it provokes the viewers out of an easy complacency about racial attitudes and double standards.

Conclusion

Both Claudette Wyms and Jon Kavanaugh are positioned as contrasting figures of policing to Vic Mackey's brutal prejudice. They are restricted by the result-oriented police department that allow officers like Mackey and his Strike Team to proceed with their extralegal methods. While Kavanaugh succumbs to the pressures of getting his target in a limited time-frame, Wyms overcomes the situation by remaining true to her ideals about policing. *The Shield* grants its white middle-aged protagonist many narrative victories through the course of the show, but those victories are undercut by his abdication of moral authority. The show's racial pecking order seems to treat African American officers with greater scrutiny for similar behavior. However, it also vests the moral authority to challenge extralegal methods with Claudette Wyms, the lone African American woman prominently featured in the show. She performs the long-suffering penance as a righteous cop who does not waver from her code of ethics. Ultimately, the final moments reveal that even in the face of her declining health and inevitable retirement, her moral victory is undeniable. These narrative journeys expose the double standards in operation for white and non-white characters within the rules of the narrative world. So, while The Shield offers narrative pleasures of outlaw justice and traffics in problematic casting practices, the two African American characters discussed here expose the show's, and in turn, the genre's hypocrisy about the double standards in representing people of color.

REFERENCES

Adorno, T. W. (1594). How to Look at Television? *The Quarterly of Film and Television,* Vol. 8, No. 3 (Spring). 213–235. Retrieved from http://www.jstor.org/stable/1209731.
Chopra-Gant, M. Masculinity, Race and Power in *The Shield.* (124–144).
Framework: The Journal of Cinema and Media (36), 68–81. Retrieved from http://www.jstor.org/stable/44111666.
Hall, S. (1989). Cultural Identity and Cinematic Representation.
Hall, S. (1993). What Is This "Black" in Black Popular Culture? *Social Justice, 20*(1/2 (51–52)), 104–114. Retrieved from http://www.jstor.org/stable/29766735.
Huff, Q. (2007). *The Shield:* The Detective and the Lieutenant. Pop Matters. Retrieved from https://www.popmatters.com/the-shield-the-detective-the-lieutenant-2496206085.html.
Nama, A. (2003). More Symbol than Substance: African American Representation in Network Television Dramas. *Race and Society.* 6. 21–38. 10.1016/j.racsoc.2004.09.003.
Ray, N. "A Different Kind of Cop" Exception and Complicity in *The Shield* (166–185).
Ray, N. (Ed.) *Interrogating* The Shield (166–185). New York: Syracuse University Press.
Ryan, S. (creator). (2002–08). *The Shield* [Television series]. Los Angeles: FX.
Vest, J. P. Gender, Sexism, and *The Shield* (145–166).
Wayne, M. (2014). Mitigating Colorblind Racism in the Postnetwork Era: Class-Inflected Masculinities in *The Shield, Sons of Anarchy,* and *Justified. The Communication Review,* 17: 183–201.

Mammies, Jemimas, Jezebels and Sapphires

Deconstructing Representations of Black Women Coroners on Crime Dramas

Tammie Jenkins

The twenty-first century witnessed a change in narratives of Black womanhood as more Black women characters began appearing on primetime crime dramas such as *Law & Order: Special Victims Unit* (1999–present), *CSI: Miami* (2002–2012), and *Bones* (2005–2017) entering spaces once occupied by white men and women. These African American female characters are perceived by co-workers in law enforcement and the forensic medical examination field as professional in reference to their job performance. However, these women are humanized only when their family life is included in the show's plot. This essay examines how the complex role of the medical examiner on primetime crime dramas, with a particular focus on Fox's *Bones*, is complicated by stereotypical representations derived from larger societal discourses of Black womanhood. Even though Black women medical examiners on primetime crime dramas seem like authentic representations of women in the field, they are anchored in reinvented stereotypical representations such as Mammy, Aunt Jemima, Jezebel, and Sapphire. It is through this lens that I explore the impact of such narratives on televised depictions of Black women medical examiners on crime dramas. Relevant examples from *Law & Order: Special Victims Unit, CSI: Miami,* and *Bones* are used to compare and contrast how Black women medical examiners are portrayed as women and medical professionals.

From *Bones*, I focus on the character of Dr. Camille "Cam" Saroyan (Tamara Taylor), a medical examiner at the Jeffersonian Institute. I explore her character through her relationships with co-workers, significant others, and her adopted child. I use intersectionality theory to reference the connection between popular stereotypical representations of Black womanhood and their recreation in the twenty-first century. Additionally, I use narrative analysis to trace the underpinning stereotypes embedded in or rejected by the character of Dr. Saroyan through the series (hooks, 2014). This essay employs the following guiding questions: What are some stereotypical representations used to portray Black women as medical examiners? How are Dr. Saroyan and other similar characters marginalized in their storylines? In what ways is this character progressive or regressive in comparison to Black medical examiners on other crime dramas?

Mammies, Jezebels, Aunt Jemimas and Sapphires

The roles assigned to Black women medical examiners on television is one steeped in a history of stereotypical representations in which these characters are presented as either a Mammy, a Jezebel, an Aunt Jemima, or a Sapphire (Thomas, McCurtis, Witherspoon, & Speight, 2004; West, 1995). Such characterizations became popular in the nineteenth century during Blackface minstrel shows. In such a venue, white men adorned darkened faces, wear women's clothing, and acted out perceived Black female mannerisms. The Mammy archetype was a docile, obese dark-complexioned, and asexual woman dedicated to her white family as a caregiver and domestic servant (Bogle, 2001; Guerrero, 1993; hooks, 2014). Filmic renderings like *Birth of a Nation* (1915) and *Gone with the Wind* (1939) are shining examples of the Mammy figure that illustrates the attributes associated with this character. The image of Mammy was juxtaposed with that of a hypersexual, light-skinned Black woman referred to as Jezebel. This representation showed the sexualized objectification of Black women at the hands of white men. From her creation, Jezebel has been portrayed as a willing participant in her own promiscuity as depicted in the films *Black Hooker* (1974) and *Action Jackson* (1988). By the turn of the twentieth century, the Mammy caricature was replaced with that of Aunt Jemima, a brown-skinned maid that lovingly cared for her white family while running her own household with an iron fist (Bogle, 2001; Guerrero, 1993; West, 1995). Depictions of Aunt Jemima were first displayed on Quaker oatmeal boxes, in 1939, however, her narrative was translated to movie theaters in cinematic offerings such as *Imitation to Life* (1959). This archetype was replaced by the more verbal and assertive Sapphire personality. The product of radio and later television, the Sapphire stereotype derives its name from a domineering female character on the *Amos 'n' Andy* (1951–1960) show. Sapphire was a loud, fast-talking, quick-tempered woman who verbally stripped her husband of his masculinity at every opportunity. Sapphire likenesses have been reintroduced in contemporary incarnations such as that of the "angry Black woman" and the "strong Black woman." These four attributes are applied to the characters I selected for this essay as contemporary interpretations of these older representations in their professional roles as medical examiners and in discussion of their personal lives.

For instance, Dr. Camille "Cam" Saroyan worked as a police officer in New York City for eleven years before enrolling in medical school. Once she completed her education, Dr. Saroyan worked as a coroner often performing autopsies under unsavory conditions before accepting a job at the Jeffersonian Institute in their Forensic Division. During her tenure, Dr. Saroyan embodied the Jezebel, Mammy, and Sapphire archetypes. Prior to her character's start on *Bones*, Dr. Saroyan had an intimate relationship with Seeley Booth (David Boreanaz), a white Federal Bureau of Investigation (FBI) Agent that she had known since they were teenagers. Their relationship on and off-screen placed Dr. Saroyan in the traditional role of Jezebel by portraying her as a white man's mistress. Upon her relocation to Washington D.C., Dr. Saroyan adopted the Jezebel archetype by resuming her romantic and sexual relationship with Agent Booth. The two maintained a close friendship after they broke-up with Dr. Saroyan assuming the traits of Mammy by acting as Booth's confidant. Newly single, Dr. Saroyan assumed the traits of Jezebel (e.g., hypersexuality; promiscuity) by having a one-night stand with Birimbau/Grayson Barasa (Sean Blakemore), her co-worker Angela's (Michaela Conlin), ex-husband. Dr. Saroyan's life changes significantly once she adopts Michelle (Tiffany Hines), the daughter of her now deceased ex-fiancée. This mother experience centers Dr. Saroyan, on a personal level, but her Sapphire mannerisms (e.g., domineering; overbearing) causes tension between her and Michelle because Dr. Saroyan must learn how to parent a teen-age girl. Their mother-daughter relationship becomes more natural once Dr. Saroyan begins dating Michelle's gynecologist and realizes that her daughter only wants her to be happy. In the show's final season, Dr. Saroyan began an intimate relationship with Arastoo Vaziri (Pej Vahdat), a laboratory assistant (intern) and her subordinate. They fall in love and Dr. Saroyan assumes the role of Sapphire as she proposes to Arastoo, he accepts, and they wed. After they marry, Dr. Saroyan and her new husband travel to Mississippi to adopt three children and Dr. Saroyan becomes an amalgamation of Jezebel, Mammy, and Sapphire.

Dr. Alexx Woods (Khandi Alexander) on *CSI: Miami* graduated at the top of her medical school class despite being reprimanded by her superior for pointing out a mistake he had made in a patient's treatment. Directed to remain silent, Dr. Woods followed orders and was present as the patient died at the hands of her superior. Upon receiving her medical degree, Dr.

Woods took a job as a part-time coroner in New York City before accepting a job opportunity in Miami, Florida, as an assistant medical examiner. Along with her unseen husband, Henry, and their two children, Dr. Woods relocated. Dr. Woods displays the Mammy and Aunt Jemima archetypes through her maternal treatment of her deceased patients as they are autopsied. Often speaking to the dead as if they are able to communicate with her, Dr. Woods uses her knowledge as a medical examiner to uncover their manner of death and help catch their murderer. Dr. Wood's motherly care extends to her co-workers who she treats as family while sometimes neglecting her own.

Conversely, Dr. Melinda Warner (Tamara Tunie) on *Law & Order: Special Victims Unit* exhibits Sapphire and Aunt Jemima attributes. Having served in the United States Air Force for two tours during the Gulf War, Dr. Warner became a medical examiner in New York City, particularly for the Special Victims Unit of the New York Police Department, after replacing Dr. Elizabeth Rogers (Leslie Hendrix). The character of Dr. Warner and that of her family contain underdeveloped narratives in which her family and home life are mentioned, but not extensively discussed. The characters of Dr. Saroyan, Dr. Woods, and Dr. Warner are physical manifestations of larger social narratives in which stereotypical representations of Black womanhood developed their storylines. Physically, Dr. Saroyan and Dr. Warner due to their light complexions, European features, and straight (sometimes curly) hair texture exhibit the attributes assigned to the Jezebel archetype. However, Dr. Saroyan is the only one of the three to display the promiscuous nature associated with Jezebel. Dr. Woods visually resembles the Aunt Jemima representation with her darker brown skin, but not in shape. Dr. Saroyan and Dr. Warner embodied the Sapphire persona (e.g., feisty, stubborn, overbearing) in their previous occupations which were positions predominantly held by men. In spite of their differences, each to varying degrees were manifestations of the Mammy archetype. These women cared for their biological families, the victims they serviced, and their co-workers in a manner most aligned with a Mammy.

Meanwhile, those associated with Mammy, Jezebel, Aunt Jemima, and Sapphire are continuously reinvented on television as new generations interpret their meanings based on the character and the actresses that portray them (Bogle, 2001; Guerrero, 1993, hooks, 2014). Although these women are beautiful, intelligent, and hard-working they each portray one or more of the tropes previously discussed in this section. Like their predecessors, Black women actresses have endeavored to offer positive depictions for their gender and their race on the small screen. Yet, their characters are often plagued by the remnants of stereotypical representations such as Mammy, Jezebel, Aunt Jemima, and Sapphire, hence, placing

Black professional women, including medical examiners, into a paradig-
matic state.

Portrayals from the Margins

On primetime television shows such as those used in this essay, Black
women professionals, specifically medical examiners, serve as props or
backdoor storylines on these series (Cartier, 2014). Often stereotypical representations are incorporated to separate Black female characters from
their white counterparts which place Dr. Saroyan, Dr. Woods, and Dr. Warner at a considerable disadvantage in the context of their shows. Their roles
and personal lives become germane when connected to events in their
series' main plot. Dr. Saroyan received her job at the Jeffersonian to replace
her predecessor Dr. Daniel Goodman (Jonathan Adams), a friendly African American man, while he was on sabbatical. Dr. Saroyan became a permanent fixture on the show after Dr. Goodman decided not to return to the
Jeffersonian Institute. An eager, hands-on boss, Dr. Saroyan was initially at
odds with Dr. Temperance "Bones" Brennan (Emily Deschanel), the show's
lead character as well as other laboratory employees which caused tension
in the workplace. The tense interactions between Dr. Saroyan, Dr. Brennan,
and other staff were accentuated by the fact that Dr. Saroyan was not only
the only medical examiner, but she was one of the only women involved in
multiple dialogues across settings. Dr. Saroyan's professionalism and thor-
oughness as a medical examiner is what propels her work relationships
forward and justifies her being their boss. Once Dr. Brennan deems Dr.
Saroyan a suitable replacement for Dr. Goodman the remaining staff con-
curs and endeavor to follow Dr. Saroyan's directives. Prior to obtaining the
approval of Dr. Brennan, Dr. Saroyan was viewed as a strict micromanager
much like the Sapphire stereotype. Afterwards, Dr. Saroyan is an accepted
member of the team which changes her status from Sapphire to Mammy.
This is illustrated particularly by her maternal instincts in caring for her
adopted daughter Michelle and co-worker Zack Addy (Eric Millegan).

Unlike Dr. Saroyan, Dr. Woods, and Dr. Warner were slowly added to
standing storylines on *CSI: Miami* and *Law & Order: Special Victims Unit*.
Dr. Woods' character began as an Assistant Medical Examiner who only
interacted with main characters such as Horatio Caine (David Caruso)
when discussing victims' wounds or the outcome of an autopsy. In this role,
Dr. Woods resembles an Aunt Jemima at times that is responsible for taking care of her work family which expands the perimeters of their relationship from strictly business to personal interactions. For instance, in season
three, Dr. Woods lectures Ryan Wolfe (Jonathan Togo) about not informing

her or his superiors of his vision issues. After Dr. Woods verbally chastises Ryan for this omission, then as a Mammy, Dr. Woods provides Mr. Wolf with the name of a specialist in the field of ophthalmology. Although Dr. Woods maintains her professionalism, she displays stereotypical components that transform her character across these representations while enabling her to reposition her narratives in these conversations.

Contrary to Dr. Saroyan and Dr. Woods, Dr. Warner separates her home-life from her professional life by discussing her family, but not identifying her immediate members by name. As a result, this places Dr. Warner on the continuum of Mammy and Aunt Jemima, where she functions as both simultaneously (Cartier, 2014; Morgan, 2005; West, 1995). Dr. Warner's role as Mammy manifests when she is providing care to her patients during autopsy while enabling Dr. Warner to transform into Aunt Jemima when offering her co-workers, the results of her post-mortem examination. The role of medical examiner is complicated on *Bones*, *CSI: Miami*, and *Law & Order: Special Victims Unit* by the stereotypical representations that construct the narratives of Dr. Saroyan, Dr. Woods, and Dr. Warner. Each began with minor storylines on their respective shows. They are presented as knowledgeable and professional; however, their conversations with white co-workers are tense and robotic. Their co-workers view them as essential sources of information, but rarely express an interest in learning about the personal lives of these women. However, their storylines become significant to their shows' respective plots when their professional statuses become elevated via a promotion such as Dr. Saroyan (Head of the Jeffersonian Institute's Forensic Division), Dr. Woods (CSI Coroner), and Dr. Warner (Chief Medical Examiner), and their personal lives interfere with their work performance. Characters such as Black women medical examiners on television in the twenty-first century are considered by many as a big step forward, but how are these characters progressive or regressive when compared to similar characters on other shows?

We're Gaining Momentum

Since the televised inception of *Bones*, *CSI: Miami*, and *Law & Order: Special Victims Unit*, there has been an influx of television shows featuring Black female medical examiners on primetime crime dramas. Series like *Castle* (2009–2016) and *NCIS: New Orleans* (2014–present), place these characters in dual roles (e.g., medical examiner/friend; coroner/landlord) in which contemporary stereotypical representations are used to demonstrate the progressive storylines in these shows (Morgan, 2005). However, it is the pervasive nature of Mammy, Jezebel, Aunt Jemima, and Sapphire archetypes that permeate these new portrayals by signifying how these ingrained social narratives continue to define female African American medical examiners in a primetime crime drama series (Gates, 1988). Crime dramas like those presented in this essay, visually demonstrate how society has changed and possibly how African American female medical examiners are viewed in these new narratives.

Still, the portrayals of Dr. Saroyan, Dr. Woods, and Dr. Warner are marred by the remnants attached to the stereotypical representations used to develop their storylines on television. However, the character of Dr. Saroyan remains progressive when recalling that she was hand-picked by Dr. Daniel Goodman to lead his team during his sabbatical. Although Dr. Saroyan's former occupations made her an unusual choice for the job, her medical knowledge, deductive reasoning skills, and hand-on approach enabled her to excel in this position. As a result, Dr. Saroyan earned the respect of the other employees at the Jeffersonian Institute as well as the admiration of Agent Seeley Booth. Contrary to Dr. Saroyan, Dr. Woods' induction into the confidence of the *CSI: Miami* detectives, evolved over a couple of seasons where she was transformed from Dr. Woods, medical examiner, to Alexx a member of her work family as declared by Lieutenant Horatio Caine. Remember prior to that, Dr. Woods had served as an adoptive mother to the patients she autopsied while maintaining her professional distance from her co-workers and detectives assigned to her cases. As their interactions increased, Dr. Woods began to relax and let down her guard which contributed to a shift in the dynamics of their working relationship, in addition, to their professional one. But, unlike Dr. Saroyan and Dr. Woods, Dr. Warner began her career as an active member of the armed forces before becoming an Assistant Medical Examiner for the state of New York. Recalling that initially, Dr. Warner much like Dr. Woods was straight by the book in her professional interactions with her co-workers and the detectives she worked with; however, these women soften as they became friends with the lead detectives on their respective series.

Like Dr. Saroyan, Dr. Woods and Dr. Warner are attractive, intelligent, and accomplished African American women who chose to enter the male-dominated field as medical examiners. When viewed collectively, these characters propel forward the notion that African American women are competent medical examiners, yet the mannerisms they exhibit are in many ways regressive expressions ingrained with the larger societal expectations used to stereotype this group as Mammies, Jezebels, Aunt Jemimas, and Sapphires (Bogle, 2001; Guerrero, 1993; hooks, 2014). Characters such as Dr. Saroyan, Dr. Woods, and Dr. Warner are indicative of unspoken social narratives regarding African American women advancements as professionals in the medical field, still each remain constant reminders of the oppressive marginalization that these women have been able to overcome as measured by their success.

Conclusion

Black women professionals have existed on television shows for over thirty years with each of these characters taking a more active role in their series' plots. Stereotypically, playing a subordinate role such as caregiver, nurse, or maid, Black women were granted storylines that reinforced prevailing stereotypes such as Mammy, Jezebel, Aunt Jemima, and Sapphire. These parts were professionally limiting until the late 1960s and 1970s. Although early shows featuring Black women in the medical profession are considered groundbreaking, these characters were constructed by the same stereotypes as their present-day counterparts. The success of these shows created pathways for future representations of Black women professionals, such as medical examiners, to enter the plot of their respective series as major characters. This trek has been difficult since such positions on popular primetime crime dramas were held by white men. The twenty-first century has presented modernization of the Mammy, Jezebel, Aunt Jemima, and Sapphire archetypes, yet their narratives are continually used to construct representations of African American female medical examiners like Dr. Saroyan, Dr. Woods, and Dr. Warner. As progressive as Dr. Saroyan, Dr. Woods, and Dr. Warner appear on the small screen, their narratives are constructed by stereotypical representations that are verbally articulated and physically acted out during their scenes. Characters such as these serve as inspiration for future African American female medical professionals while providing fertile ground for Black actresses to break the glass ceiling by deconstructing stereotypical representations that are used to construct their storylines.

REFERENCES

Bogle, D. (2001). *Toms, Coons, Mulattoes, Mammies, and Bucks: An Interpretive History of Blacks in American Films*. Bloomsbury Publishing.
Braxton, J. M., & McLaughlin, A. N. (Eds.). (1990). *Wild Women in the Whirlwind: Afra-American Culture and the Contemporary Literary Renaissance*. New Brunswick, NJ: Rutgers University Press.
Cartier, N. (2014). Black Women On-Screen as Future Texts: A New Look at Black Pop Culture Representations. *Cinema Journal, 53*(4), 150–157.
Catterall, B. (2005). Is It All Coming Together? Further Thoughts on Urban Studies and the Present Crisis:(4) Space-Time (s), Meanings, Trapped Situations and Mediations. *City, 9*(1), 150–158.

Collins, P. H. (2002). *Black Feminist Thought: Knowledge, Consciousness, and the Politics of Empowerment.* New York: Routledge.

Doriani, B. M. (1991). Black Womanhood in Nineteenth-Century America: Subversion and Self-Construction in Two Women's Autobiographies. *American Quarterly, 43*(2), 199–222.

Dube, M. (Producer). (2002–2012). *CSI: Miami* [Television series]. United States: Columbia Broadcasting System.

Dyson, A. H. (2005). Crafting "the humble prose of living": Rethinking Oral/Written Relations in the Echoes of Spoken Word. *English Education, 37*(2), 149–164.

Gabbin, J. V. (1990). A Laying On of Hands: Black Women Writers Exploring the Roots of Their Folk and Cultural Tradition. *Wild Women in the Whirlwind: Afra-American Culture and the Contemporary Literary Renaissance,* 246–263.

Gates, H.L., Jr. (2014). *The Signifying Monkey: A Theory of African American Literary Criticism.* Oxford University Press.

Gray, H. (1995). Black Masculinity and Visual Culture. *Callaloo, 18*(2), 401–405.

Guerrero, E. (2012). *Framing Blackness: The African American Image in Film.* Temple University Press.

hooks, b. (2014). *Ain't I A Woman: Black Women and Feminism.* New York: Routledge.

Mitchell, R. (2010). Cultural Aesthetics and Teacher Improvisation: An Epistemology of Providing Culturally Responsive Service by African American Professors. *Urban Education, 45*(5), 604–629.

Morgan, M. (2005). Hip-Hop Women Shredding the Veil: Race and Class in Popular Feminist identity. *South Atlantic Quarterly, 104*(3), 425–444.

Reichs, K., Deschanel, E.,Boreanaz, D., & Hong, G. (Producers). (2005–2017). *Bones* [Television series]. United States: Fox Broadcasting Company.

Wolf, D., Kotcheff, T., Jankowski, P., Smith, M., Martin, J., Starch, J., Forney, A. W., & Hargitay, M. (Executive Producers). (1999–2019). *Law & Order: Special Victims Unit* [Television series]. United States: National Broadcasting Company.

Black Woman

High-Powered but
Not Balanced in Shondaland

ADELINA MBINJAMA-GAMATHAM *and*
ELEDA MBINJAMA

Introduction

According to Warner (2014), Shonda Rhimes has established herself as a showrunner with a passion for women's stories; she thus uses her production company, Shondaland, as a space of refuge for creatives in which she carefully selects writers, creators, actors/actresses and producers for the stories that she is interested in telling. According to Everett (2015), in September 2014, Shonda Rhimes, executive producer and creator of *How to Get Away with Murder* (2014–2020) and *Scandal* (2012–2018) made a historic turn as the first African American showrunner ever (female or male) to have an entire primetime programming block of three consecutive hours for three different shows on one single night—a night dubbed "Thank God It's Thursday" (TGIT). Annalise Keating (Viola Davis) and Olivia Pope (Kerry Washington) are significant to Shonda Rhimes' opus and programming wherein viewers see Black women professionals as powerful leaders of industry.

Shonda Rhimes' first television show, *Grey's Anatomy* (2005–present) experienced popularity amongst viewers across the globe; this popularity has increased significantly since the inclusion of professional Black women leads. *How to Get Away with Murder* is centered on Annalise Keating, an attorney and professor of Criminal Law while *Scandal* focuses on Olivia Pope and her crisis management firm, Olivia Pope & Associates (OPA). This essay focuses primarily on Annalise Keating who is at the center of eye-brow raising, jaw dropping, and exhilarating content that defines a Black woman in a professional role. Rhimes' transformational work is made evident through the character representations of a dark-skinned Black woman lead actress which allows the viewer to confront various thoughts about Blackness, womanhood, leadership, professional credibility and the ability to maintain a healthy work/life balance.

While both series are popular, *How to Get Away with Murder*, to some extent, reflects the innermost secrets, ambitions, anxieties and traumas of Black women in high-profile positions—from their careers, romantic or sexual relationships, to the ways in which they navigate society's multiple obstacles to the development of, and its discursive violence against, Black women. The character of Annalise Keating allows Rhimes to tell stories through an intersectional lens, by focusing on race, gender and class in the life of a powerful, Black, woman professional.

Black, Powerful and Imperfect Stories

From a much broader view, the stories of the two leading characters in *How to Get Away with Murder* and *Scandal* share some similarities: both are well-educated Black women who are in relationships with powerful, professional, white men. They have problems steering their own personal lives and, at times, they self-destruct; however, through their internal resolve and professional excellence, these high-powered Black women thrive in their professions. Even when their work is toxic, they are both so consumed with their professional lives that this dedication is extended to others, particularly when they have to clean up the lives and protect the careers of their associates. Pope's personal life is not a major part of the show until later seasons. Viewers do not get to know much about her African American roots, aside from scenes in which she interacts with her government operative father and terrorist mother. Pope is depicted as a high-powered professional who in her personal life has to reconcile with the truth of both her parents lying to her, which has caused some imbalance in her life. The privatization of Pope's personal life is also symbolic of the way in which high-powered Black women become less concerned about sharing their personal lives with outsiders as they become more successful. Some even mute their Blackness by ensuring that they do not appear or sound "too Black."

In the series pilot of *How to Get Away with Murder*, the viewer is introduced to the excitement and admiration from all of Keating's law students, primarily because she is recognized as a living legend on the university campus. In utilizing her student's admiration, she encourages competition amongst her students in order for them to (1) impress her, and hopefully gain her approval and attention; and (2) to be mentored by her personally in her private law firm. Keating is influential and admired by younger, future professional leaders, especially Michaela Pratt (Aja Naomi King), another Black woman character in the show. When Pratt witnesses how Keating operates in the courtroom by cross examining her witness, a detective with whom Keating is having an affair, with authority and thus winning the case, she exclaims, "I want to be like her." While Pratt is naive, she shows her competitive edge much sooner than most of her peers and often tries to get the first prize from Keating. This signifies how Black women are serious and driven about their careers and are aware that, in order to succeed, one has to be prepared to compete with the best and do whatever it takes to succeed. Rhimes' Black women characters lead hardworking and meticulous lives which allow for imperfect stories to be told.

Rhimes, who is known for using a casting practice called blind casting (where the notion of a color-blind and post-racial society is reinforced), has been admired for her narratives of strong women (Warner, 2014). Since leading characters carry the narrative and flow in a series, having two series with Black female leads, telling female stories, carries meaning to an audience that has long become accustomed to markedly anti–Black tropes in television drama. For example, *Scandal*, does away with the popular "white savior" stereotype by casting a Black woman figure as the "fixer" of both the nation's and the economic elite's problems. Filoteo (2014, p. 213) argues that "[t]hrough this, the show serves to challenge representations of African American women by providing a strong female lead character played by an African American actress."

When analyzing Shondaland's productions, it is important to ask, "who is telling the stories?" Rhimes' casting practice has introduced characters through which she can tell stories about Blackness without having to make Blackness the main motif for her shows. Warner (2014) explains that blind casting, which is the "process of not writing race into the script, is often considered a progressive step toward actors' equality." This casting practice has allowed for two Black women to tell stories about highly intensive work, relationships, scandals, and politics. The fact that the lead roles in two of Rhimes' most popular television series are Black Women shapes the narratives and viewer perceptions of these stories. It also reimagines the way in which Black professional stories are told in mainstream media, through Black female lead actresses, and the challenges they encounter by being Black, high-powered but unbalanced and yet still strive to be their authentic selves.

The Real Woman: Viola Davis Requests Realness of Her Character

The protagonist in Rhimes' *How to Get Away with Murder*, Annalise Keating, a defense lawyer and professor, was a character that remained "un-raced" in script, until African American actress Viola Davis was screen tested for the part. Humanizing Black women who play leading roles is intrinsic for Davis, who agreed to play Annalise Keating only if she could be a "real woman." The original script described her character as highly sexualized and seductive, which would then rely on popular colonial and television tropes of Black women's lascivious nature, which Davis opposed. Davis wanted to represent more than that; she wanted to show parts of what it means to be a Black professional woman. In this respect, segments of the script were adapted to fit Davis' vision of the character as a "real woman." We believe that since the actress is dark skinned, (unlike Kerry Washington who is fairer in complexion), and has experienced discrimination in the industry (not to say that Washington did not), she is aware "that there are preconditions of success for Black creative workers at major media organizations namely to 'be Black but not too Black" (Erigha, 2015).

Davis' authenticity resonated with fans who became increasingly intrigued by the crossover phenomena that Keating's character represents for women of color, especially dark-skinned Black women. Historically, Black women have starred in supporting roles, such as housekeepers, and they are now lead actresses in professional roles in big productions. Contrary to many television depictions of lead women as pristine figures of feminine beauty, without any hint at the "unmasked" realities in the lives of their characters, Davis insisted that her character is seen to undergo a beauty routine familiar to many Black women: she removes her wig and hangs it up at the end of a long business day, wraps her hair in a silk bonnet/ scarf, removes her eyelashes and makeup, and applies cocoa butter before bed in episode 4, of season 2, "Let's Get to Scooping." This scene symbolizes how many Black women manage their professional presence, by shielding their true thoughts and feelings, while conforming to white ideologies and practices by wearing a wig during the day—particularly a wig of fine straight hair. However, when Black women go home, they tap into their raw feelings, and they are purely in their authentic form and state of mind.

Fans enjoy *How to Get Away with Murder* because it is centered on an older professional Black woman who is morally ambiguous. Her boldness, craziness, and attitude is refreshing and, at times, thrilling, often leaving viewers with the sense that Keating can achieve anything that she sets her mind to, which is a great motif for the show. In her interview with Robin Roberts (ABC News, 2014), Davis mentioned how her character helped her "step into her power." She explained:

Stepping into my power … being number one on the call sheet, knowing that I have to set the tone every time I walk on that stage, you know … being a woman who is mysterious and sexy and working outside of my comfort zone … and literally not being afraid of that, knowing that there is a certain amount of failure that's attached to that and knowing that there is a certain amount of scrutiny attached to that but saying, you know what, this a time in my life that I am not going to live in fear [ABC News, 2014].

Davis understands that her character embodies someone who has to be powerful, strong, caring, ruthless and dysfunctional in order to perform her best, even when this calls for unethical behavior. For Davis, the risk was shedding fear in order to portray Keating convincingly, that is, in a way that would entertain viewers and lend authenticity to the story of a Black female attorney and professor who struggles to keep her life balanced.

Upon close reading of Rhimes' lead characters, Pope and Keating, it is clear that blind casting worked well for the series as well as for her politics, especially as the shows gained popularity and momentum on Twitter. As a segue into the next section, it is important to highlight that the two Black women represent different age-groups and socio-economic backgrounds, with Pope presumably in her mid to late '30s while Keating is in her '50s. The two series have also allowed fans on Black Twitter to comment on the shows, interact with the actresses and share stories that the producers, writers, and actresses want to explore in their crafts. With regard to *How to Get Away with Murder*, Black users use Black Twitter to not only perform racial identity but to also deliberate upon discourses on Blackness (Williams & Gonlin, 2017, p. 984). This is made explicit through Keating's womanhood, as well as her high-powered professional and unbalanced personal life, which were discussion points on Twitter.

#HTGAWM and How to Get Away with Being Black

Following *Scandal's* online success on Twitter (see Goldberg, 2013; Mask, 2015; Pixley, 2015; Chatman, 2017), Black audiences could not get enough of Shondaland and, as Rhimes' next series emerged, Twitter users coined the hashtag #HTGAWM for the series *How to Get Away with Murder*. Much like the continued online dialogue on *Scandal*, the conversation on Black identity in contemporary America was enriched by the #HTGAWM hashtag on Twitter, thus converting the television show into a weekly moment of broad socio-cultural reflection. For many, Twitter provided a voice to groups that are often excluded from mainstream media and, for once, the conversation was around professional Black women in high-powered positions and what they do with that power to remain sane. Black Twitter has been a space for Black audiences of the show to engage on matters affecting Black successful women and to explore issues of mental health and self-acceptance.

Black Twitter has been described as a sort of cultural identification on Twitter. Clark (2014) describes it as a social network focused on issues of interest to the Black community. More specifically, Black Twitter can be described as a cultural movement—a way in which Black people and those who stand for the Black community can voice their opinions (see Manjoo, 2010; Ramsey, 2015). We can carefully add that *#HTGAWM* has allowed Black Twitter, particularly professional women to embrace Blackness with messages of inclusivity and non-judgment.

The various "[t]weets, hashtags, and trends associated with the *#HTGAWM* are used to demonstrate that second screening and co-viewing of the series on Twitter enables a techno cultural discourse on a shared cultural history of Black womanhood" (Williams & Gonlin, 2017, p. 984). Stereotypically, an African American woman is seen as being "cold and callous, even neglectful of her own children and family while being overly solicitous toward Whites" (Ladson-Billings, 2009, p. 89). Twitter followers often remarked about how *#HTGAWM* allows them to see themselves and to discuss their Blackness, brokenness, and un-balanced power. Keating's imperfections and inability to manage her own stereotypical characteristics reminds Black women especially that they are not the only ones having to manage these realities. Keating's character in #HTGAWM is the foci of this essay because she represents a broader base of Black, dark skinned, professional women who do their best to be in control of their private and professional lives.

From In Control to No Control

Black professional women often have to face challenges in their lives that are unique to them based on their race, cultural background, class and gender. Some of the problems can be out of their control such as the pressures to conform to the beauty standards of Hollywood. Keating would have been labeled a "mammy," someone who takes care of everyone but herself, that is, the driven, aggressive, angry Black woman (Ladson-Billings, 2009, p. 89). In the series she is a strong, relentless, and powerful woman, even though she possesses elements of the mammy archetype. She covers up for her associates and protects them from harm. However, the show manages to break this stereotype by focusing on Keating's professional work-life and how she organizes everything and everyone around her in order to fulfill her personal mandates. She is mostly in control of what she does and who she decides to help, which communicates to audiences that Black women should use their power carefully and pursue actions that serve their self-interest. Keating's sporadic meltdowns is reassuring that even high-powered Black women can operate from a place of being in control to not having any and that, that too, is enough. How she recovers from the disintegration, and focuses on her professional work is inspiring and invigorating. In comparison, in *Scandal*, Pope is usually seen with her flat ironed hair, wearing nice clothes, drinking wine and eating popcorn when distressed, thus representing a more unrealistic and "high class" attempt of dealing, but actually avoiding stress and anxiety. The two women represent different economic backgrounds. Pope is from a more affluent family, although both parents are Black, she is fairer in complexion and has softer features. She is educated by polished, private schools unlike Keating who appears to be more from a low-income household and all her access to education was gained by her ability and not money. Pope's character is quite whitewashed and often does not represent the Blackness many Black people experience. Nevertheless, both characters epitomize hardworking, Black proficient women who are at the peak of their careers and are extremely influential. Rhimes' work dares women of color to see parts of themselves through community, and authentic reflections of being Black that are often hidden from the world for the fear of 'not being taken seriously.' The messages that are associated with the characters suggest that when a Black woman reaches a certain height in her career, she becomes high-powered but unbalanced unless she undergoes a personal journey of "unraveling" or unshielding, and begins to confront her personal demons.

In "Mama's Here Now," episode 13, of season 1, after her cheating husband is murdered, and her boyfriend is falsely accused of his murder, Keating, in a depressive state, reaches out to her mother, Ophelia Harkness (Cicely Tyson), for support. Ophelia continually refers to Keating as "Anna Mae," in response to which she tells her mother that she had changed her name from Anna Mae Harkness to "Annalise" Keating. In return, Ophelia rebukes her daughter by saying "I wiped your ass and I can call you anything I want." It is clear that Keating's change from a name common for Black girls in her generation, is an attempt to fit into her professional environment more comfortably and, perhaps, to less markedly "announce" herself as "Black." In addition to this "tempering" of her Blackness through renaming herself, Keating is also married to a white man, who had previously been her psychologist.

Ophelia's visit allows the viewer insight into other aspects of her identity that Keating may have refashioned. For example, it is apparent that she comes from a poor background, as Ophelia is in awe of her daughter's "fancy, rich house." In this episode the viewer is also introduced to a Black woman's experience and communal history of self-care, intergenerational dialogue, and collective memory as Ophelia does her daughter's hair. This moment in which Keating is sitting on the bedroom floor, huddled between her mother's knees, as Ophelia scratches and oils her scalp, while combing her hair out—a scene that is strikingly familiar to Black households globally—is quite possibly one of the most endearing scenes of the intimacy and authenticity in the show's portrayal of Black womanhood. In addition, her meltdown showcased how trauma can reduce even a high-powered, professional, and resolute woman to a child who needs the healing support of a mother. This moment defies the misogynoir stereotype of the strong Black woman who must constantly be resilient in the face of trauma and endure pain. This further shows that Black professional women have problems and that they need to be loved and supported.

Conclusion

In light of this analysis of Black women professionals in Shonda Rhimes' two popular series, we acknowledge the way in which she dissects and represents her characters through use of language, plot structure and building of character. To be original, her use of dialogue—by letting her characters be intelligent—moves away from cliché stories that are not unique. Most television shows go by the slight "dumbing down" approach to tell stories, while Rhimes' creativity and freedom, prompted her to making her characters appear more intelligent than the audience. Through Rhimes' characters, Black women begin to see how things are done by professional women. Keating's character helps to understand and discover the experiences of Black women in positions of power. While noting how her character may be viewed and interpreted by various Black audiences, we appreciate her being represented as inspiring, Black, powerful, high-powered and un-balanced. It is effective that Keating represents Black women who are great at what they do while also showcasing when they are "breaking a rule," which teaches the audience to think about those rules and their significance. Such stories affirm women to be their authentic selves by embracing their imperfections; and that it is important to be unapologetic about being competitive, successful, and recognizing that there may be problems that need to be confronted and overcome. Telling stories that people are avoiding talking about, makes Rhimes more credible as a writer. Her stories get audiences following her shows and sparking conversations about realistic issues. Rhimes provides her audience with usable moments that allow for reflection and to consider different ways of approaching professional work and being cognitively present for each personal milestone. The stories that she creates and produces are honest and have helped shape the world of television. In 2015, for her portrayal as Keating, Davis became the first Black woman to win the Primetime Emmy Award for Outstanding Lead Actress in a Drama Series (Simon, 2019).

While, in comparison to other television networks, American Broadcasting Company (ABC) leads in tackling diversity, with Rhimes being one of the few Black women writers and producers who had the chance to be successful in the industry. Rhimes has in recent years moved her production company, Shondaland, from Disney-ABC Studios to Netflix in order to grow her network of writers, creators, and producers. This move allows for creative freedom and a broader audience, which begs the question, what do traditional broadcasters have to do in order to retain top talent? Even though Rhimes was criticized for moving her production company from ABC to Netflix, she remains focused on her transformational agenda to reach across cultural and religious beliefs, telling compelling stories to a new generation of viewers. Through Shondaland, Rhimes intends raising the next generation of writers and producers; and, because she understands her audience, Shondaland's move to the digital space allows for more stories to be told and shared across various age-groups, races and genders. We are sure Shondaland will continue to share stories of "real women" and all aspects of Black lives, including the high-powered and the unbalanced. This notion is complementary to what Davis said in an interview with *Variety* about Rhimes' stories and characters. She said:

> I still believe, and I will say this until I go to my grave, that Annalise Keating and Olivia Pope are the greatest characters on TV. … And I say that because the people here are not writing tentatively for people of color. And I see some of the characters that people eat up—that they love—that are just not deep, are not drawn-out; they're everything that people feel comfortable with—even biopics, maybe even some things that I've been involved in [Simon, 2019].

References

ABC News. (2014). Behind the Scenes of Shondaland [Video]. YouTube. https://www.youtube.com/watch?v=H9B5Us9zHRc.

Chatman, D. (2017). Black Twitter and the Politics of Viewing Scandal. In *Fandom: Identities and Communities in a Mediated World*. Second Edition. Edited by Jonathan Gray, Cornel Sandvoss and C. Lee Harrington. New York: New York University Press.

Clark, M.D. (2014). To Tweet Our Own Cause: A Mixed-Methods Study of the Online Phenomenon "Black Twitter." [Doctoral Dissertation, University of North Carolina at Chapel Hill Graduate School] https://cdr.lib.unc.edu/indexablecontent/uuid:1318a434-c0c4-49d2-8db4-77c6a2cbb8b1.

Erigha, M. (2015). Shonda Rhimes, *Scandal*, and the Politics of Crossing Over. *The Black Scholar*, 45(1), 10–15. https://doi.org/10.1080/00064246.2014.997598.

Everett, A. (2015). Scandalicious. *The Black Scholar*, 45(1), 34–43. https://doi.org/10.1080/00064246.2014.997602.

Filoteo, J. (2014). ABC's *Scandal*. *Humanity & Society*, 38(2), 212–215. https://doi.org/10.1177/0160597614532191.

Goldberg, L. (2013, February 7). How ABC's *Scandal* Gets 2,200 Tweets Per Minute. *The*

Hollywood Reporter. https://www.hollywoodreporter.com/news/kerry-washington-abcs-scandal-gets-418091.

Ladson-Billings, G. (2009). "Who You Callin' Nappy-Headed?" A Critical Race Theory Look at the Construction of Black Women. *Race Ethnicity and Education, 12*(1), 87–99. https://doi.org/10.1177/105678791802700303.

Manjoo, F. (2010, Aug 10). How Black People Use Twitter: The Latest Research on Race and Microblogging. Slate.com. Retrieved 2 April 2015. http://slate.com/articles/technology/technology/2010/08/how_Black_people_use_twitter.

Mask, M. (2015). A Roundtable Conversation on *Scandal. The Black Scholar, 45*(1), 3–9. https://doi.org/10.1080/00064246.2014.997597.

Pixley, T. (2015). Trope and Associates. *The Black Scholar, 45*(1), 28–33. https://doi.org/10.1080/00064246.2014.997601.

Ramsey, D.X. (2015, April 8). The Truth About Black Twitter: Complex, Influential, and Far More Meaningful Than the Sum of Its Social Justice-Driven Hashtags. *The Atlantic*. http://www.theatlantic.com/technology/archive/2015/04/the-truth-about-Black-Twitter/390120/.

Simon, J. (2019. September 25). Why Viola Davis Will "Go to Her Grave" Saying Annalise Keating and Olivia Pope Are the Greatest Characters on Television. *Shadow and Act*. https://shadowandact.com/why-viola-davis-will-go-to-her-grave-saying-annalise-keating-and-olivia-pope-are-the-greatest-characters-ontelevision?fbclid=IwAR0lNQgio0y03K4qYH1aTN7yZ8mnsGDQBYf7U85aOibspoNUhpoXtzMUFNo.

Warner, K.J. (2014). The Racial Logic of *Grey's Anatomy*: Shonda Rhimes and Her "Post-Civil Rights, Post-Feminist" Series. *Television & New Media 2015, 16*(7), 631–647. https://doi.org/10.1177/1527476414550529.

Williams, A. & Gonlin, V. (2017). I Got All My Sisters with Me (on Black Twitter): Second Screening of *How to Get Away with Murder* as a Discourse on Black Womanhood. *Information, Communication & Society, 20*(7), 984–1004. https://doi.org/10.1080/1369118X.2017.1303077.

PART VI

New Television

Awkward and Black

Redefining Representations of Black Women on The Misadventures of Awkward Black Girl *and* Insecure

Regina M. Duthely

From Online to On Television

In 2011 actor, producer, and writer Issa Rae launched her web series *The Misadventures of Awkward Black Girl,* and it went on to be a viral hit. Rae claims that she created her show to fill a need for representations of Black women that she felt would not be welcome on network television. The popularity of the show demonstrated that she was correct in that assertion and there was indeed an audience for the kinds of stories she wanted to tell. In the Kickstarter campaign to raise money for the webseries Rae (2011) writes:

> Television today has a very limited scope and range in its depictions of people of color. As a Black woman, I don't identify with and relate to most of the non–Black characters I see on TV, much less characters of my own race. When I flip through the channels, it's disheartening. I don't see myself or women like me being represented. I'm not a smooth, sexy, long-haired vixen; I'm not a large, sassy Black woman; an angry Post Office employee. I'm an awkward Black girl [Rae, 2011, Kickstarter].

Rae created a character that reflected a vision of Black womanhood that was not based only on her sexuality or alignment with stereotypes of Black women usually seen on television. In this way Rae ushered in a new representation of Black women on television, but also put herself in the vanguard of Black women creators transforming television in our contemporary moment.

Rae's webseries launched prior to the explosion of Shonda Rhimes' *Scandal* (2012) and the cult following of Mara Brock Akil's Gabrielle Union led *Being Mary Jane* (2014) on BET. There were comedies featuring Black women in the 1990s and early 2000s like the Queen Latifah led *Living Single* (1993) and *Girlfriends* (2000) featuring Tracee Ellis Ross, but these shows were still rare compared to the dearth of television shows centering white protagonists. At the time, there were a limited number of shows centering the experiences of Black women, but the creation of network dramas *Scandal* and *Being Mary Jane* signaled the beginning of a turn in network television. Shows featuring interesting, complex Black woman protagonists surged in popularity, and many of these shows centered on the professional lives of their Black woman protagonists. *Scandal's* fixer Olivia Pope and *Being Mary Jane's* highly successful newscaster Mary Jane Paul, for example, both reflect super successful and extremely ambitious professional Black women. Rae's webseries *The Misadventures of Awkward Black Girl* and her later HBO series *Insecure* both take a different, more comedic approach; the workplace also figures prominently in her protagonists' narratives, but the fictional J and Issa of *Misadventures of Awkward Black Girl* and *Insecure* respectively, are both searching for professional fulfillment, and lack the traditional capitalist markers of the ultra-successful image of their television counterparts.

Springing from the popularity of her web series, Rae created the HBO series *Insecure* that premiered in 2016. Through her own position, Rae is reimagining Black professional womanhood in her own right. As creator, writer, and actor on her own shows, Rae has worked to fight for a place for Black women's stories on television and in film. The creative control she has garnered, and the media content she has produced, is an important part of Black women's disruption of professional media spaces that they are often denied access. Using Gwendolyn Pough's theory of wreck I argue that Rae's work brings wreck to the public sphere and disrupts representations of Black professional womanhood in the media landscape both through her presence as a television executive, as well as through the characters she creates on her shows. Pough (2004) defines wreck as, "a rhetorical tool that builds on Black womanist traditions and a hip-hop present ... when Black women's discourses disrupt dominant masculine discourses, break into the public sphere, and in some way impact or influence the United States imaginary" (p. 12). Rae's work and her comedic, millennial point of view is bringing wreck to people's living rooms by challenging dominance and not being satisfied with hegemonic representations of Black professional womanhood in media. Rae's web series and television show both present alternative representations of Black professional womanhood. She has created room for a Black woman professional that is flawed and nuanced in ways that are not always seen in mainstream media.

Black Women Wrecking Television Media

Black women have sought to create and maintain spaces that challenge hegemony and empower other Black women in the face of mainstream media representations that reinforce negative stereotypes and ideologies held about Black women. Black women are working to reimagine and reconfigure safe spaces that combat dominant ideology. In *Sista Talk: The Personal and the Pedagogical* Rochelle Brock argues that ideology is the lens through which we shape our view of the world. She says, "Ideology allows and enforces the constructions of Black womanhood to be taken for granted and implies some natural state, because what is forgotten, and ignored, is that images of Black women are faulty constructions of reality, created by dominant thought, as much as it creates dominant thought" (Brock, 2005, p. 9). The way Black womanhood is constructed in our contemporary imaginations is not an accurate reflection of what it means to be a Black woman. The images and stereotypes perpetuated are not accurate reflections of the nuanced, complex, and diverse experiences of Black women. Their purpose is to continue to oppress Black women and ensure that existing hierarchies used to marginalize Black women remain unchanged. However, Black women in the public sphere disrupt these negative images of Black womanhood by, "claiming control of the public's gaze and a public voice for themselves" (Pough, 2004, p. 17). Rae does this claiming through the work of her web-series and on *Insecure*.

Issa Rae, creator of the popular web series *The Misadventures of Awkward Black Girl*, created her show to fill a need for representations of Black women that she felt would not be welcome on network television. Rae (2011) argues that her work is simultaneously specific and universal which challenges the ways Black characters are created on mainstream television. Often television shows and films with Black protagonists are seen as only appealing to Black audiences. This contributes to the lack of Black representation in mainstream media. However, Black creatives are challenging that thinking. Her presence, along with the work of many other Black women creators, is transforming the television profession. In an interview on NPR about *The Misadventures of Awkward Black Girl* and J's story Rae claims, "I think the fact that she is Black but the concepts are universal speaks volumes. Like, it shows that you can have a Black—just because she's a Black female lead doesn't mean you can't relate to her. And I think that that speaks more to mainstream media because there just is this sort of perception that, you know, if a Black person is in the lead, then it has to be for Black people. It has to only relate to them" (Martin, 2011). Rae is challenging the ways that Black people's stories are told. Her push for Black representation in the mainstream that presents diverse images of Black womanhood, particularly in the workplace, are not limited only to Black audiences. Representations of the full richness of Black lives are necessary in mainstream media. Rae's work is bringing digital wreck to mainstream media that claims that no one wants to see these stories, and that no one will watch. *The Misadventures of Awkward Black Girl* critiques existing media paradigms that insist on boxing Black women into stereotypical roles and limiting accurate representations of Black womanhood.

The success of *The Misadventures of Awkward Black Girl* signals a significant move to empower women of color to create their own identities and write their own professional narratives in media spaces where they are unwelcome. The support the show has received from viewers helped them to raise $56,000 to keep the show in production, and Rae credits the viewers for making the show a success, "*The Misadventures of Awkward Black Girl* beat out 783 other web series to win the 2012 Shorty Award for Best Web Show. For the unfamiliar, the Shorty Awards honor the best in social media and Internet content, so it was quite the honor that: (1) our viewers rallied to nominate us into the top five shows and (2) the Shorty Award committee recognized our impact on the web series community" (Rae, 2012, para. 1). Issa Rae details exactly why shows like hers are not free to exist on mainstream television. The racist responses she received for winning an online award reflect the pervasive racist ideology suppressing positive and complex images of Black professional women that Black women creators like Issa Rae struggle to promote. Black creators are treated as though they do not have stories to tell, their shows and films are too niche, and no one will watch. Rae (2012) says of this racist ideology, "This mindset is exactly why creative shows of color don't get to exist on television anymore. There's an overbearing sense of entitlement that refuses to allow shows of color to thrive. How dare we even try?" (para. 2). Through racism, both blatant and subtle, that sought to deny her access, Rae was able to provide an example of a new Black professional in media. Her professional positioning and success as a creator helped to remind people that Black women belong in media spaces. According to Gwendolyn Pough (2004), "When a woman of the hip-hop generation is able to build on the legacy of Black women's activism, expressive culture, and speech acts and grabs hold of the public sphere by bringing wreck, there must be potential for change. Ultimately, the moment of bringing wreck should bring those who witness it to a different understanding of Black womanhood, even if only momentarily" (p. 83). The telling of new stories is a way for Black women to develop counternarratives that they control.

Insecure and Representations of Black Women Professionals

After *The Misadventures of Awkward Black Girl* garnered a great deal of praise and online success Rae shot to stardom and turned the success of her webseries into a successful HBO series that she created with comedian Larry Wilmore. On the HBO series the character Issa, also played by Rae, works for a non-profit that runs after-school programming for underrepresented students. Issa is the only Black woman in her office, and similar to the webseries, she is constantly navigating the casual racism of her liberal white coworkers who imagine themselves as saving the children of color they serve. The show does a good job of representing the experiences of being the only Black person in an office of allegedly well-intentioned, but still condescending, white colleagues trying to serve people and communities that they feel they must save.

In season 3 the show moved from focusing on the end of Issa's long-term romantic relationship to focusing on her financial woes and lack of professional fulfillment. In episode 2 "Familiar-Like" Issa is in a meeting where she and her colleagues discuss the need to update the company logo. The logo is a drawing of a white hand holding up a group of Black children. As her coworkers explain to the CEO why people might find the logo racist, the CEO becomes defensive and finally quips, "It can't be racist because it is my hand!" The CEO's inability to see her racially problematic ideologies demonstrate the kinds of microaggressions Black people endure in the workplace. Sue, Lin, and Rivera (2009) argue that "Many racial microaggressions are delivered outside the awareness of perpetrators because most white Americans experience themselves as good and moral people who believe in equality and democracy" (p. 159). This subtle and paternalistic view of people of color that the CEO demonstrates in this moment puts Issa in the uncomfortable position of awareness of the act of bias while feeling pressure to not challenge her boss who imagines herself as well-meaning. Issa sits quietly throughout the meeting allowing her non–Black coworkers to take the lead on critiquing the CEO because she knows that her position as the only Black woman in the office is one of constant precarity. Her attempt at pushback in season 2 got her demoted.

According to Dickens and Chavez (2018) Black women often engage in identity shifting in the workplace which they define as, "identity shifting, also known as identity negotiation, which is the alteration of one's actions, speech, and appearance to adjust to cultural norms within a given environment" (p. 760). Issa performs this identity shifting throughout the show, and particularly in this moment where there is an aside where Issa speaks directly to her viewer/audience and colleagues while all of the action is suspended Issa says what she really thinks before she gives her answer to her colleagues. Her true answer is "oh now ya'll see it's racist but when I was saying it all along no one cared!" Out loud to her coworkers she says, "I support all that you are saying and I thank you for saying it." This moment where the action freezes and Issa is able to speak her truth is a profound moment of this identity shifting in action. Issa is very aware that even when her opinion is solicited her honest answer is not actually welcome. Later when she is having lunch with her coworkers they admonish her for not speaking up during the meeting because she is the only Black person in the office. Issa pushes back saying that she does not want to be the spokesperson for Black people in the office. Her queer colleague says, "I have to represent all gay people. You have to represent all Black people. That is just the way it is." In this moment the show demonstrates the challenge of being a member of a marginalized group in the workplace. Underrepresented people become the de facto spokesperson for their entire group while also being at risk for challenging those in power on their racism, sexism, homophobia, and other forms of bias.

Insecure also does important work around reimagining Black professional womanhood in media by allowing Issa to be "regular." She is a woman in her early '30s who still has not figured it out. She does not have to be the super powerful and successful Olivia Pope of *Scandal* or Mary Jane Paul of *Being Mary Jane*, nor does she fall into stereotypical roles of the sassy comic relief. Allowing Issa to be a flawed young woman is similar to the ways that white characters are allowed to be imperfect while not being a caricature. Issa is unhappy at her job, but is afraid to explore other options. She has become professionally complacent in a position that doesn't satisfy her. It is a common experience among millennials who are graduating from college with huge student loan debt, limited job prospects, and stagnant wages in the jobs that they do find. Wanzo (2016) calls these types of narratives "precarious-girl comedy" whereby abjection is a space for freedom. Issa's experience is not uncommon in the new millennium, but it is rarely seen from the perspective of a Black woman. Rae's ability to capture these relatable universal themes, while also being specifically Black, is part of what makes the show work so well.

Counter to Issa's professional perspective is her best friend Molly. Molly is a successful attorney. She is professionally and financially secure. However, the framing of Molly's character reflects an oft used trope of the successful Black woman unable to find a suitable partner. *Insecure* reimagines that trope by providing more nuance and development beyond the basic stereotypes of Black women being unmarriageable. This is not to say that all women should aspire to be married, but Molly does aspire to marriage. Her parents are in a long-term seemingly happy marriage and Molly desires the same. This complicates what Wanzo (2016) describes as the "liberal feminist mold, in which women move forward professionally or contest traditional domestic roles" (p. 30). Molly is a well-developed character, so her romantic struggles are not a reflection of aggressive, angry, or qualities that are typically framed as emasculating which are the usual stereotypes imposed on professional Black women on television, nor does she completely reject the roles of wife or mother in her pursuit of professional success. Molly's inability to find a suitable partner is complicated and complex. The show uses Molly's shortcomings as well as those of her potential suitors to reflect the struggles with dating that many women have. *Insecure's* depiction of Molly demonstrates the ability to tell Black women's stories as "universal" and not just a repackaging of stereotypes when the story is told by a Black woman creator and writer. Molly is allowed to have the very relatable dating struggles that are common for all women without it relying on racist tropes to explain the narrative.

In season 2 Molly's character is not just struggling with her dating life. She is also countering the struggles of unequal pay in her workplace. After accidentally finding the pay stub of a white male colleague she realizes that despite being her junior and having less success at the job, he is making significantly more money than she is. As Molly is vying to become a partner at her firm based on her accomplishments, this man that would not even be a suitable option for that position has a much higher salary already. The show grapples with Molly's attempts to advocate for a pay increase and recognition from the largely white male power structure at her job. She demands not just financial compensation from them, but she also demands that they acknowledge her valuable contributions to the firm. This is particularly significant because Black women's labor is often undervalued and unrecognized but always expected. Molly's refusal to have her work at the firm ignored is a significant moment on television. Molly approaches the partners with data about her work at the firm and concrete facts about her performance. When the partners do not meet her demands she leaves.

Season 3 begins with Molly beginning a new job at a law firm that is made up of a team of predominantly Black lawyers and staff. Molly is enthusiastic about the possibility of working with people that look like her, and she assumes she will be treated as a respected and valuable member of the team. Molly quickly realizes that her new firm is behind the times with regards to best practices in the profession. Her disappointment with how the law firm conducts its business reflects a common intraracial critique that Black owned businesses are often mismanaged to their detriment. This is a recognizable conversation that would be familiar to a Black viewer of the show. When Molly is complaining to her girlfriends over drinks two of them agree with her, with one of them even stating "I use a white accountant!" to which they all exclaim, "But you're an accountant!" Issa is the lone holdout and reminds them that Black people are held to an unfair standard that is often not imposed on their white counterparts. Even in the midst of this comedic moment *Insecure* is able to adeptly illuminate the struggles of Black professionals. The notion that Black people must be above and beyond the standards that white people are held to is one that is commonly held by the Black community. The show is able to complicate Molly's criticism of her new law firm in ways that do not lose the humor, erase the intraracial challenges within the Black community, or allow that critique (often unfairly directed) to be the only position presented. In this moment viewers get a depiction of the challenges of being Black in a workplace that is very different from Issa's experiences in her predominantly white workplace. *Insecure* juxtaposes these moments to demonstrate that being a Black woman in a professional setting is always fraught with complex interactions and dynamics. The seemingly simple answer, work with or for Black people, is still not the easy answer that Molly expected it to be.

Rewriting Black Womanhood on Television and Online

Issa Rae's *The Misadventures of Awkward Black Girl* transformed narratives of Black womanhood in the digital public sphere. The popularity of Rae's show indicated that viewers were open to new visions of Black professional womanhood, and Rae's own positioning as producer, writer, and actor transformed the possibilities for her as a Black professional in television. As the show moved from YouTube into its current iteration on HBO viewers have been able to see Rae develop more complexity and in-depth narratives for her protagonist while staying true to telling the story of a regular Black woman who does not have it all figured out professionally but is kind of trying. The flawed, awkward, and unsure Issa who raps to herself in the mirror to work out her feelings reflects a more complex Black womanhood than is often present on television. Issa's interiority on the show allows viewers insight into the universal theme of insecurity through a Black woman character. Rae created a space for the awkward Black girl to be seen. These counternarratives, and Rae's own professional trajectory, perform the "wreck" that Pough (2004) calls for. Rae and her work on both *The Misadventures of Awkward Black Girl* and *Insecure* reframe Black professional womanhood in the public sphere and disrupts dominant ideologies of Black womanhood, particularly in the workplace.

REFERENCES

Brock, R. (2005). *Sista Talk: The Personal and the Pedagogical*. New York: Peter Lang.

Dickens, D. D. and Chavez, E. L. (2018). Navigating the Workplace: The Costs and Benefits of Shifting Identities at Work Among Early Career U.S. Black Women. *Sex Roles, 78,* 760–774. doi: 10.1007/s11199-017-0844-x.

Martin, M. (Interviewer) & Rae, I. (Interviewee). (2011). "Awkward Black Girl" Garners Laughs [Interview transcript]. Retrieved from https://www.npr.org/2011/09/01/140113 809/awkward-Black-girl-garners-laughs.

Pough, G. (2004). *Check It While I Wreck It. Black Womanhood, Hip-Hop Culture, and the Public Sphere*. Boston: Northeastern University Press.

Rae, I. (2011). The Misadventures of AWKWARD Black Girl Kickstarter. Retrieved from https:// www.kickstarter.com/projects/1996857943/the-misadventures-of-awkward-Black-girl.

Rae, I. (2012). People on the Internet Can Be Hella Racist. *xoJane*. Retrieved from https:// www.xojane.com/issues/people-internet-can-be-hella-racist.

Sue, D.W, Lin, A., and Rivera, D.P. (2009). Racial Microaggressions in the Workplace: Manifestation and Impact. In Chin, J. (Ed.), *Diversity in Mind and in Action [3 volumes]* (pp. 157–172). Santa Barbara: Praeger.

Wanzo, R. (2016). Precarious-Girl Comedy: Issa Rae, Lena Dunham, and Abjection Aesthetics. *Camera Obscura*, 31(2), 27–59.

Behind Their Masks

*Complex Black Superheroes
on the Small Screen*

CHRISTOPHER ALANYE COVINGTON

In the superhero genre, Marvel and Detective Comics (DC Comics) are the two biggest comic distributors in the world. Their characters have worldwide recognition by any generation. When it comes to representation of Black characters in the superhero genre, there has been some advancement in the quantity of Black superhero characters, but not by much in the overall grand scheme of comics. It can still be easily visualized that the superhero genre is still very much populated by white males. Although Black mainstream superheroes started in the 1960s with Marvel's comic books, there has been much progress over the decades to bring Black superheroes and characters to live-action media. Bringing Black superheroes and characters to a live-action format allows viewers to observe the performance of various levels of Blackness as well as the professionalism these characters portray. The one thing that goes unnoticed are the roles the characters portray as professionals within the superhero genre such as professions in the medical field, law enforcement, education, STEM, and service professions. This is especially important when it comes to Black superheroes and characters, because it is important for African Americans to see these positive portrayals of characters as professionals with various jobs or careers. It is equally important that these images and portrayals combat the typical and oversaturated negative image portrayals of African Americans in media.

The first Black mainstream superhero started with the Black Panther in *Fantastic Four #52* in 1966. Black Panther, king of the fictional African country of Wakanda, was created by Stan Lee and Jack Kirby. In 1969, The Falcon made his first appearance in the comic *Captain America #117*, making him the first African American superhero. As years went on more

African American superheroes were created. Marvel's character Luke Cage appeared in Marvel's *Hero for Hire #1* in June of 1972. Additionally, DC Comics had their first Black superhero in 1972, with the first appearance of John Stewart as the Green Lantern in *Green Lantern #87*. The character Black Lightning, who appeared in his self-titled comic book *Black Lightning #1* debuted April of 1977. Blaxploitation was a major influence in the creation of characters such as Luke Cage, Black Lightning and Black Goliath who appeared in the 1960s and 1970s. (Howard, S. C., and Jackson II, R. L., 2013).

African Americans have more frequently been seen in more superhero productions within film and television as characters and leads. In the '90s, Black superheroes had some appearances in film and television. As for film, in 1993, Robert Townsend brought the world *Meteor Man*. Meteor Man was about Jefferson Reed (Robert Townsend), a high school teacher in Washington D.C. who encounters a meteor that crashes to Earth and gives him superpowers to save his neighborhood. In 1997, *Spawn* came to theaters. Spawn, based on the same self-titled comic book (1992) and television series *Spawn* (1997–1999) by Todd McFarlane, is about a mercenary named Al Simmons (Michael Jai White), who is killed and recruited to serve in the devil's army, but wants revenge on the people who betrayed him. The following year, the film *Blade* came out in theaters in 1998. *Blade* is a movie that features a Black half-human, half-vampire-being named Blade (Wesley Snipes) who hunts evil vampires. Blade is on the mission, to not only rid the world of evil vampires, but also to find the vampire that killed his mother. The character launched on the small screen in 2006 based on the same premise as the film. The show's Blade character was played by Sticky Fingaz, however the series was short-lived lasting only one season. Earlier in the '90s, in 1994, Fox premiered a superhero show that had an African American male lead called M.A.N.T.I.S., Mechanically Augmented Neuro Transmitter Interception System. MANTIS' lead, Miles Hawkins (Carl Lumbly), was a wealthy scientist and founder of the Hawkins Institute who had been paralyzed after being shot in his back, damaging his spine (Muir, 2008). A wealthy Black male scientist broke all stereotypes for Black men in media. The show's pilot originally had a predominantly Black cast, but after the series started, that was no longer the case. Fox struggled with how to handle these issues, ultimately deciding to pull the plug in 1995 (Brehmer, 2017).

Along with these superhero moments of the '90s, African American television in the '90s had a visual shift in their representation in sitcoms. Throughout the '90s, African American television viewers could enjoy primetime television programming such as *The Cosby Show, A Different World, The Fresh Prince of Bel-Air, Family Matters, Martin,* and *Living Single* to name a prominent few. These shows allowed viewers access to characters that not only were African American but also, had professional careers that included law enforcement, medicine, judicial law, educators, and entertainers. Moving ahead into the 2010-decade African Americans have been able to enjoy the increase of Black characters in not just sitcoms, but in superhero shows as well. It can be noted that the Black characters in superhero shows have evolved from sidekick roles to more central and contributing characters. They also have skills and professions that make their roles much more relevant to the overall premise of the show.

Streaming Services

Netflix, Hulu, YouTube Red, and other streaming services or non-cable or satellite-based viewing services are taking over the way television is viewed and how it is made. Streaming services have opened doors and gateways for television programming that can be more diverse in casting and less restrictive in content. In the article, "How Online Streaming Has Improved Diversity in the Television Industry," Gee says "What this has really demonstrated to TV execs though is that beyond Hollywood there is a whole world of audiences who want to see everything on their televisions. From complex LGBT issues to more Black female leads (shockingly *Scandal* was the first network drama with a Black female protagonist in a network drama in nearly 40 years)—we want entertainment that is as interesting and as diverse as the world we live in" (Gee, 2017). What these streaming services have also taken on is the development of more superhero related programming. Much success has come from the Netflix Marvel series of *Daredevil, Jessica Jones, Luke Cage, Iron Fist*, and *The Punisher*. These shows, unlike the superhero shows on broadcast television, have allowed superhero shows to have a more graphic approach than broadcast television. This gives these shows the possibility to have darker themes, more violence, include sexual intimacy, stronger language, and the ability to broaden casting and characterizations. This is especially important when looking at racial and ethnic character diversity in superhero television shows. Superhero shows have previously been an untapped resource for showcasing professional African Americans, but now especially with these shows having a diverse audience viewership, representation expands.

The purpose of this essay is to highlight the African American characters in contemporary superhero shows to showcase their professionalism and how their character fits in the category scheme of representation. With their popularity, shows such as *Luke Cage* and *Black Lightning*, which have predominantly Black casts, showcase Black characters in various roles in the superhero genre. The following shows have been identified for their Black character representation and will be categorized in the role they serve, and the professionalism they display. Those shows include FOX's *Gotham* (2014–2019), CW's *The Flash* (2014–), *Arrow* (2012–2020), and *Supergirl* (2015–) along with Netflix's *Luke Cage* (2016–2018) and CW's *Black Lightning* (2018–). These two streaming series have broken the supporting and sidekick molds, and because they are predominantly Black casted shows, the focus will be on a few characters. For *Luke Cage*, the main focus will be on Luke Cage (Mike Colter) and Misty Knight (Simone Missick), and *Black Lightning* will focus on Jefferson Pierce/Black Lightning (Cress Williams), Anissa Pierce (Nafessa Williams), and Lynn Stewart (Christine Adams).

Superhero Television and African Americans: Categorizing the Types of Representation of African Americans and Highlighting Professionalism

In contemporary television, African Americans have come to be represented as medical and legal professionals, law enforcement, heads of military, in STEM fields, and even President. Even with this being the case, African Americans are still highly visible in roles that are negative and stereotypical. Nevertheless, it has become more common to see them in roles that sometimes counter Black stereotypes.

In an overview of African Americans in superhero genres it has been determined that their representation resides in four major categories. For the purposes of this essay they are entitled the following: The STEM, The Renaissance Man, The Moral Compass, and The Conflicted Hero. The definitions of each come from an analysis of various superhero shows over time that have displayed these reoccurring representations. Typically, a superhero group or team has one of these characters, but it is more important to highlight when African Americans take on these positions because it defies negative representations. The STEM, who is typically a science or techie person, has evolved from being the nerdy assistant to being the scientific brains behind the superhero's operations. This all-around technology and science person possesses a type of professional capability not often associated with African Americans. The Renaissance Man/Person is the everything person. They are good at almost anything they put their hands on or mind to; the Jack and Jill of all trades. They typically have multiple skill sets or qualities and switch back and forth between them. There are times in many shows where everyone looks to the one person that seems to know what should be done as opposed to what should not be done; that's the Moral Compass. This person typically serves as the voice of reason for a group or the superhero, and may or may not have special abilities. Lastly, The Conflicted Hero, the one who understands that right and wrong is not as simple as Black and white, and they consistently navigate the grey area. This category is usually helmed by Black hero leads. It is important to note that at times some characters can be defined by more than one category representation. The Conflicted Hero can embody, The Renaissance Man and the Moral Compass, which makes the hero conflicted. In the following shows, *Gotham, Arrow, The Flash, Supergirl, Black Lightning*, and *Luke Cage* its important how each African American character's category and their profession, supports their role within the show. These categories outline one way to understand and analyze Black television characters in the superhero genre. The analysis of the shows *Luke Cage* and *Black Lightning* will showcase a more in depth look of Black characters as professionals in predominantly Black-casted superhero shows. Preceding this deep analysis this essay will discuss the shows previously stated and the professionalism showcased by African American characters.

The STEM

Often in superhero series, when the television show has a mixture of characters, one character tends to stand out, who is especially smart, tech savvy, or a genius—this is The STEM. The STEM character most likely went to a four-year college or skipped college and taught themselves because they decided college was a waste of their talent. In *Gotham*, Lucius Fox (Chris Chalk) is the STEM person. Lucius Fox is one of the main (probably the only) recurring African American characters on *Gotham*. Lucius Fox works in the Gotham City Police Department. While he is not always a consistently present character on the show, when important or extreme matters arise, he is always consulted. As the show progressed, he has helped Bruce Wayne (David Mazouz) take on the Batman persona by creating armor and materials as he began becoming the unofficial Batman.

The Renaissance Man

The series *Arrow* has a Renaissance Man. As defined earlier, they are good at almost anything they put their hands on or mind to. In some instances, they are put in compromising situations which sometimes has their role going from support person to leader or even an advisor. At times they can function as the Moral Compass character, which sometimes can appear seamless. What sets the Renaissance Man and Moral Compass apart are the Renaissance Man's skill sets. For *Arrow*, it's John Diggle (David Ramsey) who is usually referred to as Diggle. Diggle is a former soldier turned bodyguard, turned hero, turned family man, turned leader in a secret government organization known as A.R.G.U.S. He is the original recurring African American character on *Arrow*, and unfortunately Diggle began with the role of the sidekick but later breaks out of that role and into the position of support/partner character. Diggle being a trained military professional has used his skills to help The Arrow also known as Oliver Queen (Stephen Amell) fight crime initially by planning and strategizing, and only later does he join the team. As the show continues Diggle breaks away from the team to become the head of A.R.G.U.S.

The Moral Compass

In *Supergirl*, the alien Jonn Jonz (David Harewood) is Hank Henshaw when in human form, a Black man, but when in his green natural alien form he is known as Martian Manhunter. Hank Henshaw is the director of the Department of Extra-Normal Operations (DEO), which means he also supervises Supergirl, and runs an organization dedicated to monitoring and protecting Earth from extra-terrestrial presence or invasion. While there are moments in the show when Jonn Jonz is in green alien form, there are times when he shape-shifts into other people or characters in the show. The reason he is being discussed is because during the majority of the show Jonn Jonz, is seen as Hank Henshaw, an African American man. Hank Henshaw is the moral compass of the show because he is the reasonable and level-headed character on the show. Despite frequent extra-terrestrial and non-extra-terrestrial issues that arise, he is not quick to act and takes time to plan and strategize. Hank's ability to be the moral compass continues after his tenure of being director of D.E.O. is over.

The television series *The Flash* and the concept of professionalism, go hand and hand. This CW television series has an African American family that are all professionals in their own right. To start, you have the father, Detective Joe West (Jesse L. Martin), the moral compass. Joe is the character that knows his skills as a detective are a vital part of the Team Flash. He makes the moral compass category because he knows his skills and lived experience make him the voice of reason at times. Once his daughter, Iris West (Candice Patton) starts to be more involved with Team Flash she becomes more of a renaissance woman/moral compass hybrid. She started working as a journalist for the newspaper, yet later she becomes Team Flash's leader because she was able to make more sound decisions than The Flash himself. This was most vital when The Flash had to leave due to going into the speed force to save the team. Following his exit, Iris became the permanent team leader. It should also be noted that Iris continues to lead Team Flash as well as founding and owning The Central City Citizen newspaper agency.

Conflicted Heroes in Luke Cage and Black Lightning

Marvel's Luke Cage on Netflix at first sight is a show about a strong, Black man, with a moral compass, but later becomes conflicted. This show follows the journey of Luke Cage, a wrongly convicted police officer who manages to escape prison after being experimented on to supposedly save his life, which also gave him special abilities. After his escape, Cage, makes his way back to Harlem, where he attempts to maintain a low profile and hide his special abilities. By assisting Pop (Frankie Faison) in Pop's barbershop, Luke Cage ideally wants to be left alone. It was not until Pop was murdered in his barbershop in front of Luke Cage, that Cage changed his disposition and not only wanted to avenge Pop, but also save Harlem from drugs and violence. Luke Cage uses his former law enforcement skills, along with his special abilities of unbreakable/bulletproof skin and super strength, to avenge Pop and stop crime and violence in Harlem. Because of Luke Cage's moral sensibilities and past life as law enforcement and his understanding of how the criminal justice system works, Cage defies this system and its processes, by taking the law into his own hands. Having to work outside the law and resorting to violence Luke Cage becomes a conflicted hero. A series which involves drugs, violence, and organized crime is bound to include law enforcement. Misty Knight (Simone Missick) is a detective for the Harlem police department, and is a true moral compass to begin, but also later becomes a conflicted hero. Early in season one, Detective Knight wants to ensure she, along with others, do the right thing. Knight later discovers that her former partner was a corrupt officer and she begins to question what she believes—she becomes conflicted. In season two, Knight truly is Luke Cage's moral compass, whether she is successful or not is perhaps in the eye of the beholder.

With *Black Lightning*, there is a family dynamic in which each character is defined as a lead: Jefferson Pierce, Anissa, and Lynn are all conflicted heroes. Black Lightning takes place in the fictional city of Freeland, where now the gang *The 100* have taken over the streets with crime and violence, and are prime sellers of a special drug called Green Light. Jefferson Pierce (Cress Williams), also known as Black Lightning, is the principal of Garfield High School, and is from Freeland. Jefferson saw his father murdered in front of him when he was younger, which was also when his powers started to manifest. The show starts off 10 years after Black Lightning retired his hero persona, because he thought that after avenging his father's death, Black Lightning was no longer necessary. The first episode titled "Resurrection," reveals that Black Lightning has returned to help the city of Freeland once again.

Jefferson's representation can appear to be that of the renaissance man category, because he is a principal, father, friend, and superhero. But it is because of those identities which makes him a conflicted hero. His oldest daughter, Anisa Pierce (Nafessa Williams), is currently teaching part-time at Garfield High School, while she attends medical school. After she gets more familiar with the superhero work/life balance, she obtains a Robin Hood type persona of robbing the rich and giving to the poor. Anisa is a conflicted hero because although she has her heart in the right place, she has to balance her multiple identities much like her father, of being a daughter, friend, lover, superhero, and vigilante.

A lot of the conflict of these two heroes have come from difference of opinions between Jefferson and Anisa. In one perspective, there is the familial dynamic of father and daughter. This dynamic also plays into their superhero characters as Black Lightning and Thunder, in which the father identity is always present and guides how the duo operates together. In another perspective, Jefferson/Black Lightning is shown to have a more passive and law-abiding method than Anisa/Thunder, who tends to have a more aggressive "Malcolm X" approach, by any means necessary. These two varying ideologies create conflict for them as family, superheroes, and how they view their work in the community. Being portrayed on screen also shows the complexities of family dynamics and additionally ideologies among different generations in Black families.

Conclusion

African Americans in the comic industry have made progress since the '60s. They have gone from being sidekicks in comics to breaking cinematic records, to having predominantly Black casted live-action series. Along with progress in representation of African Americans in television sitcoms, so too has been the same with African Americans in the superhero genre. Looking back at African American shows in the '90s, it was easily visible seeing positive representation of professionalism in television from different shows in which they were involved in. Most of those shows were predominantly Black casted shows that allowed for an array of African American characters to be viewed. There is a sense of progress to be able to see superhero shows having African Americans contributing to the show as opposed to unimportant roles. Such progress is further enhanced by seeing a Black casted superhero series with a range of representation. There are multiple professions that can be observed in the superhero television genre such as law enforcement, government officials, STEM, and educators. These representations are pivotal in changing the negative representation and the lack of African American representation that has oversaturated television for decades. It will be exciting to see how much more progress will be made, as superhero films and shows dominate the box office and find more space in the realm of streaming platforms.

References

Brehmer, N. (2017, December 08). 16 Superhero Shows Canceled for Strange Reasons. Retrieved December 15, 2018, from https://screenrant.com/superhero-shows-canceled-shocking-reasons/

Chow, K. (2016, May 13). Waiting for Superman: The Beginning of the End of Smallville. Retrieved September 2, 2018, from https://thenerdsofcolor.org/2016/05/13/waiting-for-superman-the-beginning-of-the-end-of-smallville/

Gee, T. J. (2017, February 16). How Online Streaming Has Improved Diversity In the Television Industry. Retrieved September 2, 2018, from https://graziadaily.co.uk/life/tv-and-film/online-streaming-improved-diversity-tv/.

Howard, S. C., & Jackson II, R. L. (Eds.). (2013). *Black Comics: Politics of Race and Representation*. A&C Black.

McPherson, T. (2013, December 15). The Era of Superheroes: TV's Dominating Genre. Retrieved September 2, 2018, from https://the-artifice.com/tv-superheroes-era/.

Muir, J. K. (2004). *The Encyclopedia of Superheroes on Film and Television*. Jefferson, NC: McFarland.

Nama, A. (2011). *Super Black: American Pop Culture and Black Superheroes*. Austin: University of Texas Press.

Rearick, L. (2018, April 08). *Black Panther* Broke ANOTHER Box Office Record. Retrieved September 2, 2018, from https://www.teenvogue.com/story/Black-panther-is-the-third-highest-grossing-film-in-north-american-box-office-history.

About the Contributors

Mia L. **Anderson** is an associate professor at Azusa Pacific University. She received her Ph.D. from the University of Alabama. Her interests include the history of African American magazines, minority images in the media, and communication and sport. Her work has been published in the *Journal of African American Studies,* the *Journal of Sports Media,* and *The Media in America: A History (9th ed.).*

LaToya T. **Brackett** is an assistant professor at the University of Puget Sound. She earned her Ph.D. in African American and African studies from Michigan State University. Her interests include popular culture and the African diaspora. Her work has appeared in *Black Culture and Experience,* and *Race Still Matters* among other scholarly collections. She is the founder and executive director of the Phyllis Marie Brackett Memorial Scholarship.

Malika T. **Butler** is a graduate of the University of North Carolina at Chapel Hill, having earned her BA in elementary education. She earned her MS in student affairs from Indiana University. She earned her Ph.D. in Educational Leadership and Policy Studies from Iowa State University. Her work is interdisciplinary and investigates the ways Black educative spaces have been utilized to foster social justice, Black liberation, and freedom.

Christopher Alanye **Covington** is an alumnus of Michigan State University. His research focuses on popular culture as it pertains to Black characters, representation, underrepresentation, stereotypes, and Black masculinity. He teaches computer science and gaming for a charter school in Detroit and runs his non-profit, S.A.V.E.T.H.E.M. (Stomping Away Various Epidemics by Teaching Health Education and Mentoring).

Kristal Moore **Clemons** earned her Ph.D. from the University of North Carolina at Chapel Hill and a graduate certificate in women's studies from Duke University. Her research centers on the activism of Black women in various spaces ranging from Chicago tenement housing projects to the Civil Rights Movement in the American South. She is the national director of the Children's Defense Fund Freedom Schools.

Phokeng Motsoasele **Dailey** is an assistant professor at Ohio Wesleyan University. Her research focuses on health disparities among U.S. immigrant and refugee populations in the areas of sexually transmitted infection, cancer prevention and decision-making. She has been published in *Health Communication*, *Communication Studies* and the *Journal of Cancer Education*.

Darnel **Degand** is an assistant professor at the University of California–Davis. He has an Ed.D. in instructional technology and media from Teachers College, Columbia University. His two decades of experience as a multimedia producer includes roles as an online game developer for Sesame Workshop and multimedia designer for the City University of New York.

Regina M. **Duthely** is an assistant professor at the University of Puget Sound in Tacoma, Washington. She specializes in Black feminist digital rhetorics, and uses Black feminist readings of popular culture and Black women's digital rhetorics to argue that the use of (dis)respectability politics in the public sphere is a means of liberation for Black women.

Amir Asim **Gilmore** earned his Ph.D. in cultural studies and social thought in education at Washington State University. His background in cultural studies, Africana studies and education allows him to traverse the boundaries across the social sciences, the arts, and the humanities. As an assistant professor at WSU, he works in teacher education and the application of Afrofuturism and Afropessimism to educational practices within the K–12 education system.

Natalie J. **Graham** earned her MFA in creative writing at the University of Florida and her Ph.D. in American studies at Michigan State University. Her collection, *Begin with a Failed Body*, was selected for the 2016 Cave Canem Poetry Prize. Her work has appeared in the *San Francisco Chronicle*, *Southern Humanities Review*, and *The Journal of Popular Culture*, among others. She is a Cave Canem Fellow, Sewanee Fellow, and associate professor at California State University, Fullerton.

Tammie **Jenkins** holds a doctorate degree in curriculum and instruction from Louisiana State University. Her research interests include Black Atlantic studies, women and gender studies, and African American history. She serves as an associate editor for *The Criterion* and sits on the advisory board for *Epitome*. She works as a special education teacher in her local public school system.

Saravanan **Mani** holds a doctoral degree from NTU, Singapore. His thesis was on twenty-first century American crime TV series. His research interests are television studies, picture theory, cultural studies and ethics. He has written and presented on the topics of police procedure, criminal justice and seriality in TV and film. He teaches English language and literature at a secondary school in Singapore.

Eleda **Mbinjama** holds a bachelor's degree in dentistry (BChD) and a post graduate diploma in oral surgery from the University of Western Cape (UWC) in South Africa. She is a civil servant in the Eastern Cape Department of Health and has been practicing for ten years. She is an independent researcher with interests in behavioral science and cultural relativism.

Adelina **Mbinjama-Gamatham** is a lecturer in the Department of Media Studies at the Cape Peninsula University of Technology in Cape Town, South Africa. Her teaching and research interests are in social media-communications, cyber-ethics,

Black feminism and representation of women in the media. She holds a doctoral degree in media studies from the Nelson Mandela University.

Dominick N. **Quinney** is an assistant professor of ethnic studies at Albion College in Albion, Michigan. His qualitative research interests include understanding racial dialogue among diverse groups and race pedagogy. He has extensive research in community engagement and the development of urban high school students. He earned a Ph.D. in African American and African studies from Michigan State University

David **Stamps** received his Ph.D. from the University of California, Santa Barbara, and is an assistant professor at the Manship School of Mass Communication at Louisiana State University. His research focuses on representations of marginalized groups in mass media and the impact of mass media imagery on audiences.

Index

216   Index